CISCAUCASIA

UCASUS

MOUNTAINS

TRANSCAUCASIA

Kura River

▲ *Mount Ararat*

Lake Sevan

Araxes River

Lake Van

TU

Greater Zab River

Lake Urmia

○ Hasanlu
○ Dinkha Tepe

Nineveh
Kalkhu

ZAGROS

○ Nuzi

Tigris River

Diyala River

○ Godin Tepe

LURISTAN

○ Eshnunna

AKKAD

Sippar ○

○ Babylon
○ Kish
○ Nippur
○ Isin
○ Umma
○ Lagash
BABYLONIA
Uruk ○ Larsa
River
○ Ur
Eridu ○

Euphrates

Tigris River

SUSIANA
○ Súsa
ELAM

SUMER

Karun River

MOUNTAINS

ELBURZ MOUNTAINS

Caspian Sea

MEDIA

PARTHIA ○ Tepe Hissar

Dasht-i-Kavir Desert

○ Tepe Sialk

IRAN

SIMASHKI

Anshan ○ ○ Pasargadae
○ Persepolis

TURKMENISTAN

Kyzyl Kum Desert

Kara Kum Desert

Atrek River ○ Anau

KOPET DAG

○ Namazga-Depe
○ Altyn-depe
MARGIANA

Tedzhen River

Amu Darya River (Oxus)

○ Yaz-depe

Kuchuk Tepe ○

BACTRIA

Murgab River

Helmand River

Dasht-i-Lut Desert

Failaka Island

Persian

Bahrain

DILMUN

QATAR

Gulf

○ Tepe Yahya

○ Bampur

○ Shimal

Gulf of Oman

○ Hili

ARABIAN

ENINSULA

MAGAN

OMAN PENINSULA ○ Maysar

Arabian Sea

The Ancient Near East

An Encyclopedia for Students

Ronald Wallenfels, *Editor in Chief*

Jack M. Sasson, *Consulting Editor*

Volume 2

CHARLES SCRIBNER'S SONS
An Imprint of The Gale Group
NEW YORK   DETROIT   SAN FRANCISCO   LONDON   BOSTON   WOODBRIDGE, CT

Developed for Charles Scribner's Sons by Visual Education Corporation, Princeton, N.J.

For Scribners
PUBLISHER: Karen Day
SENIOR EDITOR: Timothy J. DeWerff
COVER DESIGN: Lisa Chovnick, Tracey Rowens

For Visual Education Corporation
EDITORIAL DIRECTOR: Darryl Kestler
PROJECT DIRECTOR: Meera Vaidyanathan
WRITERS: Jean Brainard, John Haley, Mac Austin, Charles Roebuck, Rebecca Stefoff
EDITORS: Dale Anderson, Carol Ciaston, Linda Perrin, Caryn Radick
ASSOCIATE EDITOR: Lauren Weber
COPYEDITING MANAGER: Helen Castro
COPY EDITOR: Marie Enders
PHOTO RESEARCH: Sara Matthews
PRODUCTION SUPERVISOR: Marcel Chouteau
PRODUCTION ASSISTANT: Brian Suskin
INTERIOR DESIGN: Maxson Crandall, Rob Ehlers
ELECTRONIC PREPARATION: Cynthia C. Feldner, Christine Osborne, Fiona Torphy
ELECTRONIC PRODUCTION: Rob Ehlers, Lisa Evans-Skopas, Laura Millan, Isabelle Ulsh

Library of Congress Cataloging-in-Publication Data

The Ancient Near East : an encyclopedia for students / Ronald Wallenfels, editor in chief; Jack M. Sasson, consulting editor.
     p. cm.
    Includes bibliographical references and index.
    ISBN 0-684-80597-9 (set : alk. paper) — ISBN 0-684-80589-8 (vol. 1) — ISBN 0-684-80594-4 (vol. 2) — ISBN 0-684-80595-2 (vol. 3) — ISBN 0-684-80596-0 (vol. 4)
    1. Middle East—Civilization—To 622—Dictionaries, Juvenile. [1. Middle East—Civilization—To 622—Encyclopedias.] I. Wallenfels, Ronald. II. Sasson, Jack M.

DS57 .A677 2000
939'.4—dc21

00-056335

TABLE of CONTENTS

VOLUME 1 Abraham–Cities and City-States

VOLUME 2 Clay Tablets–Inheritance

VOLUME 3 Inscriptions–Phoenicia and the Phoenicians

VOLUME 4 Phrygia and the Phrygians–Zoroaster and Zoroastrianism

MAPS & CHARTS

COLOR PLATES

iii

A Time Line of the Ancient Near East

	Neolithic Period ca. 9000–4000 B.C.	Chalcolithic Period ca. 4000–3000 B.C.

Mesopotamia	Neolithic culture in northern Mesopotamia
	  Earliest permanent farming settlements, ca. 7000 B.C.
	  Earliest evidence of pottery, ca. 6500 B.C.
	Ubaid settlements in southern Mesopotamia
		Late Ubaid period
		Uruk and Jamdat-Nasr periods
		  Development of city-states
		  Invention of writing

Anatolia	Earliest permanent farming settlements, ca. 7000 B.C. Çatal Hüyük inhabited Earliest evidence of pottery, ca. 6300 B.C.	Development of agricultural and trading communities
Syria and the Levant	Agriculture first practiced, ca. 8500 B.C. Settlement of Jericho Domestication of animals, ca. 7300 B.C. Earliest evidence of pottery, ca. 6600 B.C.	Development of agricultural and trading communities
Egypt	Earliest permanent farming settlements in northern Egypt, ca. 5200 B.C. Earliest evidence of pottery in northern Egypt, ca. 5000 B.C. Evidence of predynastic graves in southern Egypt, suggesting the existence of permanent settlements, ca. 4000 B.C.	Predynastic period Invention of hieroglyphics
Arabia	Earliest evidence of pastoralism and pottery in western Arabia, ca. 6000 B.C. Contact between eastern Arabia and southern Mesopotamia	Permanent settlements established Contact between western Arabia and Syria and the Levant Continued contact between eastern Arabia and southern Mesopotamia
Iran	Earliest permanent farming settlements in southwestern Iran, ca. 7000 B.C. Earliest evidence of pottery in southwestern Iran, ca. 6500 B.C. Susa founded	Proto-Elamite culture
Aegean and the Eastern Mediterranean	Earliest permanent farming settlements on Crete, ca. 7000 B.C. Earliest permanent farming settlements on the mainland, ca. 6700 B.C. Earliest evidence of pottery on the mainland, ca. 6300 B.C. Earliest evidence of pottery on Crete, ca. 5900 B.C.	Development of agricultural and trading communities

Early Bronze Age ca. 3000–2200 B.C.	Middle Bronze Age ca. 2200–1600 B.C.

Sumerian Early Dynastic period
Akkadian empire
   Sargon I (ruled ca. 2334–2278 B.C.)
   Unification of Sumer and Akkad
	Gutian and Amorite invasions
	Second Dynasty of Lagash
	   Gudea of Lagash (ruled ca. 2144–2124 B.C.)
	Third Dynasty of Ur
	   Ziggurat of Ur
	Dynasties of Isin and Larsa
	Old Assyrian period
	Old Babylonian period
	   Hammurabi (ruled ca. 1792–1750 B.C.)
	Hurrian immigrations

Development of city-states
   Troy
   Alaca Hüyük
	Old Assyrian trading colonies
	Old Hittite period
	   Khattushili I (ruled ca. 1650–1620 B.C.)
	Hittites invade Babylon

Development of city-states
Sumerian-style urban culture
   Kingdom of Ebla
      Akkadians conquer Ebla
	Rise of Amorite city-states

Early Dynastic period
Old Kingdom period
   Djoser (ruled ca. 2630–2611 B.C.)
      First pyramids
   Great Pyramid of Giza
	First Intermediate period
	   Civil war between dynasties at Thebes
	   and Heracleopolis
	Middle Kingdom period
	Second Intermediate period
	   Hyksos conquest

Levantine, Mesopotamian, and Iranian influence in the northwest Magan and Dilmun trade with Mesopotamia	Mesopotamian and Iranian influences along coast of Arabian Gulf
Old Elamite period Wars with Mesopotamia Susiana under Akkadian and Sumerian domination	Sukkalmakh dynasty Susiana allies with Elam Babylonians control Elam
Early Cycladic culture	Minoan culture on Crete Mycenaeans invade Peloponnese Volcanic eruption at Thera

A Time Line of the Ancient Near East

	Late Bronze Age ca. 1600–1200 B.C.	Iron Age ca. 1200–500 B.C.

Mesopotamia	Hittites invade Babylon
	Dark Age
	Middle Babylonian (Kassite) period
	Hurrian kingdom of Mitanni
	Middle Assyrian period
		Second Dynasty of Isin
		Neo-Babylonian period
		Neo-Assyrian empire
		   Sargon II (ruled 721–705 B.C.)
		Late Babylonian period (Chaldean dynasty)
		   Nebuchadnezzar II (ruled 605–562 B.C.)
		Persians conquer Babylonia

Anatolia	Hittite empire
	   Shuppiluliuma I (ruled ca. 1370–1330 B.C.)
	   Hittite wars with Egypt
	Destruction of Khattusha
		Dark Age
		Rise of Neo-Hittite states
		Kingdoms of Urartu and Phrygia
		Cimmerian invasion
		Kingdoms of Lydia and Lycia
		Median expansion
		Greek city-states in western Anatolia
		Persians conquer Lydia

Syria and the Levant	Canaanites develop aleph-beth Egyptian domination Hittite invasions Hurrian domination Sea Peoples	Aramaean migrations Israelites settle in Canaan Philistine and Phoenician city-states Kingdoms of Israel and Judah Assyrian conquests Babylonian conquests

Egypt	Expulsion of Hyksos
	New Kingdom period
	Expansion into Syria, the Levant, and Nubia
	Invasion of the Sea Peoples
		Third Intermediate period
		   Libyan dynasty
		   Nubian dynasties
		      Taharqa (ruled 690–664 B.C.)
		Assyrian conquest
		Late period
		   Saite dynasty

Arabia	Decline of Dilmun Qurayya flourishes Arabia dominates aromatics trade	Qedar tribe dominates northern Arabia Syria dominates in the east Neo-Babylonians control trade routes Sabaean rulers

Iran	Middle Elamite period
	Aryans (Medes and Persians) enter Iran
		Neo-Elamite period
		Median kingdom
		Zoroaster (lived ca. 600s B.C.)
		Persians overthrow Medes
		Cyrus the Great (ruled 559–529 B.C.)
		   Conquest of Babylonia
		Persian empire established
		   Darius I (ruled 521–486 B.C.)

Aegean and the Eastern Mediterranean	Decline of Minoan civilization Rise of Mycenaeans Mycenaeans colonize Aegean	Trojan War Dorian invasions Fall of Mycenae Dark Age Greek colonization Competition with Phoenician trade

Persian Period ca. 500–324 B.C.	Hellenistic Period 323 B.C.–A.D. 1
Persian domination Alexander the Great (lived 356–323 B.C.) enters Babylon	Seleucid empire Parthian empire
Persian domination Macedonian conquest	Roman rule

Persian domination
   Jews return from Babylon
   Second temple of Jerusalem
Macedonian conquest
	Ptolemaic kingdom and Seleucid empire
	Maccabean Revolt
	Hasmonean dynasty
	Roman rule

Persian domination
Local dynasties of native Egypt
Macedonian conquest
	Ptolemaic dynasty
	   Ptolemy I (ruled 305–282 B.C.)
	   Cleopatra (ruled 69–30 B.C.)
	Roman rule

Nabatean kingdom in Jordan Persian domination	Trade with Hellenistic world Roman conquest
Persian empire dominates the ancient Near East Greek invasions Macedonian conquest Alexander the Great	Seleucid empire Parthian empire
Persian wars Classical period Peloponnesian War Macedonian conquest	Hellenistic dynasties Roman conquest

CLAY TABLETS

The earliest forms of writing were symbols scratched on tablets made of clay for recording quantities of goods. Soon people made impressions in damp clay to record business deals, keep accounts, recognize treaties, or set down laws. The clay was then dried in the sun to harden it and preserve the inscribed message. Only rarely were tablets baked in an oven. This early form of WRITING, which was used in much of the ancient Near East, was very durable. Almost half a million clay tablets have been found throughout the region so far, and new discoveries are reported regularly. The tablets provide invaluable and detailed insights into life in the ancient Near East.

Before Tablets. Before tablets, there were tokens. As far back as 8000 B.C., people were using clay to keep records. They pressed small lumps of clay between their fingers to make a token about one-half to one inch across. The tokens came in many shapes, including spheres, discs, cones, and rods. Some were plain; others had markings. Each token represented a commodity, such as a bushel of grain, a sheep, or a jar of oil. People used tokens to keep track of supplies, to make calculations, and to conclude transactions.

Although the tokens were small, they could be rather cumbersome when large numbers of them were needed. People therefore started to make clay "envelopes" to contain them. The tokens were placed inside a hollow clay ball, called a bulla, which was then sealed with a cylinder SEAL.

A drawback of the envelopes was that they concealed the contents. Once they were sealed, nobody could see how many tokens were inside until the envelope was broken open at its final destination. To overcome this problem, people developed a system of markings. Tokens like those inside were pressed onto the outside of the envelope while it was still soft to indicate how many of each type of token the envelope held. By about 3500 B.C., solid clay tablets had replaced the envelopes. The token impressions that had been placed on the envelopes were soon replaced with drawings of the tokens on the tablets. Now instead of repeating the information contained inside the envelope, the markings themselves gave the message.

How the Tablets Were Made. People made clay tablets by patting damp clay into the desired shape. The most common shape was that of a rectangle with rounded corners, but tablets were also square, circular, and oval. Some tablets were formed in the shape of barrels, others prisms with as many as ten sides. The tablets varied greatly in size, depending on the amount and importance of the information to be recorded. The smallest tablets were just a few centimeters in length and width. The larger tablets, which contained literary or historical records, may measure as much as 45 by 30 centimeters.

The writing was done by scribes*, who in most societies were the only people who knew how to write. After the surface of the tablet was made smooth, the scribe used a reed with a wedge-shaped tip called a stylus to impress triangular-shaped marks in it. For long scholarly texts, several tablets were used. For some long texts, scribes might also draw lines on the tablets to divide them into sections. In most cases, scribes wrote on both sides of a tablet, flipping it over from top to bottom.

* **scribe** person of a learned class who served as a writer, editor, or teacher

Clay Tablets

The cuneiform clay tablets, shown here, date from the third to the first millennium B.C. Initially, the tablets were inscribed from top to bottom and from right to left. In later years, the direction of writing changed, and the tablets were inscribed from top to bottom and from left to right. The sizes of the inscriptions also changed over the years. When scribes ran out of space on the tablet, they sometimes inscribed the edges or squeezed words between lines.

See color plate 5, vol. 2.

* **stylized** referring to art style in which figures are portrayed in simplified ways that exaggerate certain features, not realistically

Once the marks were made, the tablets were placed in the sun to dry. If the message was especially important, the tablet was baked in a kiln—an oven used for hardening pottery. This ensured that the tablet hardened properly and would then last a long time.

What the Writing Was Like. The form of writing used on clay tablets is called CUNEIFORM. The name comes from two Latin words—*cuneus,* meaning "wedge" and *forma,* meaning "shape"—and refers to the kind of marks made by the scribe's stylus. Each mark was made by pressing the stylus into the clay, not by drawing it across the surface. As a result, the marks retained the basic shape of the part of the stylus that was pressed in, either the wedge-shaped end or the straight edge. A remarkable number of different symbols could be created by varying the number of wedges and their orientation.

Cuneiform was developed by the Sumerians at URUK in about 3100 B.C. Initially, the symbols were closely related to the objects they represented. As time passed, however, cuneiform symbols became more and more stylized*. They began to "stand for" something rather than "be" a picture of it. Eventually, some symbols were used to represent sounds instead of objects. These changes were significant developments; with them, written language could now express many more ideas.

What the Tablets Were Used For. Initially, clay tablets were used mainly for recording the movement of goods and people administered by the central temple at Uruk. As the tablets' use widened, they were employed to keep track of inventories, to itemize expenditures, and to record laws and treaties. Some kings had scribes write about their accomplishments to keep the gods and future rulers informed. These records were called royal INSCRIPTIONS. In addition, people used clay tablets for sending letters.

Clay tablets were also used to record numerous myths and legends, even prayers to the gods. In most nonliterate societies, these stories and prayers were passed down by word of mouth and thus are often no longer available. The tablets were also used in schools, where students practiced the equivalent of spelling and composition, as well as mathematics, on them.

How Tablets Were Kept. Sometimes tablets were stored in large clay containers. They might also be stored in wooden boxes or even stacked on wooden shelves almost like modern books. Not all tablets were stored, of course. Many were discarded once they were no longer needed. Because they were usually rectangular and because of their hardness, they might be used as building material and placed under new pavements or within new walls. This made them that much easier to be found by archaeologists* many centuries later.

Royal inscriptions received better treatment. Mesopotamian kings had these tablets buried under the foundations of buildings or stored in special rooms. The tablets were, in a sense, the first time capsules, waiting to reveal their contents to future generations.

Why Clay Tablets Were Replaced. Clearly, clay tablets had their drawbacks as well as their advantages. They were time-consuming to make, bulky to store, and heavy to carry (one tablet that has been found weighs 11 pounds). Tablets were also difficult to change. If a scribe made an error in recording information, the clay could be smoothed over and new marks made. However, if a change needed to be made in the text after the tablet had dried, there was no way to do this. In some periods of Mesopotamian history, scribes used wax spread on wooden boards, instead of clay, to record information that was needed only briefly. After the text was no longer required, they could smooth over the wax and reuse it.

Despite these difficulties, ancient cultures used clay tablets with satisfaction for about 3,000 years. During all that time, however, written language was evolving, and methods for recording language were being refined. Eventually clay tablets and the cuneiform system of writing gave way to alphabets inked on animal skins and papyrus*. The last known cuneiform tablets date from at least the first century A.D. and perhaps even as late as the A.D. 200s. (*See also* **Alphabets; Record Keeping; Scribes.**)

* **archaeologist** scientist who studies past human cultures, usually by excavating material remains of human activity

* **papyrus** writing material made by pressing together thin stripes of the inner stem of the papyrus plant; *pl.* papyri

CLEOPATRA

lived 69–30 B.C.
Queen of Egypt

Cleopatra VII (klee•uh•PA•truh) was a queen of ancient Egypt and one of the most fascinating women in history. She was born in 69 B.C., daughter of King Ptolemy XII, the Macedonian ruler of Egypt. In 51 B.C., when Cleopatra was just 17, her father died and she became queen. As was the custom in ancient Egyptian royal families, Cleopatra married her brother, the new king, Ptolemy XIII, who was 15, and the two of them ruled together.

Cleopatra and her brother shared an uneasy rule. In 48 B.C., Ptolemy XIII and his supporters seized power and removed Cleopatra from the throne. Cleopatra, however, was ambitious. She wanted not only to rule

Climate

Cleopatra, shown here in the guise of the Egyptian goddess Isis, was a woman of keen intellect. Although she was descended from the Macedonians, she learned the Egyptian language. In fact, Cleopatra was the only member of the Ptolemaic dynasty to do so.

* **dynasty** succession of rulers from the same family or group

Egypt but also to return it to its previous status as a world power. To this end, when the Roman leader Julius Caesar visited Egypt in 48 B.C., Cleopatra set out to charm and influence him to gain his political backing. Subsequently, civil war broke out in Egypt between Cleopatra and her brother. With the help of Caesar's army, Cleopatra won the war, and her brother died while trying to escape. Cleopatra then married her other brother, Ptolemy XIV, and she again became coruler of Egypt. Shortly thereafter, she gave birth to a boy, Caesarion, who she claimed was Caesar's son.

Caesar and Cleopatra had fallen in love, so soon after Caesar left Egypt for Rome in 47 B.C., Cleopatra joined him. She was still in Rome when he was assassinated by his enemies in 44 B.C. Cleopatra returned to Egypt until the Roman political crisis caused by Caesar's murder was resolved. Three men—Gaius Octavian, Marcus Lepidus, and Marcus Antonius, or Mark Antony—came to power in Rome in 43 B.C. as corulers. Antony, however, wished to rule Rome alone. Cleopatra saw another chance to achieve her own aims. Consequently, when Antony summoned her to Tarsus, she set out with gift-filled ships to win Antony's heart and gain his backing. She succeeded. The two fell in love, and in 40 B.C., Cleopatra gave birth to twins. By 37 B.C., Antony and Cleopatra were married, and the following year, she bore another son by him.

Their marriage was unpopular in Rome, and by Roman law, it was invalid—Antony already had a wife. The Roman government stripped Antony of his title, and Octavian sent an army to destroy Antony and Cleopatra. In 31 B.C., their navy was defeated by Octavian's at the battle at Actium, off the west coast of Greece.

Shortly thereafter, both Antony and Cleopatra committed suicide to avoid being humiliated and probably executed during the anticipated celebration of Octavian's triumph in the battle. Antony stabbed himself, and Cleopatra took her own life by allowing an asp, a poisonous snake, to bite her. She died in 30 B.C., in Alexandria, Egypt, at the age of 39. She was the last ruler of the Ptolemaic dynasty*, which had ruled Egypt since 323 B.C. After Cleopatra's death, Egypt fell under Roman domination. (*See also* **Egypt and the Egyptians; Ptolemy I.**)

CLIMATE

Climate is the pattern of weather in an area over a long period. The climate of a region is typically described in terms of the average temperature and precipitation during the year. The climate of the Near East in ancient times was generally similar to that of the area today. The region was primarily arid or semiarid, with hot summers and mild winters. Rainfall, usually light, occurred mostly in the winter months.

However, these general comments do not give a full picture of the climate of the ancient Near East. First, the period under consideration is vast, and there were changes in climate during those thousands of years. Second, because the Near East is a large region, climate varied locally. Geography, plant life, and nearness to the sea all affected the climate of a particular locale—as did human activity.

Studying Ancient Climates. Studying climate in the ancient Near East is not an easy task. The best tools for studying climate are long-term records of what weather occurred. However, such records are not available for ancient times. Although people there created writing systems thousands of years ago, they did not keep regular weather logs.

Scientists study ancient lake beds to determine the water levels in ancient times and measure the oxygen trapped in layers of polar ice to find the global temperatures at that time. Geologists measure sediment* deposited by rivers and streams to determine how heavy a river's flow was. By analyzing pollen grains, botanists find what plant life existed in ancient times, which hints at the climate in those periods. Botanists also use the width of a tree's growth rings to determine weather patterns. Wider growth rings suggest better climatic conditions; narrower ones represent poorer conditions. By comparing many trees, botanists can assemble a picture of climate conditions of a period. Ancient records can also help in this search. Accounts of floods, crop yields, and activity such as hunting or forestry give an idea of what weather was like. Comparing texts across time and place produces a picture of climate.

Changes Over Time. In the Pleistocene epoch, which lasted until about 9000 B.C., the overall climate of the earth cooled and warmed several times. The periods of cooler climates are called ice ages because vast amounts of water were trapped in sheets of ice called glaciers. Some glaciers formed in the high mountain ranges of ANATOLIA (present-day Turkey), in the CAUCASUS Mountains, and in the mountains of IRAN. Lakes and inland seas were larger then than they are now because the cold air temperatures prevented lake water from evaporating. With little evaporation and cold temperatures, there was little rainfall.

As the last Ice Age ended about 10,000 years ago, temperatures rose. Until about 6000 B.C., temperatures were mild and rainfall was somewhat higher than it is today. Vegetation thrived and forests expanded from the foothills into mountain areas. Grasses spread on the plateaus, inviting game animals. The large numbers of animals and the thriving grasses lured people, who hunted the animals and gathered plants. People also began to domesticate* plants and animals to have a reliable food supply. The climate changes brought about by the end of the ice ages created the circumstances for this important change in human life. Gradually, climate changed again, but at different times in different places. Even as late as 3000 B.C., the deserts of the Near East were moister than they are today. Eventually, the climate in the ancient Near East became much like it is today.

Climate Zones. Egypt lies in a desert zone, where little grows except near a river or an oasis*. The hot season is from May to September, and the cool season is from November to March with transitional periods in between. Near the coast, temperatures range from 99°F to 57°F. Inland desert areas vary from 114°F during the day to 42°F at night. In winter, the temperature often drops below freezing. The wettest area of Egypt lies along the coast, but even there, rainfall is only eight inches per year. Rainfall is much less toward the south. Modern Cairo gets only an inch per year, and it may not rain for years in the desert.

* **sediment** material deposited by water or wind, usually in layers

See map in Geography (vol. 2).

* **domesticate** to adapt or tame for human use

* **oasis** fertile area in a desert made possible by the presence of a spring or well; *pl.* oases

Clothing

CLOTHING

* **steppe** large semiarid grassy plain with few trees

* **Levant** lands bordering the eastern shores of the Mediterranean Sea (present-day Syria, Lebanon, and Israel), the West Bank, and Jordan

Ancient MESOPOTAMIA consisted of three climate zones. The mountainous north had cool summers and cold winters. The dry central region was in a steppe* climate zone. Its mild winters and hot summers supported the growth of large grasslands. Southern Mesopotamia was—and still is—an arid region. Some of the world's highest temperatures have been recorded in southern Iraq. Iran shared these three climate zones.

On the southern edge of Anatolia stand the Zagros Mountains, where cold, wet winters and dry summers support the growth of thick stands of trees. Near the Mediterranean and Aegean coasts, the summers are warm and the winters mild and rainy. The central plateau is a steppe region with a climate similar to that of central Mesopotamia. Southeastern Anatolia is driest and hottest, with summer temperatures averaging more than 85°F.

The climate of ancient SYRIA and the Levant* was similar to that of Anatolia. Hot dry summers and mild winters were typical, with little variation in temperature. Further inland, there were more extremes of temperature. The plateau areas, though dry, were fertile. Rainfall, which generally came in winter, was light, except near the coast.

The Impact of Human Society. The climate of the Near East has changed little in the last 6,000 years. The long history of human activity in the region, however, has added to the difficulty in farming caused by the dryness of the region. Cutting trees and allowing domestic animals to graze extensively have combined to remove valuable roots that hold the soil in place. When rain does fall, then, it runs off quickly instead of seeping into the earth and refilling underground reserves of water. Changing the courses of rivers and building canal systems have contributed to this effect as well. Heavy irrigation has raised the level of salt in the soil, making it nonproductive. (*See also* **Agriculture; Building Materials; Canals; Irrigation; Water.**)

CLOTHING

Most of our knowledge about the clothing of the peoples of the ancient Near East comes from sculptures, cylinder SEALS, and artworks, as well as written descriptions. Because few fabrics have survived the several thousands of years since they were made and worn, little is known about clothing before the development of sculpture and writing. These artworks tend to portray the costumes of the rich and royal, and more men than women and children, except in religious works, where women do appear.

* **fourth millennium** B.C. years from 4000 to 3001 B.C.

Mesopotamia. In the second half of the fourth millennium B.C.*, priest-kings wore a kiltlike skirt woven with a crisscross pattern and a fringe around the hem. Priestesses wore long pieces of fabric draped over the left shoulder and around the body, leaving the right arm bare. From about 3000 to 2300 B.C., men and women wore long sheepskin skirts called *kaunakes*. The wraparound skirts were worn with the wool, which was combed into decorative tufts, on the outside. They were pinned into place and worn down to the knees or to the ankles. Men and women

See
color plate 1,
vol. 2.

wore headdresses of leather or felted wool (thick, tightly woven animal hair), wigs, and elaborate JEWELRY. They went barefoot or wore simple leather sandals.

As evidenced by images on cylinder seals, fashions in Mesopotamia changed around 2300 B.C., when men began to cover their chests with one-shoulder robes similar to those worn by women. Wool fabric with elaborately knotted fringes replaced sheepskin garments. Artwork from about the same time also depicts men wearing robes and kilts of finely pleated material and shoes with upturned toes. They put their hair in a distinctive bun. These new forms of dress were adopted by the Akkadians under Sargon I.

During the Old Babylonian period (ca. 1900–1600 B.C.), with the introduction of tailoring, people began to wear closely fitted garments. Robes became short-sleeved dresses, held in place with belts. Mesopotamians also began to dye fabrics in vivid colors or embroidered geometric patterns. They wore heavy and highly ornamented jewelry. For underwear, women wore a short skirt; men wore a loincloth. Men and women wore sandals or boots made from soft leather or fabric.

Assyrians draped long fringed pieces of fabric around their bodies. Men also wore robes and horizontally patterned woolen kilts that were fastened with belts or sashes. Little is known about women's clothing in Assyria because women were rarely shown in art and sculpture. Assyrian men and women sometimes wore a shawl over the right shoulder, fastened with a fibula, a fancy safety pin, and slippers on their feet.

Remember: Words in small capital letters have separate entries, and the index at the end of this volume will guide you to more information on many topics.

Egypt. Most Egyptian clothing was made of natural-colored linen, a fabric woven from the FLAX plant. Much of the Egyptians' clothing was also made from wool. They sometimes used natural dyes to color their garments, although this was more common during the time of the New Kingdom (ca. 1539–1075 B.C.). From an examination of artwork from the Old and Middle Kingdoms (ca. 2675–1630 B.C.), it is evident that men wore a pleated kilt wrapped around the hips and tied at the waist. Women were generally depicted wearing a plain sheath dress with shoulder straps that often left their breasts exposed. Both men and women wore cloaks.

Around 1500 B.C., Egyptian women began wearing longer, looser garments, which covered one shoulder and fell to the ankles. The robes were fastened beneath the breasts with a sash or belt. They decorated these garments with colorful embroidery, or by creating collar and apron areas. With time, the kilt and draped tunic were decorated with fringes, and embroidered bands adorned hems, sides, and necklines.

Accessories were also quite common in ancient Egypt. Men and women wore shawls, belts, scarves, caps, and gloves. Both sexes wore headdresses, usually in the form of elaborate wigs. Most people went barefoot, but important people wore sandals made from papyrus, palm leaves, or leather.

Members of the royal family wore similar clothing, but the linen used to make their clothes was finely spun and bleached. Their garments were sewn with special care and decorated with beads and metalwork. The wardrobes of the royal family and the wealthy generally included richly

Clothing

This wall painting, from the tomb of Egyptian official Sobekhotep, shows the typical dress of Syrian men during the 1400s B.C. The men are clothed in long-sleeved, close-fitting robes with embroidery and tassels adorning the edges and seams. However, in the next century, perhaps due to the increased popularity of the tapestry loom, dark-colored, patterned robes became the garments of choice among Syrians.

* **archaeologist** scientist who studies past human cultures, usually by excavating material remains of human activity

* **faience** decorated object made of quartz and other materials that includes a glaze

* **Levant** lands bordering the eastern shores of the Mediterranean Sea (present-day Syria, Lebanon, and Israel), the West Bank, and Jordan

embroidered garments, several loincloths, and fringed tunics. In the tomb of the architect Kha, for instance, archaeologists* have found 26 knee-length kilts, 17 sleeveless tunics, and 50 loincloths.

Anatolia. Vases and drinking vessels show that Hittites during the 1300s B.C. wore short, belted tunics (some with sleeves) with fringed or dyed borders. They wore high boots or shoes with upturned toes. Men and women decorated their robes and tunics with pleats, fringes, elaborate embroidery, and knots. In fact, woolen textiles found at ÇATAL HÜYÜK reveal that several techniques of weaving and knotting existed in the region from very early times. Archaeologists have also excavated textiles at Acemhuyuk with blue faience* beads sewn with golden threads.

Syria and the Levant. In both Syria and the Levant*, clothing was similar to that of their more powerful neighboring states, but it was also often quite distinctive. Syrian cylinder seals from the 1700s B.C. show kings wearing wraparound robes with thick edges, perhaps a fur trim. Egyptian tomb paintings from about the same time show Canaanite men and women in brightly colored, full-length woolen dresses with bold geometric patterns. The dresses were draped over one shoulder and pinned with a metal toggle (pin). Women wore high-top closed shoes with laces, while men wore sandals.

Tombs from about 1500 B.C. show people wearing long, white, close-fitting, long-sleeved garments, with seams and edges trimmed with colored, patterned braids and with small tassels at the hem. Later they wore linen garments, perhaps dyed blue and trimmed with multicolored wool.

In Israel, priests wore linen underpants beneath robes or tunics with a fringe or tassel on the bottom four corners. This style was stipulated in the Hebrew BIBLE, along with the requirement that the fringe include a blue thread as a reminder to obey God. Laws in the Bible specified that Israelites could not wear clothing made from a combination of linen and wool. In most periods, working-class men wore the simple short skirt.

Iran. Between 3000 and 1000 B.C., people in Susa in southwestern Iran wore clothing resembling that of their Mesopotamian neighbors, with some local variations. Unlike most peoples of the ancient Near East, who draped lengths of fabric, the Persians of the middle of the first millennium

* **first millennium** B.C. years from 1000 to 1 B.C.

B.C.* wore close-fitting garments. Scholars believe that fitted clothing was practical because the Persians hunted extensively, especially on horseback. They wore animal skins and later made garments from woven cloth. Both men and women wore trousers that were tight at the ankles and tunics or coats with sleeves. They also wore leather shoes and boots. Women additionally wore long veils that covered their heads. (*See also* **Textiles**.)

Coins

See *Money*.

Commerce

See *Economy and Trade*.

In these days of e-mail and telephone, it is hard to imagine a time when long-distance communication was a matter of sending a messenger who might take months to deliver a message and just as long to return with a reply. For most people of the ancient Near East, this kind of communication was impossible—and unnecessary. For rulers and certain businessmen, however, it was crucial.

The Function of Messengers. In the ancient Near East, the messenger between kings played a vital role. The Akkadian word for messenger, *mar shipri,* can be translated as "envoy," "ambassador," "agent," "diplomat," "deputy," and even "merchant," depending on the situation being described. Some messengers simply brought information from one ruler to another. A messenger might be sent to deliver tribute* from a weaker to a stronger power or to bring news of events at a faraway royal court.

* **tribute** payment made by a smaller or weaker party to a more powerful one, often under the threat of force

More important messengers were those who were given a certain amount of authority to make judgments about the responses to the message and to act on the ruler's behalf. These messengers, who were really diplomats, were necessary because of the length of time any negotiation and travel between two lands might take. Such messengers were used to arrange marriages, funerals, and religious ceremonies or to negotiate treaties or the sale of goods.

Messengers could be anyone, male or female, from slaves to members of the royal family. They were valued for their loyalty, speed, and trustworthiness. Women typically carried messages between queens. In some cases, one ruler requested a specific person—someone known and trusted—to bring messages from another ruler.

The choice of messenger was dictated by the situation. If the message was of a personal nature, a king might choose a family member or a trusted member of the royal court. If someone was available who was related to the recipient of the message, that might be a good choice. If danger was foreseen, the messenger might be a soldier.

In the ancient Near East, the position of messenger or diplomat came with many benefits. When visiting kings, messengers received a place to stay as well as normal rations of food. Sometimes, a diplomat might be invited to dine with the king. Some messengers also received gifts, such as clothes and shoes. This relief shows a Median diplomat presenting himself to King Darius of Persia.

The Trials of a Messenger

Around 1080 B.C., an Egyptian messenger named Wen-Amun was sent to the Phoenician city of Byblos to buy timber to build a sacred boat. His journey suggests the difficulties of being a messenger. While traveling by sea, he was robbed in the port of Dor. Though without goods to pay for the timber, he sailed on. Encountering a ship from Dor, he seized silver equal to what had been stolen from him. When he reached Byblos, the prince refused to see him at first. When the prince finally did grant an audience, Wen-Amun did not have the right papers from his master, and he did not have enough silver. The prince was furious. Wen-Amun sent back to Egypt for better gifts, and when he received them, the agreement was made. Just as Wen-Amun was ready to start back, 11 ships from Dor arrived in Byblos and demanded that the prince arrest Wen-Amun for theft. The prince decided in the Egyptian's favor, but on the way home, a storm forced Wen-Amun to land in Cyprus. Threatened by the local people with death, he pleaded for—and won—his life and was allowed to leave. At this point, the account is broken off. How much longer it took Wen-Amun to get home is unknown.

Travel. Messengers often traveled in CARAVANS, so that they could carry supplies and gain protection from bandits. One inscription tells, for example, of a caravan that consisted of 2 messengers and 22 other people that was attacked and robbed. The messengers and 12 others in the caravan were killed. As some protection against this kind of danger, messengers often carried "passports" written by their ruler to all others. The text of one passport is typical:

> To the kings of Canaan, servants of my brother: Thus [says] the king: "I herewith send Akiya, my brother. No one is to hold him up. Provide him with safe entry into Egypt and hand him over to the fortress commander of Egypt. Let him go immediately, and as far as his presents are concerned, he is to owe nothing."

Notwithstanding these precautions, messengers were not always well treated. Many letters containing complaints about the mistreatment of royal messengers have been found in Egypt and elsewhere.

Presenting the Message. When a messenger finally arrived at the destination, the task had only begun. Some messages were admitted, and some were turned away. Some messengers were forced to wait for a long time before they gained an audience with the king.

At last, the messenger stood before the king—and the scribes* and sometimes a translator. If the message did not require negotiation, the messenger would deliver it verbally and then hand over a clay tablet sealed inside a clay "envelope" that had another version of the message written on it. The scribe would read the tablet aloud, and the king would compare the two messages for consistency. When the message was more complex, so was the presentation. A diplomat might present the king's request for some good, such as timber, and then negotiate a price, for example. This could require an extended visit, during which the messenger and any companions stayed at the palace.

Returning Home. The trip to a distant palace was only half of the messenger's job. In order to leave, messengers needed the permission of the ruler of the land they had visited, and they did not always get it. Some found themselves held hostage for years. Those who were allowed

* **scribe** person of a learned class who served as a writer, editor, or teacher

to return were often given escorts by the ruler who had received the message. These escorts might carry responses to the original message, and they, in turn, would be escorted back to their own land when their mission was completed. Not sending an escort was seen as an insult.

The journey home was marked by the same difficulties that plagued the messenger on the first leg of the trip. When the messenger did manage to return home, however, he was often richly rewarded by the king for a difficult job well done.

Communication Within an Empire. As the empires of the ancient Near East grew larger, their governmental organization became more complex. Rulers named local governors to oversee government functions in far-flung territories. Communication between the central government and these distant outposts took on growing importance. Rulers used messengers to deliver edicts*, to order the assembling of an army, or to try to learn about developments in the governors' lands. To make it easier for messengers to travel, rulers built systems of roads that were dotted with inns where their messengers could rest along the way. The PERSIAN EMPIRE included an elaborate system of imperial messengers for these purposes. (*See also* **Government.**)

* **edict** pronouncement of the government that has the force of law

Contracts, Legal

See *Law.*

Copper

See *Metals and Metalworking.*

COSMETICS

* **third millennium** B.C. years from 3000 to 2001 B.C.

* **frankincense and myrrh** fragrant tree resins used to make incense and perfumes

In the ancient Near East, cosmetics were initially used for religious purposes. Over time, people employed them for two other functions: to make themselves more attractive and to heal and protect the skin. The first use of cosmetics, as long ago as the third millennium B.C.*, was ceremonial. Egyptian priests applied cosmetics to the face, especially the eyes, of their statues and other images of their gods. Oils and other preparations were used in embalming to protect and preserve the body after death. Cosmetics were applied to the face of the deceased and were included in the tomb for use in the AFTERLIFE. In coronation ceremonies in Israel and Judah, new kings were anointed with oil.

The hot, dry, and sunny climate caused a great deal of wear and tear on exposed skin, especially the face, hands, and arms. Oils and ointments were used to protect the skin from sun and wind and to make the skin smooth and soft. These ointments were made from plant (thyme, oregano, frankincense and myrrh*, saffron, rosewater) or animal (ground ants' eggs) products. These substances were mixed with almond, saffron, or olive oils or with cat, hippopotamus, or crocodile fat. Egyptians also invented a wrinkle remover, made of oil, beeswax, incense, and cypress

The most information on the use of cosmetics in the ancient Near East comes from Egypt. In ancient times, Egyptian women used an eye makeup called kohl to line their eyes, as seen on this statue of Lady Nofret, which dates from Egypt's Fourth Dynasty. Kohl was made of soot and minerals and was usually stored in tiny stone pots.

See color plate 10, vol. 2.

berries. Cosmetics were expensive, but they were considered a necessity rather than a luxury reserved for the rich. During the reign of RAMSES III (from the 1180s to the 1150s B.C.), tomb workers at Thebes went on strike when their allotment of oils was reduced. Among the Egyptians, cosmetics were worn by both men and women.

Egyptian women used makeup to enhance the beauty of their eyes. They darkened their eyebrows, colored the upper lids, and outlined their eyes with black or gray kohl. Kohl was an eye makeup made of soot and two minerals—antimony and galena, a type of lead. They outlined the lower lids with a green paste made from the mineral malachite. In addition to enhancing beauty, this makeup protected the skin from the sun and repelled flies, which were annoying and carried diseases.

Egyptian women used red ocher to color their cheeks and lips. They used reddish henna, a dye, to color their palms, fingernails, and the soles of their feet. Henna was also used as a hair dye. Another dye (no longer in use) was made of oil mixed with the boiled blood of a black cat or black bull. The Egyptians made abrasives—stones or minerals very finely ground—to whiten their teeth.

Although evidence for the use of cosmetics in Mesopotamia is limited, women did use cosmetics for their eyes and complexion. From the Sumerian royal burials at UR dating from the middle of the third millennium B.C. come cockleshells containing pigments in assorted colors, including yellow, red, green, blue, black, and white. A second millennium B.C.* Mesopotamian text describes the goddess Inanna-Ishtar applying an eye ointment called "Let him come, let him come," prior to her descending into the underworld. Babylonians also used red pigments on their faces. Israelite women used a white face powder made of flour and red coloring on

* **second millennium** B.C. years from 2000 to 1001 B.C.

12

their cheeks. According to religious teachings, a husband was required to give his wife an allowance to buy cosmetics.

Because cosmetics were expensive, they were made a little at a time and stored for long periods. An industry arose to manufacture small containers to store ointments and perfumes. Making these containers became an art form, with containers made of precious stones and carefully decorated. A wealthy woman might own more than half a dozen cosmetics jars, all kept in a painted cedar box. Containers, some with a residue of the contents, have frequently been discovered in tombs. Recipes, too, have been found, explaining what ingredients, and in what combinations, produce the best results.

Egypt became well known for its cosmetics and developed an export industry. Not all cosmetics were purchased, however. Many women prepared their own, assembling the ingredients, grinding them up, and mixing them with oils and fats. A related industry was PERFUMES. Because of the hot temperatures in the ancient Near East, body odor was common. The Egyptians bathed for pleasure, and the Hebrews had ritual bathing requirements, but this did not solve the problem. Perfume helped by covering over natural odors. Perfume manufacture was often kept secret, which increased the cost of scents. Perfumes were a major industry in Mesopotamia, where they had cosmetic, medicinal, and religious uses. Women were the major manufacturers of perfumes in Mesopotamia. Fortunately, a little goes a long way, and if stored in a sealed container in a cool place, perfume lasts. Open perfume bottles were buried in tombs to keep the air fresh and sweet. Not all cultures approved of widespread use of perfume, however. Israelite priests used it as incense* in the temple, but because it had sacred purposes, they were forbidden to give away the secret of making it. They were even forbidden to give any perfume to their wives. (*See also* **Hair.**)

* **incense** fragrant spice or resin burned as an offering

CREATION MYTHS

Myths are stories that give form to a culture's beliefs and values. Among the most recurrent of any culture's myths are its creation stories, which tell how the world came into being. These myths include cosmogonies—accounts of the creation of the physical universe—and occasionally, stories of human origins. Creation myths offer people a way of imagining their place in the universe and their relationship to the gods, other people, and nature. Creation stories in most of the ancient Near East cultures recount that before the world was made, everything was covered with water. This theme can be found in Egyptian, Babylonian, and Hebrew creation myths.

Egypt. A basic Egyptian creation story centered on Atum, a creator god who existed at the beginning of all things, floating in primeval* waters like "he who is in his egg." Just as the waters of Egypt's Nile River receded every year at the end of the flooding season, exposing fertile new soil, the primeval waters drew back from Atum, exposing a mound where he began to create aspects of his own being. This brought about the gradual unfolding of the world. First he sneezed, producing air and the male and

* **primeval** related to the earliest times

* **deity** god or goddess

female deities* Shu and Tefnut. Then he created the earth god Geb and the sky goddess Nut to form a permanent boundary between the newly created world and the surrounding primeval waters.

Atum became the sun god Re, whose rising and setting brought time into the world and mirrored the cycle of life and death. Geb and Nut gave birth to two pairs of deities: OSIRIS and ISIS, who represent order and fertility (and whose son HORUS was associated with kingship), and Seth and Nephthys, representing the necessary opposite qualities of confusion (disorder) and barrenness.

Over time, the priests at different religious centers developed varying versions of the basic story. In MEMPHIS, for example, the primeval creative force of Atum-Re took the form of the god Ptah, the divine craftsman—who was also the local god of Memphis. The version of the story that came from THEBES singled out AMUN as the great creator. As Amun-Re, he became the chief god of Egypt.

Mesopotamia. For the Sumerians and the Babylonians, creation began with an act of separation in which a single body of primeval matter took on different aspects. A Sumerian fragment says that the god ENLIL separated heaven and earth and created the universe. Related myths describe the origin of the sun, moon, cities, temples, and humans. One story describes the god Enki's creation of the pickax and brick mold as gifts to the human race to enable humanity to build its cities.

The best-known Mesopotamian cosmogony is the Babylonian poem *Enuma Elish,* in which an underlying Sumerian story becomes a celebration of the Babylonian god MARDUK, the city of Babylon, and the festival of the New Year. It begins with these words: "When above the heavens were not named, Below, the earth was not called by name."

In this account of creation, the primeval water includes a male part named Apsu and a female part named Tiamat whose mingling produced the gods. The Babylonian *Epic of Creation* is mainly concerned with explaining how Marduk became the supreme god when Tiamat and a host of monsters threatened the gods. Marduk defeated Tiamat in a legendary battle. He and the god EA then organized the universe. There are two versions of the creation of the human race: that people grew out of the

This detail from an Egyptian papyrus dating from the Twenty-first Dynasty depicts Nut, the sky goddess, arching over the earth god Geb. According to one myth, the sky and earth were created when Nut and Geb were separated for eternity after they were seen sharing an embrace. The oceans and seas were created with Geb's tears of despair, when he cried inconsolably at being separated from his beloved Nut.

ground like plants and that the gods molded them from clay mixed with divine blood.

Israelite Culture. The Israelite culture developed a cosmogony that shared elements of myths from Mesopotamia, CANAAN, and the Levant*. The Hebrew Bible contains several accounts of creation. In each case, the universe and its contents are created by the all-powerful god YAHWEH, but details differ in the different versions.

According to the first chapter of the book of Genesis, when Yahweh began to give order to the universe, there were water, earth, wind, and darkness, making this version very close to Greek accounts of creation. The second chapter of Genesis describes the universe before creation as a rainless desert. This may reflect conditions in the Levant, where people depended on rainfall as a source of water. Other accounts say that Yahweh defeated a sea monster named Leviathan before creating an orderly universe. These actions echo those of Marduk and of the Canaanite deity Lotan, who was defeated by BAAL, another Canaanite god.

Mesopotamian elements may also underlie other myths that shaped the main Israelite cosmogony in Genesis. One such Mesopotamian element may be seen in the description of Yahweh molding the first person from earth. Moreover, the paradise that Yahweh planted in Eden for the first humans resembles ancient Sumerian accounts of Dilmun, a peaceful, divine garden in which death and age did not exist. (*See also* **Bible, Hebrew; Gods and Goddesses; Literature; Mythology; Poetry; Religion.**)

* **Levant** lands bordering the eastern shores of the Mediterranean Sea (present-day Syria, Lebanon, and Israel), the West Bank, and Jordan

Cremation

See *Death and Burial.*

CRETE

The largest of the Greek islands, Crete was a thriving trade center in ancient times. Lying between Greece and the Near East, Crete took advantage of its location to establish trade links with its neighbors. These contacts led to the development of the MINOAN CIVILIZATION, which reached its peak between about 1800 and 1400 B.C. At that time, Crete was the chief trading power in the Aegean region.

Geography and Early Settlement. Crete is a long, narrow island in the Mediterranean Sea. Mountains running east to west form the interior. These mountains fall to plains near the northern and southern coasts, which have several good harbors. The climate is Mediterranean, with hot, dry summers and cool, rainy winters.

Crete was first inhabited around 6000 B.C. by Neolithic farmers who probably came from ANATOLIA (present-day Turkey). During the next 3,000 years, pottery making was introduced, and the people became skilled in the use of copper tools. By about 3000 B.C., Cretan farming communities were growing grapes and olives and raising sheep for trade.

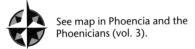

See map in Phoencia and the Phoenicians (vol. 3).

Being able sailors, the Cretans traded wine, oil, and textiles for tin, copper, gold, silver, precious stones, and timber. Trade gave them enough wealth to construct public buildings and homes that comprised some of the earliest towns in the Aegean region.

The Minoan Civilization. Crete's wealth from farming and trading led to the rise of a rich and accomplished civilization around 2000 B.C. Historians call it the Minoan civilization, after King Minos of Greek legend. The development of new towns and villages gave rise to a class of skilled artisans*, such as metalworkers, potters, and weavers. Metalworkers used bronze, an alloy of tin and copper, to make jewelry, tools, and weapons. They used gold, silver, and precious stones to make jewelry worn by Crete's growing upper class. All the metals had to be imported to Crete, but the finished products created by Minoan artisans were traded throughout the Mediterranean. For a time, Crete controlled the trade routes that crossed the eastern Mediterranean.

The Minoan civilization was centered on enormous palaces on the island. The largest of these was at KNOSSOS near the northern coast. It served as Crete's religious, social, and trading center. The palaces reveal the island's prosperity and suggest that Minoan civilization had developed into an ordered, hierarchical society run by a wealthy elite.

In about 1700 B.C., most palaces on the island were destroyed, probably by an earthquake. The Minoan culture continued to flourish, however, and the palaces were reconstructed on an even grander scale. The architecture of the new palaces was sophisticated. There were grand stairways and courtyards. Graceful columns, wide at the top and narrow at the base, supported roofs. An elaborate plumbing and drainage system used clay pipes to carry rainwater from the roof and set pipes and channels beneath the floor to carry water away from the palaces.

In these palaces, archaeologists* have found CLAY TABLETS inscribed with writing. Around the time that the palaces were rebuilt, the style of writing changed from the use of picture symbols to a system using horizontal and vertical lines. This system has been called Linear A, but it has never been fully deciphered. A later form of Cretan writing—called Linear B—was deciphered in the A.D. 1950s and was found to be an early dialect of Greek. Most of these texts that have been translated are accounts—records of the thriving Cretan trade.

The walls of the palaces on Crete were decorated with magnificent frescoes* illustrating palace ceremonies. Among the first frescoes discovered was a procession of people carrying pottery and other goods. The hairstyles and clothing of these figures were remarkably like those seen in tomb paintings in Egypt. Egyptian writing in these tombs said the people came from Keftiu, "the isles in the midst of the sea." With the discovery of the paintings on Crete, archaeologists concluded that Crete was the origin of the figures in those Egyptian paintings.

The frescoes in Crete also reveal that women held an important position in Minoan society. Their religion centered on a mother goddess, and priestesses played important roles in cults*. Some scholars have suggested that Minoan society was matriarchal*, though that view is not widely held.

* **artisan** skilled craftsperson

* **archaeologist** scientist who studies past human cultures, usually by excavating material remains of human activity

* **fresco** method of painting in which color is applied to moist plaster so that it becomes chemically bonded to the plaster as it dries; also, a painting done in this manner

* **cult** system of religious beliefs and rituals; group following these beliefs

* **matriarchal** society in which women hold the dominant position

A popular fresco motif throughout the ancient Near East was that of the bull-jump. This fresco, dating from the 1500s B.C., adorns a palace wall at Knossos, a Cretan city rich in frescoes. Other popular Cretan motifs include bird, cat, ape, and deer scenes, as well as seascapes with dolphins and octopuses. Human figures are rare.

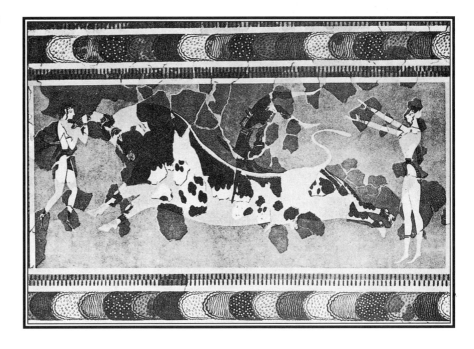

Finding the Minoans

Minoan civilization was unknown until about A.D. 1900 and was only discovered by accident. British archaeologist Arthur Evans was shown some ancient objects that he was told were found in Crete. Recognizing them as unusual, he went to the island to look further. Searching at the site of Knossos, he found a large mound of earth, where he began to dig. Evans's work uncovered the palace at Knossos, which he proceeded to excavate for several years. Eventually, Evans decided not only to excavate the palace but also to restore large parts to its original splendor. This decision to reconstruct was highly controversial. Evans defended it by saying that "without restoration the Palace would be a meaningless heap of ruins."

* **first millennium B.C.** years between 1000 and 1 B.C.

* **city-state** independent state consisting of a city and its surrounding territory

Minoan frescoes contain almost no scenes of battles or warriors. This, coupled with the fact that the palaces had no defense systems, suggests that the Minoans lived in peace. They were probably aided in this by the fact that Crete was a sea power in an age when most Near Eastern kingdoms focused on building their power on land.

By about 1600 B.C., the Minoans had reached the height of their wealth. Wealthy people built spacious homes around the palaces and in the surrounding countryside. Smaller towns had clusters of houses for farmers, fishermen, sailors of the Minoan merchant ships, and artisans. Life for the Minoans appears to have been peaceful and pleasurable.

These pleasures came to a sudden end, however, around 1500 B.C., when the nearby volcanic island of Thera exploded. The eruption generated powerful earthquakes and sent enormous tidal waves crashing into Crete. The damage to towns and palaces was repaired; however, around 1400 B.C., a new catastrophe occurred, one in which many coastal towns and palaces were burned, perhaps as a result of an invasion from the mainland. Although the island remained an important center of trade, power in the Aegean passed to the Mycenaean Greeks on the mainland.

Greek and Roman Rule. Sometime after 1200 B.C., a northern Greek tribe, the Dorians, took control of the island. During the first millennium B.C.*, numerous city-states* came into being on the mainland and struggled with each other to gain power. Following the Macedonian conquest and the death of Alexander the Great, Crete became for many years the base of operation for pirates throughout the Aegean and eastern Mediterranean Seas. Toward the end of the first millennium B.C., Rome became the dominant power in the Mediterranean. In 67 B.C., the Romans took over the island of Crete and made it a Roman province. (*See also* **Aegean Sea; Mediterranean Sea, Trade on; Mycenae and the Mycenaeans; Palaces and Temples; Shipping Routes.**)

Croesus

See *Lydia and the Lydians*.

CULTS

Today the term *cult* is commonly used in reference to an untraditional religion or to a group that is committed to unusual teachings or practices. Modern cults are also associated with the extreme behaviors of their members and are not viewed as legitimate religions. When discussing religion in the ancient Near East, this use of the word *cult* is not valid. Rather, it refers to the links ancient peoples felt with their gods and how they expressed their devotion and beliefs.

Religions of the ancient Near East included various cultic activities. In terms of the ancient Near East, a cult refers to the act of worship by a group of people united in its devotion to a particular god or belief. The term also refers to the system that unites the people in their beliefs. This devotion was demonstrated in routine acts of worship, which could include prayers, processions, the adoration of images, gestures, and sacrifice. These rituals sometimes took place in sacred places, such as temples or shrines.

Many ancient Near Eastern cults focused on deities*. The Mesopotamians, for example, recognized many gods, but certain cults were devoted to individual gods such as ENLIL, god of the earth and air. Their cult activities followed a regular pattern based on sacred calendars. Other cults concentrated on a single aspect of general religious belief. An example is the cult of the dead, which was widespread in Egypt and called for elaborate burial practices to ensure peaceful life after death.

Some cults were official; that is, they were supported by the government and were meant to solidify the connection among a god, a ruling elite, and the people. For instance, the Mesopotamians believed that the purpose of the government was to provide the gods with everything they needed so that the gods, in turn, would help the people flourish. The ruler, who represented his subjects before the gods, was responsible for carrying out the important rituals. These rituals guaranteed the survival of both the state and its inhabitants because a god might turn vengeful if not worshiped properly.

Throughout the ancient Near East, all people attended public processions involving images of the gods. An important part of the cult festival took place within the temple. Only priests were allowed in the sanctuary*. However, some people had opportunities to take part in these special acts. In Egypt, high-ranking people could temporarily serve as assistants to the priests for periods of up to a month.

Rituals conducted by cult priests and priestesses in some societies, such as those of the Babylonians and the Elamites of ancient IRAN included animal blood sacrifices to the gods. Often these rituals took place not in temples but in holy groves, fenced-in areas of sacred forest with altars at their centers. Elamite cult activities always included music. Music and dance were also involved in the cult festivals and processions of the Hittites of Anatolia (present-day Turkey).

Archaeologists* have unearthed many artifacts* related to cults. These include bowls used to hold OFFERINGS to the gods and knives used to conduct

* **deity** god or goddess

* **sanctuary** most sacred part of a religious building

* **archaeologist** scientist who studies past human cultures, usually by excavating material remains of human activity

* **artifact** ornament, tool, weapon, or other object made by humans

the ritual killing of sacrificial animals. Many of these objects are images representing the gods themselves. Egyptian cult images, generally small and made of wood, depicted the gods in human form, sometimes with animal heads. They were kept in mysterious darkness in the sanctuary. The priest's task was to worship, clean, clothe, and protect these images from evil.

Mesopotamian cult figures were also represented by wooden statues in human form. Their faces and hands were plated with gold, and their beards were made of precious stones. Such a statue was considered a manifestation of the god. Priests fed it twice a day and supplied it with music, fragrant incense, and clothing. (*See also* **Gods and Goddesses; Religion; Rituals and Sacrifice.**)

CUNEIFORM

The world's oldest form of writing, cuneiform (kyu•NEE•uh•fawrm) takes its name from the distinctive marks used to create its signs. Cuneiform originated around 3100 B.C. in Sumer in southern MESOPOTAMIA. Eventually, it was adopted throughout that region and remained in use for more than 3,000 years. When cuneiform was deciphered* in the A.D. 1800s, it was a major breakthrough in ancient Near Eastern studies.

The Beginnings. From as early as the ninth millennium B.C.*, people had been using small variously shaped pieces of clay, called tokens, in a system of accounting where each token stood for units of goods. The use of tokens increased rapidly after 3500 B.C., when large-scale trade began, especially in Sumer. During the next 400 years, accountants went from placing the tokens inside hollow clay balls to drawing diagrams of the tokens on flat, palm-sized clay tablets. This change first occurred in the southern city of URUK. The illustrations were scratched onto the tablets and ranged from abstract to realistic drawings of the objects they represented. For example, the symbol for sheep was a circle with an *X* in it, and the symbol for a bull resembled a bull's horned head.

Soon scribes* began to use a stylus—a reed with a triangular-shaped tip—to press the shape of the symbol into the surface of the clay. It was from the shape of the mark left by the stylus that the system gained its name. In Latin, the term *cuneus* means "wedge" and *forma* means "shape." This marked the beginning of cuneiform writing.

Each push of the stylus into the clay created a wedge-shaped impression with a tail, which was formed when the stylus was drawn across the surface. Over time, the signs became more stylized* and consisted of a specific number of wedges. Each wedge, with or without a tail, could be oriented vertically, horizontally, or diagonally. For example, the sign for sheep became a square with a cross in it.

By 3100 B.C., about 1,200 signs were in use, but they did not represent the sounds of any ancient Near Eastern language. Instead, they were ideographs that conveyed an idea to the viewer, much like a red eight-sided sign at any street corner around the world today tells the driver to stop no matter what language the driver actually speaks.

According to Sumerian mythology, Enmerkar, the king of Uruk during the early third millennium B.C.*, was the first to use cuneiform signs

* **decipher** to decode and interpret the meaning of

* **ninth millennium** B.C. years from 9000 to 8001 B.C.

* **scribe** person of a learned class who served as a writer, editor, or teacher

* **stylized** referring to art style in which figures are portrayed in simplified ways that exaggerate certain features, not realistically

* **third millennium** B.C. years from 3000 to 2001 B.C.

Cuneiform

to represent actual speech. Enmerkar might have used the signs to represent spoken sounds in the Sumerian language and not just objects or ideas. The Akkadians adopted cuneiform shortly after 2400 B.C., soon after they rose to power in Mesopotamia. They needed only half as many signs, most of which represented the sounds of syllables, such as /ab/, /ib/, /ba/, and /bi/, to spell out the words of their language. Around the same time, the direction in which scribes wrote began to change. The signs on the earliest tablets were written in columns from top to bottom and from right to left. Toward the end of the third millennium B.C., the signs were written from left to right in horizontal rows from top to bottom.

Who Used Cuneiform? Cuneiform was used by many cultures in the ancient Near East, especially in Mesopotamia. The Akkadians used one-syllable Sumerian words to stand for sounds in their own language, added symbols for sounds that did not exist in Sumerian, and adopted

This table shows the evolution of cuneiform writing and the phonetic values associated with cuneiform signs. Initially, the symbols were drawings of the objects they represented, such as the symbols seen in the first column. Over time, the signs became more stylized and represented the sounds of syllables used to spell out the words.

DEVELOPMENT OF THE CUNEIFORM SCRIPT

Early Pictograph	Later Pictograph	Early Cuneiform (Babylonian)	Later Cuneiform (Assyrian)	Original or Derived Meaning	Phonetic Value
				bird	khu
				fish	kha
				donkey	—
				ox	gu
				sun day	ud tam tu
				grain	she
				orchard	shar
				to plow to till	pin
				boomerang to throw to throw down	ru shub
				to stand to go	du

20

some Sumerian words. The royal inscriptions of SARGON I, who founded the Akkadian empire, were written in cuneiform. The Babylonians of central Mesopotamia and the Assyrians of northern Mesopotamia also used the system for writing their Akkadian dialects*. Akkadian cuneiform was used in other regions as well.

During the 1300s B.C., the Egyptians, the people of CANAAN, and others in the Levant* used the Akkadian language and cuneiform to communicate among themselves and with foreign rulers. The script was also used to record the languages spoken by the Hittites and others of central ANATOLIA (present-day Turkey) and by the Hurrians of northern Mesopotamia. During the early first millennium B.C. (1000–1 B.C.), the script was used by Urartian kings in Anatolia. Other cuneiform systems with unique sign-forms were developed in the early 2000s B.C. in Elam in southern IRAN, in the 1300s B.C. in Ugarit in north SYRIA, and in the mid-500s B.C. by scribes in the PERSIAN EMPIRE.

How Many Characters? The number of symbols used in the ancient Near East varied tremendously. Sumerians and Babylonians each used about 600 cuneiform symbols, or characters. Some consisted of a single wedge, or mark of the stylus, while others required up to 30 wedges. Other cuneiform scripts had fewer characters. The Hittites used about 350 characters, the Elamites 163, the Persians 36, and just 30 at Ugarit.

Scribes did not always use all the signs available when writing a particular text. During the rule of the Babylonian king HAMMURABI in the 1700s B.C., scribes wrote messages using only 80 or so signs. Assyrian traders who traveled from Mesopotamia to Anatolia maintained their accounts using only 60 or 70 signs. Managing to communicate with fewer signs enabled more people to learn to read and write.

Discovery and Decipherment. Clay tablets are durable, and almost half a million of them have been found during the last two centuries. For the longest time, though, nobody knew what they said because nobody could decipher the script. In the A.D. 1760s, a Danish traveler returning from PERSEPOLIS brought back to Europe the first accurate copies of the BEHISTUN INSCRIPTION, which was written in three styles of cuneiform—Old Persian, Elamite, and Akkadian. It took more than 40 years for scholars, including the German Georg Grotefend and the Irishman Edward Hincks, to decipher the Old Persian—the simplest of the three writings. Almost simultaneously, the Englishman Henry Rawlinson, working with copies he himself had made of the Behistun inscription, also deciphered the Old Persian portions. The second type of cuneiform, Elamite, remains only imperfectly understood to this day. The third and most complex type of cuneiform—Akkadian—was deciphered only in the 1800s, when large numbers of inscriptions were excavated at Assyrian capital cities, enabling Hincks, Rawlinson, and others to decipher the script.

Scholars face many problems in deciphering cuneiform. One problem is that each symbol had many uses. To understand, consider an example in English. Suppose a symbol is derived from a pictograph* for eye. This symbol could mean "eye" or the long *i* sound heard in *bite* and *fight* or the word *I*. The principle was the same in cuneiform. A sign could

* **dialect** regional form of a spoken language with distinct pronunciation, vocabulary, and grammar

* **Levant** lands bordering the eastern shores of the Mediterranean Sea (present-day Syria, Lebanon, and Israel), the West Bank, and Jordan

See color plate 5, vol. 2.

* **pictograph** graphic character used in a picture writing system

represent one or more syllables or one or more words. The sign could also be a "determinative," which helped the reader identify the type of the word with which it was written. A determinative tells the reader if the word next to it is a god, a person's name, an occupation, the name of a city, or the name of a country.

Moreover, cuneiform was used by many peoples over a long period of time, resulting in regional differences both within and between regions. Scribes had distinctive styles for particular kinds of texts. They followed certain rules when writing government texts and other rules for writing letters. For this reason, many scholars focus their study only on particular kinds of texts. (*See also* **Alphabets; Decipherment.**)

Cylinder Seals

See *Seals.*

CYPRUS

* **Levant** lands bordering the eastern shores of the Mediterranean Sea (present-day Syria, Lebanon, and Israel), the West Bank, and Jordan

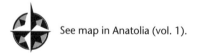

See map in Anatolia (vol. 1).

The island of Cyprus (SY•pruhs) is located in the Mediterranean Sea to the south of ANATOLIA (present-day Turkey) and to the west of the Levant*. The island is dominated by two mountain ranges separated by fertile plains. Around its coastline, it has many natural harbors—safe havens for trading vessels. In ancient times, Cyprus was a thriving trade center because of its location. Moreover, the island had rich deposits of copper at a time when demand for copper was high. Trade brought wealth to Cyprus, but this wealth attracted conquerors. As a result, Cyprus was ruled by many groups of people during its long history.

The first people to settle on Cyprus are believed to have come from Anatolia, perhaps as long ago as 6000 B.C. However, little is known about these early settlers. Over time, more settlers reached the island, including HURRIANS, SEMITES, HITTITES, and Egyptians. Settlements increased in size and number, and the island's economy grew. People raised cattle, sheep, and goats and produced textiles, pottery, and other specialized goods. From the abundant copper on the island, they made tools, weapons, and jewelry. As demand for copper grew, trade with other areas increased. By 1400 B.C., Cyprus had developed a city-based complex society and was the hub of a thriving trade network.

Around 1200 B.C., Cyprus was colonized by Mycenaeans from Greece, who left a pronounced Greek influence that remains to the present day. Soon after, raids by the so-called SEA PEOPLES, not only on Cyprus but throughout the eastern Mediterranean, interrupted trade. The invasions had less of an effect on Cyprus than on many other areas, perhaps because the island had a stable political and economic system. Cyprus opened new trade routes, began to work in iron (which replaced bronze as the preferred metal for tools and weapons), and continued to prosper.

By 800 B.C., Phoenicians, and then Assyrians, began to settle on Cyprus. Within 200 years, the island was divided into at least ten separate kingdoms, all of which were very wealthy. Short-lived conquests by Egypt and Persia followed, and in 330 B.C., Cyprus was conquered by ALEXANDER

THE GREAT. After the death of Alexander in 323 B.C., Egypt took control of the island again. Then in 67 B.C., Cyprus was taken over by Rome. The Romans drained the island's great wealth by demanding high taxes from its residents. (*See also* **Greece and the Greeks; Mediterranean Sea, Trade on; Metals and Metalworking; Mycenae and the Mycenaeans; Shipping Routes.**)

CYRUS THE GREAT

ruled 559–529 B.C.
King of Persia

* **Levant** lands bordering the eastern shores of the Mediterranean Sea (present-day Syria, Lebanon, and Israel), the West Bank, and Jordan

* **vassal** individual or state that swears loyalty and obedience to a greater power

* **propaganda** communication deliberately shaped or slanted toward a particular viewpoint

* **imperial** pertaining to an emperor or an empire

* **nomad** person who travels from place to place to find food and pasture

Cyrus the Great (SY•ruhs) founded the PERSIAN EMPIRE, which extended from ANATOLIA (present-day Turkey), through the Levant*, MESOPOTAMIA, and IRAN, to northern Arabia and present-day Pakistan and Afghanistan. Cyrus was known as a benevolent king because he treated conquered peoples kindly.

The details of Cyrus's early life are sketchy. He was born into a noble family and became king of the Persians in 559 B.C. At the time, the Persians had a small kingdom in southern Iran. They were vassals* of the MEDES, whose kingdom stretched from Iran and the Persian Gulf to the border of Lydia, a kingdom in Anatolia.

In support of the Babylonian king NABONIDUS, who wanted to retake a city in Syria, Cyrus created a diversion by rebelling against the Median king Astyages, who was his grandfather. Cyrus succeeded in 550 B.C., in part because a portion of the Median army changed to his side. Hearing of the Medes' defeat, King Croesus of Lydia tried to expand his own territory, but Cyrus moved his army west and defeated Croesus in 547 B.C. Cyrus also conquered Greek settlements on the Aegean coast of Anatolia and then turned his attention to Babylonia. Cyrus's conquest of that region was completed in 539 B.C., when he marched triumphantly into BABYLON, then considered the greatest city in the world. In just over ten years, Persia had gained a huge empire.

Cyrus used propaganda* to win the favor of the peoples he conquered. For instance, he spread rumors that Astyages tried to kill him as an infant. He also said that Nabonidus abandoned the worship of the god MARDUK, suggesting that he deserved to fall from power.

Cyrus shrewdly followed policies aimed at winning support. Rather than putting his own people in charge of conquered territories, he kept their local rulers in place. He won the favor of the Babylonians by following the customs of the temple of Marduk. He allowed the many peoples in his empire to keep their own religions and worship their own gods. The Jews supported him because he allowed them to return home after they had been forced from their homes in Judah by the Babylonian king NEBUCHADNEZZER II and had lived in Babylonia for about 50 years.

Cyrus was open to borrowing ideas from other peoples. His imperial* government followed the model of the Median empire. The capital that he built at Pasargadae shows the influence of many cultures, including those of the Elamites, Assyrians, Greeks, and Egyptians.

Cyrus died in 529 B.C. while trying to defeat a tribe of nomads* in Central Asia, although the exact circumstances are in dispute. One version of the story says Cyrus was killed by the nomads' queen after defeat

in battle. At his death, the Persian empire passed to his son CAMBYSES. For the peoples of the ancient world, Cyrus became a model of a wise ruler. Persians considered him the founder of their greatness, but his reputation extended beyond his own people.

DAMASCUS

* **second millennium** B.C. years from 2000 to 1001 B.C.

See map in Syria (vol. 4).

* **provincial** having to do with the provinces, outlying districts, administrative divisions, or conquered territories of a country or empire

Situated in southwestern SYRIA, the city of Damascus (duh•MAS•kuhs) has been inhabited since the middle of the second millennium B.C.* However, evidence of its existence can only be found in texts because Damascus has never been excavated. At the edge of a desert and near an easy route to the Mediterranean Sea, Damascus was well positioned to allow its inhabitants to control TRADE ROUTES. The city was also in a fertile region and could produce enough food to support a growing community.

Between about 1400 and 1000 B.C., Damascus was influenced by Egypt, but local rulers remained in power. By the 800s B.C., the city had become the center of one of the kingdoms of the ARAMAEANS. The people of Damascus joined forces with other Aramaeans and repulsed several attacks by the Assyrians. Still, in 732 B.C., the Assyrians seized the region and incorporated Damascus into their empire. After the collapse of Assyrian power in the 600s B.C., control of the city passed to the Babylonians, and in the 500s B.C., to the Persians.

In 333 B.C., Damascus became part of the empire of ALEXANDER THE GREAT. Later the city became a provincial* capital of the SELEUCID EMPIRE. In 85 B.C., the Nabateans took over and controlled Damascus until about 65 B.C., when it was incorporated into the Roman Empire. Damascus then flourished as a commercial center. It later became an important center of Christianity until it was conquered by Muslims in the A.D. 600s. Today Damascus is the capital and largest city of Syria.

DANCE

* **second millennium** B.C. years from 2000 to 1001 B.C.

Pictures painted on the walls of tombs and on POTTERY, engravings on SEALS, and descriptions in texts are the main sources of information about dance in the ancient Near East. They show or describe the kinds of dance steps, the occasions for dance, and the formations for dancing. Ancient Near Eastern peoples danced for entertainment, recreation, and during religious celebrations.

Mesopotamia. Images of dancing in ancient MESOPOTAMIA date back to the times before writing, which began around 3000 B.C. Most dance images are from the early second millennium B.C.*, but there are few pictorial depictions of dance after 1000 B.C. Mesopotamian dance shaped dance in ancient Egypt and Greece, and some dance forms performed in ancient Mesopotamia can be seen today.

Dance was performed on many occasions, including religious and other celebrations, such as weddings and harvest festivals. Sometimes

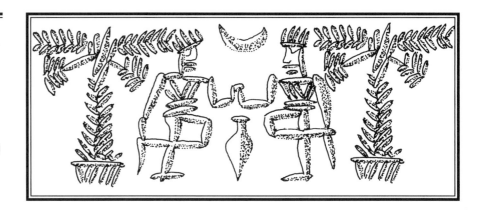

How do scholars determine from looking at an ancient painting or seal that a figure is dancing? They look for clues that identify dance movements, such as one or more feet in the air, raised arms, exaggerated postures, conga line, and flying hair. Movements such as these are evident in this drawing of a seal from the Old Babylonian Period, which shows dancers doing the "foot-clutch" step.

See
color plate 2,
vol. 2.

dancers performed special dances to repel sickness or to protect people in mourning from demons. In these cases, the dancers might form a circle around the person as they danced.

People danced alone, in pairs, and in groups. Both men and women danced, but instead of dancing together, they took turns dancing. While one group danced, the other sang. Dancers also performed a variety of steps including jumping and leaping, kneeling and bending, and dancing on pointed toes. Line dances and circle dances were performed mainly by women. Men only performed three dances. In the squat dance, they danced with their knees bent, alternately thrusting one leg to the side (similar to the famous folk dance of the Russian Cossacks). In the foot-clutch dance, a group of dancers danced on one leg while holding the other leg bent in front or back. In the "whirl," they spun around in circles, like the whirling dervishes of one branch of Islam.

Some dancers were musicians too. There are pictures of women dancers striking small, handheld drums while they danced. Other illustrations show women dancers playing lyres and male dancers playing lutes. Dancers also clapped their hands and snapped their fingers as they danced.

Egypt. The first evidence of Egyptian dance dates from the Old Kingdom (ca. 2675–2130 B.C.). At the time, dances were part of the ceremony that marked the rebirth of the god Osiris. They were also important in the worship of Hathor, goddess of love.

Temples retained groups of professional dancers who danced to honor particular gods in regular observances and at special festivals. Most of the dancers were women, although they dressed and wore their hair like young men. In fact, the picture of a male dancer was the hieroglyphic sign for "to dance."

The oldest dances in Egypt were formal and stately. The movements followed a set pattern, with groups of dancers performing the same movements in formation. For example, in one dance to Hathor (who was associated with the cow), women dancers held their arms aloft, like the horns of a cow. In another dance, female dancers held mirrors and handheld instruments called clappers (both associated with Hathor) as they danced. Sometimes acrobatics formed part of the dance—indeed, the same word was used for both dance and acrobatics.

Dance

During the time of the Middle Kingdom (ca. 1980–1630 B.C.), many dances were performed outdoors. Performers danced as the statue of a tomb owner was brought in a procession to the tomb. They also danced at the funeral rites. As in the earlier period, performances included both stately formal dances and more vigorous acrobatic moves.

While these religious dances continued to be practiced, a new stage for dancing appeared in Egypt during the period of the New Kingdom (ca. 1539–1075 B.C.). During this period of conquest and prosperity, some wealthy people began to maintain their own permanent group of musicians and dancers, who were considered valuable possessions. Others hired dancers when they needed them for special occasions such as banquets. Written records detail the fact that some dancers were brought in from other regions of Africa, such as Nubia, or from as far away as India. These dancers often wore few clothes, which emphasized the grace of their movements.

Anatolia. Information on Hittite dance comes mainly from written records; only a few pottery fragments have been found to give any visual information. These texts relate only to sacred dance. Nothing is known about the role of dance in people's daily lives. Some of the texts are not completely clear. They speak of performers dancing "in the style of the city of Lakhshan"—but scholars have no idea what that style was.

What is known is that there were many variations of dance steps and movements. These included leaping, turning, running, bending the knees, standing on the head or hands, and mime dancing ("in the manner of a leopard," for example).

Both men and women danced. There were professional dancers and those who just danced occasionally. Many of the dances were performed in groups in which all the participants made the same movements. In some cases, though, a single dancer would separate from the group to perform acrobatic movements.

Occasions for dance included important religious festivals. At the spring festival, for example, dancers surrounded the king and queen as they led a parade of dignitaries to the temple. When the procession arrived at the temple, a solo dancer performed a spinning dance to welcome them. At a procession initiating a hunt festival, special mime dancers re-created hunting scenes, portraying animals and archers.

* **Levant** lands bordering the eastern shores of the Mediterranean Sea (present-day Syria, Lebanon, and Israel), the West Bank, and Jordan

The Levant. In the Levant*, celebrations such as weddings and royal coronations gave people a chance to dance to the sounds of instruments such as tambourines, lyres, and harps. In addition, processions of women with hand drums often performed dances following military victories, joining triumphant soldiers in their march to the sanctuary of Yahweh.

The use of dance for religious purposes can be seen, for example, in the frenzied dancing of the Israelites in their worship of the golden calf. In addition, several books of the Hebrew Bible describe prophets as dancing ecstatically while prophesying. People also danced at times of sickness, the idea being that singing and dancing would cure the ill by driving away the demons that caused the malady. (*See also* **Entertainment; Music and Musical Instruments.**)

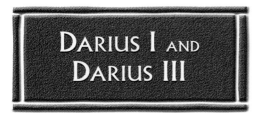

DARIUS I AND DARIUS III

Darius I
ruled 521–486 B.C.
King of Persia
Darius III
ruled 336–330 B.C.
King of Persia

* **nomadic** referring to people who travel from place to place to find food and pasture

* **satrapy** portion of Persian-controlled territory under the rule of a satrap, or provincial governor

* **eunuch** man who has been castrated, or has had his testicles removed

Darius I respected the religious beliefs of the peoples in his kingdom. Instead of trying to unite his empire under one religion, he built a temple to Amun in Egypt and allowed the Jews to rebuild their temple in Jerusalem.

Darius I (duh•RY•uhs), also known as Darius the Great, was one of the greatest rulers of the Achaemenid dynasty. He extended the PERSIAN EMPIRE and created an enduring political structure. About 150 years after the death of Darius I, the last king of the dynasty, Darius III, inherited a weakened empire that was eventually conquered.

Although Darius I was not the rightful successor, he seized the throne after the death of CAMBYSES. He strengthened his frontiers to prevent nomadic* tribes from overrunning the borders. He conquered the Indus Valley to the east, and Thrace, Macedonia, and several Aegean islands in the west. He hoped to conquer Greece as well but failed in 490 B.C., when the Athenians defeated his forces at Marathon. Darius recorded his version of his rise to power in the BEHISTUN INSCRIPTION.

Darius I was an able administrator. He organized the empire into 20 satrapies*. Each was required to pay taxes in the form of money, horses, and other items, as well as to provide ships or soldiers for the Persian military. Darius was also known for his achievements as a builder. He oversaw the construction of a network of roads radiating from his capital at SUSA, including the Royal Road, which stretched 1,500 miles from SARDIS on the Aegean Sea to Susa. Around 510 B.C., he began his most ambitious project, a royal complex at PERSEPOLIS, which included the king's palace, smaller palaces, and meeting halls.

Darius I was succeeded by his son XERXES. Several other rulers followed, until Darius III came to power in 336 B.C. By that time, the Persian empire was weak and vulnerable. The satraps had been rebelling, and there was general unrest. Darius III had been raised to the throne by the powerful eunuch* Bagoas, who had poisoned the two previous kings. When Darius tried to free himself of Bagoas's control, Bagoas tried to poison him. Instead, Darius forced Bagoas to drink the poison.

In 337 B.C., King Philip of Macedonia sent his forces into ANATOLIA (present-day Turkey) to liberate the Greek cities there from Persian rule. Philip was murdered before he could accomplish this. In 334 B.C., his son ALEXANDER THE GREAT led an army into Anatolia. Darius was not prepared for this invasion, and despite having a much larger army, he was defeated at the battle of Issus. Hoping to avoid further battles, Darius sent Alexander letters offering friendship. His offers were rejected, and Alcxander led his armies into Mesopotamia. Darius fought him again in 331 B.C. but was defeated and forced to flee. Soon after, Darius III was killed by his satrap Bessus. With his death, the Achaemenid dynasty ended, enabling Alexander to declare himself king of Persia.

DATE PALMS AND DATES

Date palms grow very well in the arid, desert climate of the Near East. Dates—the fruit of the date palm—were an important food crop in the region in ancient times, as they are today. Other parts of the date palm, including the trunk and leaves, were used for a variety of purposes.

Cultivated since the fourth millennuim B.C.*, date palms are among the earliest domesticated fruit crops. The peoples of the Levant* and MESOPOTAMIA probably first began to cultivate date palms, and from those

David

* **fourth millennium** B.C. years from 4000 to 3001 B.C.

* **Levant** lands bordering the eastern shores of the Mediterranean Sea (present-day Syria, Lebanon, and Israel), the West Bank, and Jordan

* **oasis** fertile area in a desert made possible by the presence of a spring or well; *pl.* oases

regions, their cultivation quickly spread throughout the river valleys of the Near East and along the NILE RIVER of Egypt.

Date palms grow as tall as 100 feet and have clusters of long, feather-like leaves atop slender trunks. Dates are sweet and nutritious fruits that grow in large clusters of up to 1,000 per bunch. A single date palm can produce more than 100 pounds of fruit each year. Although date palms grow best in an arid climate, their roots need a regular supply of water. Consequently, dates were grown along rivers, at oases*, or on irrigated sites. Date palms were also grown in orchards and vegetable gardens, where they provided shade for other plants.

The cultivation of date palms required time and money. It took 4 to 5 years before a tree would bear fruit, and about 20 years for the tree to reach full productivity. However, they were valuable and every part of the tree could be used. The trunks, leaves, and other parts of the palm were used as building material or fuel and for making rope and baskets. Dates were also used to make an alcoholic beverage.(*See also* **Agriculture; Food and Drink; Irrigation.**)

DAVID

ruled ca. 1000–970 B.C.
King of Israel

Searching for David

Most of what is known about King David comes from the Bible, which some would argue is not an accurate historical record. There is very little archaeological evidence to prove that David, or other early kings of ancient Israel, really existed or to reveal much of their real lives. One important piece of evidence comes from an ancient site known as Tel Dan (present-day Tell al-Qadi), located in the northernmost part of present-day Israel. The Tel Dan site contains ruins of an early religious complex, including a two-room temple. Among the finds at the site was a fragment of a large inscribed stone slab with the words *House of David*. The temple complex dates from a later period than that of David's rule. Nevertheless, the artifact does refer to King David and his descendants.

As king of Israel, David united the 12 tribes of Israel and founded a strong kingdom for his people. David, whose story is told in the Hebrew BIBLE, holds an important place in JUDAISM as an ideal king who achieved great things and who founded an enduring dynasty*.

David was the son of Jesse, a wealthy landowner of the tribe of Judah in the land of Judah. The youngest of eight sons, he grew up tending his father's sheep and learning to play the harp. A prophet* named Samuel told the young David that he would one day be king over all of Israel.

While still a youth, David won a place as a harpist at the court of King Saul of Israel. He was a favorite of Saul, became a good friend of Saul's son Jonathan, and later married the king's daughter Michal. At this time, Israel was struggling with the PHILISTINES, a neighboring people. David joined one of Saul's armies and distinguished himself by killing a giant named Goliath with a single stone from a slingshot. This feat made David famous, but his growing popularity aroused the jealousy of King Saul, who plotted to kill him.

Learning of the plot, David fled. While in exile, he assembled a powerful fighting force. Returning to the land of Judah, David became popular by protecting the local population against bandits and restoring possessions stolen by raiders. He also won the support of the leaders of Judah by paying them respect. In time, the people of Judah chose David to be their king.

Meanwhile, King Saul and his son Jonathan were killed in battle against the Philistines. David then returned to Israel to claim that throne, but he had to fight the forces of another of Saul's sons Eshbaal (Ishbosheth), who also claimed the throne. Ultimately, Eshbaal was assassinated by his followers, and the war ended. David conquered the city of JERUSALEM and made it the capital of his kingdom. He brought to it the ARK OF THE COVENANT, a sacred relic and symbol of the Israelites' religion.

* **dynasty** succesion of rulers from the same family or group

* **prophet** one who claims to have received divine messages or insights

Jerusalem's central location, nearly midway between Israel and Judah, helped unite the two regions.

Early in his reign, David reorganized the army and launched a series of wars. Decisive victories over the Philistines ended their threat, and David extended Israelite rule over many small neighboring kingdoms. He also reorganized the administration of his kingdom. In later years, he worked on plans to build a great temple in Jerusalem.

David was a successful warrior and effective ruler, but his achievements were marred by family problems and political rebellions. Like many kings who used marriage to forge political alliances, he took several foreign wives to cement relationships with other kingdoms. However, competition and rivalries among these women and the sons they bore to David led to instability. One of the most serious revolts was led by David's son Absalom, who held power for a time before his forces were eventually defeated. SOLOMON, David's son by his wife Bathsheba, eventually succeeded his father on the throne. (*See also* **Hebrews and Israelites; Israel and Judah.**)

DEATH AND BURIAL

* **funerary** having to do with funerals or with the handling of the dead

The peoples of the ancient Near East observed a variety of customs and rituals when someone died. Many of these customs were designed to prepare the body of the dead person, as well as his or her spirit, for the AFTERLIFE. People generally believed that some part of each individual continued to exist after death, although in a different world from that of the living. They also believed that the dead had the power to help or harm the living. For this reason, many funerary* practices dealt less with soothing the grief of the living than with the proper carrying out of duties toward the dead.

Mesopotamia. In ancient Mesopotamia, the afterlife was not particularly joyous, but it was better than ceasing to exist after death. One who had not been buried and mourned according to the rites could not enter the afterlife. Ideally, death occurred at home, in the presence of family and friends. After death, a spell freed the soul from the body. The soul then rested on a chair that was placed to the left of the funerary bed, waiting for offerings from the family.

Before burial, the body was washed and the mouth tied shut. Then the body was oiled or perfumed and dressed in clean clothing. The body was then displayed for public view alongside many grave goods, such as weapons, jewelry, and provisions for the journey to the underworld, or world of the dead. Royal families spent large amounts on their funeral displays. Excavations of the burial sites of Assyrian queens at Nimrud have yielded several extravagant offerings to the dead, such as gold cuffs inlaid with many semiprecious stones. Some burials even included chariots to carry the deceased to the underworld. The dead from more humble classes might get a pair of sandals. Grave goods also included gifts for the gods of the underworld so that they would welcome the deceased.

Those who could afford to do these things buried their dead in wooden or metal coffins or stone sarcophagi*. The sarcophagi of kings could be quite impressive; that of ASHURNASIRPAL II was made of dolerite

* **sarcophagus** ornamental coffin, usually made of stone; *pl.* sarcophagi

(basalt) and measured about 12.5 feet long, 6 feet wide, and 6 feet high. Commoners wrapped the dead in cloth or reed mats and buried them with simple grave goods. Kings and some commoners were buried in chambers beneath their palace or house. Others were laid to rest in public cemeteries, but the accompanying ceremonies were often costly. Reforming kings, such as Uru-inimgina of Lagash, who ruled around the 2400s B.C., did their best to ensure that the amounts charged for such services were not excessive.

The Mesopotamians believed that the well-being of the deceased in the afterlife depended on the performance of special mourning rites. If the deceased was an important person, these rituals could last a week. Close friends and relatives were expected to display their grief publicly, by wearing old clothes, tearing their garments, fasting, and going about unwashed and ungroomed. The family might hire professional mourners to add to the crowd or lead the laments in which people expressed their grief and praised the deceased. A fine example of what the ancient Mesopotamians called "exalting" the dead is the *Epic of Gilgamesh,* in which the hero mourns the death of his friend Enkidu.

Once the dead person was safely buried, the mourners purified themselves in a special ceremony and returned to their normal clothes and grooming habits. Mesopotamians believed that to speak of death was to summon it. As a result, they avoided the words *death* or *dying* and instead spoke of "going to one's fate," "being invited by one's gods," or "going on the road of one's forefathers."

Egypt. The Egyptians loved life and considered 110 years to be an ideal lifetime. Death was not the fate they feared most, however. They were more afraid of nonexistence. The goal of Egyptians was to ensure that their bodies existed for as long as possible after death. They provided their dead with supplies for the afterlife and took precautions to protect the dead and their treasures. They also went to much trouble to recover the bodies of Egyptians who died abroad. Drowning and being eaten by a crocodile was an Egyptian's nightmare because it destroyed all traces of the body. This fate was said to lay in store for people who offended the gods or swore false oaths.

The Egyptians developed a way of preserving dead bodies by turning them into MUMMIES. This process duplicated the drying process that was natural when a body was placed in dry sand, but not when a body is placed in a relatively damp tomb. There were different levels of mummification. At its most complete, the process required many months. The mummifiers removed the body's organs and fluids and stored them in special containers called canopic jars. They wrapped the heart in linen and set it in the body. They then removed the brain, applied drying chemicals to the body, and wrapped it in hundreds of yards of linen. Amulets* and guidebooks to the afterlife, such as the BOOK OF THE DEAD, were also placed in the wrappings. These procedures were too costly for the poor, who simply wrapped their dead in cloth and buried them. The burial involved many complex rituals, such as the Opening of the Mouth. This ritual involved touching the mummy's eyes, ears, nostrils, and mouth to symbolize their reopening and the deceased's return to life.

Servants of the Dead

The ancient Egyptians often included small statues of servants among the grave goods they buried with their dead. These models, along with painted scenes of daily life, represented things that the deceased might need. The Egyptians believed that these representations could magically become real. After about 1550 B.C., a new type of figurine appeared—the *ushabti,* or "answerer." These small statues were supposed to answer, "I am present" and to do any work that the deceased was asked to do in the afterlife. Some burials included boxes containing more than 400 *ushabtis*—one for every day of the year—plus foremen to supervise them.

See
color plate 9,
vol. 3.

* **amulet** small object thought to have supernatural or magical powers

Death and Burial

The Egyptian funerary papyrus of Djedkhon-sefankh, the priest of Amun, shown here, dates from about 950 B.C. Because Egyptians saw death not as an end, but simply a continuation of life, they mummified the dead and buried them with guidebooks and goods for a comfortable afterlife. This papyrus contains depictions of funerary rights and some illustrations of goods that the dead might need in the afterlife.

In the earliest known Egyptian burials, people were buried in the fetal position, curled up as they are in a mother's womb. Later, the bodies were straightened, and the arms were crossed over the chest. Written texts, which might include lists of foods and other items, were buried with prominent people. Written on the walls of tombs and on the insides of coffins, the lists were believed magically to take the place of the items. Idealized biographies of the dead person and painted scenes from the person's life, work, and even her funeral were also included.

The elite were buried in wooden coffins, often decorated with gold leaf or paint, inside stone sarcophagi. It became customary to place the bodies of kings and high-ranking nobles in a series of coffins. The innermost of these coffins was molded to the shape of the body. The coffins were elaborately painted, sometimes with images of gods who might protect the dead, and some were overlaid with gold. The Egyptians buried their elite with items for the afterlife, such as food, furniture, clothing, weapons, tools, utensils, musical instruments, and toys. Much of what is known about ancient Egyptian culture has been learned from the excavation of tombs and the study of grave goods and burial texts.

Anatolia. The HITTITES of ancient ANATOLIA (present-day Turkey) practiced cremation*, after which they buried the remains. Funerary rituals were meant to ease the dead person's passage from the society of the living to the underworld of the dead. Without proper burial, the dead person might roam the world of the living as a dangerous ghost.

Knowledge of Hittite funerary practices is based largely on royal deaths. A text from KHATTUSHA, the Hittite capital, describes in detail the 14-day ritual that followed the death of a king's brother. The participants included the king, high officials and their wives, religious officials, people connected to the royal family's cult* of ancestor worship, and women whose job was to wail and lament. The ritual began with a fast and the sacrifice of an ox as an offering to the deceased's soul. On the second day, the corpse was taken to the site of the cremation. The corpse was probably cremated on the third day. The following day, the bones were wrapped in linen and brought to a meal attended by everyone who had taken part in the ritual. The meal takers offered drinks to the soul of the dead. On the fifth day, priestesses made an image of the dead person out of tasty foods and performed a ritual to attract the soul to the image.

* **cremation** burning of the body of a dead person

* **cult** system of religious beliefs and rituals; group following these beliefs

31

Death and Burial

* **first millennium B.C.** years from 1000 to 1 B.C.

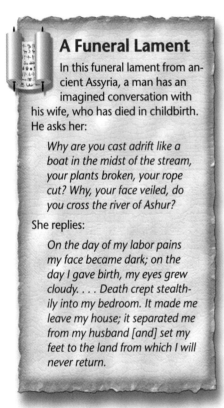

A Funeral Lament

In this funeral lament from ancient Assyria, a man has an imagined conversation with his wife, who has died in childbirth. He asks her:

Why are you cast adrift like a boat in the midst of the stream, your plants broken, your rope cut? Why, your face veiled, do you cross the river of Ashur?

She replies:

On the day of my labor pains my face became dark; on the day I gave birth, my eyes grew cloudy. . . . Death crept stealthily into my bedroom. It made me leave my house; it separated me from my husband [and] set my feet to the land from which I will never return.

See color plate 5, vol. 3.

The remaining days involved more ceremonial meals, more animal sacrifices, offerings to the deceased and ancestral spirits, and rituals such as cutting a grapevine with a silver hatchet. Finally, live seagulls and images of gulls were cremated in the burial chamber along with the bones. Later, at a feast, the mourners addressed the deceased: "Don't be angry any more. Be good to your children. . . . It shall come about that your 'god's house' will receive honor, and offerings will be set for you."

During the first millennium B.C.*, Phrygians laid their royal dead on beds in wooden chambers and buried them in enormous tumuli, or burial mounds. Excavations in Phrygia have yielded tombs containing grave goods, such as wood spoons, plates, bowls, and boxes, as well as many pieces of fine furniture. The largest mound in the region, called the Midas Mound, is thought to have belonged to King Midas. The king had been buried in a massive log coffin with at least 14 pieces of furniture, including 9 tables, 2 serving stands, 2 stools, and a chair.

The Levant. In ancient times, the region that comprises present-day Syria, Lebanon, Israel, the West Bank, and Jordan was home to many peoples, most of whom had their own practices. Many of these peoples believed that death was not the end of the deceased person's existence. Their funeral practices reflected this belief.

During the Late Bronze Age (ca. 1600–1200 B.C.), the people of UGARIT expected children to properly bury and mourn their parents. They believed that it was vitally important to leave behind descendants who could attend to these responsibilities. Mourners demonstrated their grief by sprinkling ashes or dirt on their heads, rolling in the dirt on the ground, wearing special garments, and sometimes even injuring themselves. Wailing was a very important part of the funerary process. The wailers called out the name of the deceased and complained of their loss. Sometimes professional mourners carried out these duties. Ugaritic society believed that the dead, properly mourned and honored, could play a positive role in the survival of the living. There is evidence that some of the dead were worshiped as gods.

The Phoenicians, a Canaanite people who lived along the Mediterranean coast, practiced both cremation and burial and made offerings to their dead. Some of the dead were buried in anthropoid sarcophagi (sarcophagi made with clay and in the shape of a human) or stone. The final resting place of a corpse was a permanent reminder of the dead's existence. Anyone who disturbed a burial site was cursed with a dreadful fate: to be without descendants and forgotten by all.

The Israelites believed that the existence of the soul depended on the correct treatment of the body, especially the bones. The early Israelites buried clothed corpses with personal possessions and offerings. They prohibited cremation and preferred burial in a cave or tomb dug out of rock. The tomb was a resting place for the corpse, the place where deceased individuals met their ancestors and "gathered unto their kin." The Israelites believed that the dead resided in Sheol, a pale copy of their existence on earth. Sheol was conceived as a subterranean, gloomy, and dusty afterlife, in stark contrast to the world of the living.

Those who had lost relatives or friends displayed their grief during a mourning period that usually lasted for seven days. Like the Canaanites,

Israelite mourners tore their clothes and sprinkled themselves with ashes or dust. Funerals featured lamenting, weeping, and sometimes singing and dancing. Fasting followed by a funeral banquet seems to have been part of the mourning. Eventually, the practices were codified, leading to modern Jewish practices of mourning the dead for a month ("sitting *shiva*") and immediate kin refraining from pleasurable activities for long periods.

Other Regions. The people of BACTRIA, a kingdom in CENTRAL ASIA, buried their dead in shallow graves with grave goods. No splendid "royal tombs" have been found. This suggests either that there were no great differences in social class or that burial goods were not used as an indicator of status.

The Saka, a nomadic* people of Central Asia, buried their dead in kurgans, graves under mounds of earth or stones grouped in cemeteries. Some of the deceased lay on their backs in pits, resting on beds of reeds and grasses, and others were cremated. In at least one kurgan, the body of the deceased was burned in a huge bonfire of brushwood.

Some cultures in the CAUCASUS, east of Anatolia, also buried their dead in kurgans. Since most kurgans contain few skeletal remains, it is possible that the deceased were cremated and that the cremated remains were buried. (*See also* **Burial Sites and Tombs; Religion.**)

* **nomadic** referring to people who travel from place to place to find food and pasture

DECIPHERMENT

Because so much is now known about the civilizations of the ancient Near East, it is difficult to grasp the fact that less than 250 years ago they were a great mystery. Scholars interested in the ancient world found tablets, scrolls, and wall paintings with ancient writings, but for many decades they could not read or understand these texts.

Beginning in the A.D. 1700s, scholars began to decipher ancient Near Eastern texts. First, they determined how to read the script by identifying the phonetic values assigned to each sign. Then they tried to identify the language encoded in the script. The second step was essential to the decipherment of these texts because, for example, the same set of cuneiform signs was used to render such diverse languages as Sumerian, Akkadian, Hittite, Luwian, Hurrian, Urartian, and Canaanite. Once the process was complete, many mysteries were solved.

Palmyrene. The first ancient language to be deciphered in modern times was used in the city-state* of Palmyra in SYRIA. Texts written in Palmyrene were known to Europeans as early as 1616, but the key to deciphering them was not developed until the 1750s. Palmyrene was deciphered on the basis of drawings of bilingual INSCRIPTIONS that contained the Palmyrene and Greek scripts. The Greek script could be read at that time. With the help of the Greek and some assumptions, a French scholar named Jean-Jacques Barthélemy deciphered Palmyrene. He assumed that the script was related to the Hebrew and Aramaic aleph-beth—a system of writing that contains symbols for consonants but not vowels—and that the language encoded in the script was a dialect* of Syriac, itself a late dialect of Aramaic. Barthélemy published his results in 1754.

* **city-state** independent state consisting of a city and its surrounding territory

* **dialect** regional form of a spoken language with distinct pronunciation, vocabulary, and grammar

Decipherment

* **scribe** person of a learned class who served as a writer, editor, or teacher

* **cuneiform** world's oldest form of writing, which takes its name from the distinctive wedge-shaped signs pressed into clay

* **stela** stone slab or pillar that has been carved or engraved and serves as a monument; *pl.* stelae

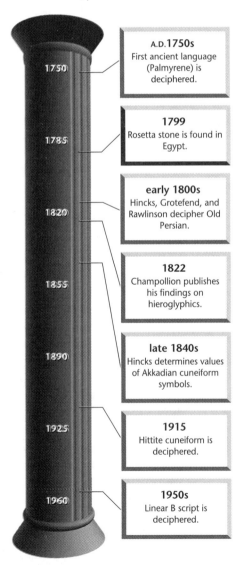

A.D. 1750s
First ancient language (Palmyrene) is deciphered.

1799
Rosetta stone is found in Egypt.

early 1800s
Hincks, Grotefend, and Rawlinson decipher Old Persian.

1822
Champollion publishes his findings on hieroglyphics.

late 1840s
Hincks determines values of Akkadian cuneiform symbols.

1915
Hittite cuneiform is deciphered.

1950s
Linear B script is deciphered.

Old Persian, Elamite, and Akkadian. Scribes* in MESOPOTAMIA and neighboring lands wrote in cuneiform*, using a stylus, a reed with a triangular tip. The first language written in cuneiform to be deciphered was Old Persian. The key to understanding Old Persian depended on the availability of accurate copies of ancient texts. In the late 1700s, a Danish explorer brought back copies of texts he had made in PERSEPOLIS, the capital of the PERSIAN EMPIRE. The copies showed three different sets of characters: a simple set that used only 40 or so signs, a more complicated one that employed about 100 signs, and a third set that used several hundred signs. Scholars assumed that the three texts conveyed the same message; what varied was the language used.

It took more than 40 years for the German Georg Grotefend and the Irishman Edward Hincks to decipher the simplest of the three writings, the Old Persian. Grotefend noticed that one set of symbols was repeated often in these texts. He thought that this set might represent the word *king*. He guessed that the other characters near *king* might be the names of kings. Since he knew the names of Persian kings from histories written in other languages, he compared the names to the characters. By matching them, he cracked the code. He published his findings in the early 1800s. Almost simultaneously, the Englishman Henry Rawlinson, working with copies he himself had made of the BEHISTUN INSCRIPTION, carved on a mountainside in western Iran, also deciphered the Old Persian portions.

The second type of cuneiform, Elamite, remains only imperfectly understood to this day. The third and most complex type of cuneiform, Akkadian, was deciphered only in the late 1800s, when large numbers of inscriptions were excavated at Assyrian capital cities, enabling Hincks, Rawlinson, and others to decipher the script.

Egyptian Hieroglyphics. For many centuries, travelers to Egypt had seen on monuments the pictures and symbols that form HIEROGLYPHICS. The meaning of these symbols was unknown, however. The breakthrough took place in 1799, when during the Egyptian campaign of the conqueror Napoleon, French engineers unearthed an inscribed stela* in the Nile Delta. This stela—the ROSETTA STONE—contained inscriptions in three scripts, one in the ancient Greek language and script and two in the Egyptian language—the hieroglyphic script and a cursive script called demotic.

When Englishman Thomas Young compared the Greek and hieroglyphic texts, he identified the name *Ptolemy* written in hieroglyphics. Ptolemy V was the Macedonian-descended king of Egypt in 196 B.C., when the stela had been carved. However, Young could not take the decipherment of hieroglyphics farther. The task fell to a French linguist named Jean-François Champollion, who had determined as a schoolboy that he would learn to read hieroglyphics. At age 16, he had written a paper arguing that Coptic—the language used in the Egyptian church—was derived from ancient Egyptian. Champollion used Coptic for hints when deciphering ancient Egyptian writing.

Champollion began by taking advantage of the way the king's name had been written. The name *Ptolemy* was enclosed in an oval called a cartouche. The presence of a cartouche always signaled that the person

* **pictograph** graphic character used in a picture writing system
* **linguist** person who studies languages
* **Egyptologist** person who studies ancient Egypt
* **archaeological** referring to the study of past human cultures, usually by excavating material remains of human activity

The Envelope, Please

In 1857, scholar W. H. Fox-Talbot suggested what has been called a translation competition to check on the accuracy of the newly developing understanding of cuneiform writing and the Akkadian language. He and four other scholars examined a text that had never been made public. Each submitted his translation, sealed, to the Royal Asiatic Society of Great Britain, where they would be compared. The idea was that if different scholars came up with the same results, that would be evidence that the translation was correct. When the sealed translations were opened, one of the judges declared that "agreement does appear to me to be satisfactory." Continued work on the ancient languages and scripts has extended scholars' understanding. Yet the 1857 test showed that the pioneers were on the right track.

named within was a ruler. (The suggestion of this link had originally been made by the Palmyrene decipherer Barthélemy.) Champollion found some of the symbols used in the name *Ptolemy* in another Egyptian monument that mentioned CLEOPATRA. This confirmed that he had correctly identified the sounds represented by these symbols. He went on to identify many other names from the times that the Macedonians and Romans held Egypt, beginning around 330 B.C. Champollion published his findings in 1822. Two years later, he published another, larger book that revealed the key to Egyptian hieroglyphics. He explained that some symbols were meant to represent the consonant sounds of the words they showed, while others were pictographs* representing the objects shown.

By the mid-1800s, two other linguists* had added to the understanding of hieroglyphics. German Egyptologist* Carl Richard Lepsius revealed that some symbols stand for more than one consonant sound. Edward Hincks—who helped in the decipherment of Old Persian—pointed out that hieroglyphics only record consonant sounds, not vowels.

Mesopotamian Cuneiform. Many more texts still remained to be decoded, however. The largest body of cuneiform texts was created in Mesopotamia and began to surface in archaeological* digs in Assyria—a region of northern Mesopotamia—in the A.D. 1800s. The language of many of these texts, Akkadian, had two dialects: Assyrian and Babylonian. Although the two dialects have almost the same symbols, there are significant differences between them. In addition, several other languages were written in cuneiform symbols. These complications made the work of deciphering cuneiform much more difficult.

Edward Hincks studied the texts in the hope of finding clues to understanding cuneiform. By the late 1840s, he had identified the values of about 236 Akkadian symbols. He established that some symbols were logograms, which meant that they derived meaning from abstract or realistic pictorial representations of the words. Other symbols were phonograms, which stood for sounds. Hincks also determined that scribes spelled the same words differently in different texts, often depending on the space available. He learned that some symbols represented vowels alone but most were consonants paired with vowels. He determined that the encoded language belonged to the family of SEMITIC LANGUAGES, which includes ancient Hebrew. Finally, Hincks realized that the signs sometimes had more than one pronunciation because the script was originally created for a non-Semitic language. Today scholars know that this language was Sumerian, the first language written in cuneiform.

Later Achievements. The decipherment of ancient languages continued in the 1900s. The first Hittite cuneiform inscriptions were found in the A.D. 1890s. They were easily deciphered because they used cuneiform signs with values known from Akkadian-language texts of the same period. One linguist, seeing the word *wa-a-tar* in a clear reference to water, identified this ancient language as Indo-European. His decipherment of Hittite was published in 1915.

Tablets written in Ugaritic—the language used in the Syrian port city of UGARIT—were first discovered in the 1930s. Ugaritic was written in a

Demons

peculiar form of cuneiform that used only 29 different signs, suggesting that the script was like an aleph-beth. The script also suggested that the language was probably a West Semitic* dialect.

Another more recent decipherment was that of Linear B. This script recorded the language spoken by the Mycenaeans during the Late Bronze Age (ca. 1600–1200 B.C.) on Crete and the Greek mainland. In the 1950s, this language was recognized as a form of ancient Greek and deciphered.

Remaining Mysteries. Despite many successes, linguists have not been able to decipher every known ancient language. Some—such as Luwian and Elamite—have been deciphered to an extent but are imperfectly understood. With others, the initial breakthrough has yet to be made. Examples are Linear A—a precursor of Linear B on Crete—and the script found in the SINAI PENINSULA that many scholars think underlies the alphabets of the Semitic languages. Texts from the ancient Phoenician city of BYBLOS include an unusual system of writing that seems to combine Egyptian hieroglyphics with the alphabet of Canaanite languages. This, too, has yet to be understood. There are several more of these known but not understood languages—and perhaps new languages yet to be discovered as archaeologists continue to unearth new texts. It is possible that these texts will also contain writing that at first seems strange but later becomes clear through the flashes of insight and close attention to detail that make up decipherment. (*See also* **Akkad and the Akkadians; Alphabets; Egypt and the Egyptians; Elam and the Elamites; Indo-European Languages; Languages; Scribes.**)

DEMONS

Ancient Near Eastern peoples believed that in addition to the gods, there were other supernatural beings or forces that could affect the world. Scholars refer to many of them as demons. These beings could do good or evil, although generally demons were associated with evil. Many aspects of ancient MAGIC were meant to protect people from demons.

In ancient Mesopotamia, people recognized at least two types of demonic forces: supernatural spirits and ghosts of the unhappy dead. Demons often appeared in groups of seven, but there were also individual demons. The best-known demon was Lamashtu, daughter of the sky god ANU. She was said to attack pregnant women, young mothers, and babies. People wore amulets* bearing her likeness or in the form of the head of the demon god Pazuzu or recited incantations* to ward her off.

Demons were represented as half human and half animal, a four-legged animal, a two-legged bird, or a fish. Examples include a figure with a lion's body and a man's head; the merman and mermaid, who had human heads on fish bodies; and the griffin demon, which combined a human body and an eagle's head and wings.

Deceased people who were improperly buried or mourned were thought to return as restless ghosts that roamed the world of the living. Those who had died sudden or violent deaths or whose bones had been scattered by animals were believed to be especially angry. Texts listed other restless ghosts, such as those of people who were killed by a weapon, died of thirst while in prison, or as a result of a sin against a god or an offense against the king.

The ghosts of unmarried people joined a special class of demons. These restless demons slipped through windows into houses, searching for men and women to become the husbands and wives they had never had. Such a demon could be very persuasive, tempting the victim with such words as, "I am the son of a prince, I will fill your lap with silver and gold." Victims of these demons could be carried into the underworld, where they, too, became spouse-seeking ghosts.

Babylonian ideas about demons were similar to some ancient Jewish beliefs. Bowls and talismans used in Jewish healing rituals contain words similar to those found on artifacts* related to demons from Babylonia. One bowl describes a demon as a lion with flashing eyes that breathes fire, similar to some of the combined creatures of Babylonia.

Egyptians also believed that demons caused illnesses and other misfortunes. SETH, murderer of the god OSIRIS, was worshiped as the god of confusion for many centuries until beliefs changed and he was seen as a demon. Also feared were the demon servants of Sekhmet, the lioness goddess. Called murderers, they were thought to be especially dangerous during the last five days of each year.

As did Mesopotamians, Egyptians also believed in the evil-roaming dead and feared them. They could lurk in any out-of-the-way place and harm the living. The Egyptians believed that "any loss is due to [the roaming dead]: the game seized in the field—it is [they] who [do] a thing like that." To protect themselves from harm, people conducted ceremonies dedicated to appease the roaming dead. (*See also* **Death and Burial; Gods and Goddesses; Mythology; Religion.**)

This detail from a cast copper or bronze plaque, dating from the Neo-Babylonian period (612–539 B.C.), depicts the demon Lamashtu. She is shown fleeing along the river of the underworld pursued by Pazuzu and tempted by various offerings. The plaque was probably used as an amulet.

* **artifact** ornament, tool, weapon, or other object made by humans

Deportations

See *Migration and Deportation.*

Diet

See *Food and Drink.*

DISASTERS, NATURAL

A natural disaster is a devastating event or series of events caused by the forces of nature. These catastrophes cause loss of life, large numbers of injuries, and major damage to property. Natural disasters may be sudden events, such as EARTHQUAKES, eruptions of VOLCANOES, FLOODS, and storms or fires. They may also occur over a long period of time. Changes in environmental conditions, such as desertification* or the buildup of salt in soil are also disasters with serious social and economic consequences. DROUGHT, disease, and insect plagues* could also bring disaster to societies.

Throughout history, the Near East has experienced natural disasters that caused direct damage to people and property and disrupted societies

* **desertification** change of useful land into desert through natural processes or human activity

Disasters, Natural

* **plague** contagious disease that quickly kills large numbers of people

by destroying farming, travel, and trade patterns. Disasters weakened once-strong societies, leaving them open to invasion and conquest or forcing their people to migrate elsewhere in search of better land.

Sudden Disasters. The fall of some ancient Near Eastern civilizations can be attributed to sudden disasters. The geologically unstable areas in and around the Mediterranean Sea have been frequent sites of earthquakes and volcanic activity. On the island of CRETE, in about 1700 B.C., an earthquake destroyed the early palaces. Around 1500 B.C., the nearby island of THERA in the AEGEAN SEA was completely destroyed by a volcanic eruption. Not only did the eruption cause destruction to Thera, but it also caused volcanic ash to fall on Crete, destroying parts of that island. Scholars believe that the eruption on Thera may have caused earthquakes as well as tsunamis (large, high-speed waves created by underwater earthquakes or volcanic eruptions) that also damaged Crete and disrupted shipping activity on the Aegean Sea. The eruption of Thera has been suggested as a possible source for the story of Atlantis, a legendary island continent that sank into the sea. In the 700s B.C., a particularly strong earthquake struck ancient Israel. The event had such as powerful impact on those who survived it that it was remembered for many generations.

Floods occurred frequently in the ancient Near East, especially in the regions near the TIGRIS RIVER. Faster flowing than the EUPHRATES RIVER and greatly affected by local, often violent, storms, the Tigris frequently destroyed lives, property, and crops as they neared harvest. In Egypt, floods caused by the NILE RIVER were more predictable and less damaging. However, in the years of high flood, the river could still submerge towns and villages. A greater problem in ancient Egypt was a low flood. Without the life-giving waters of the great annual flood, Egyptian AGRICULTURE suffered greatly. If a period of years of consistently low floods occurred, famine* could be the result. In fact, some scholars believe that the period of decline at the end of the Old Kingdom in Egypt (ca. 2675–2130 B.C.) was the result of internal weaknesses caused by low-flood-induced crop failure and famine.

* **famine** severe lack of food due to failed crops

Sometimes ancient peoples were faced with the problem of hordes of insects destroying the food supply. Plagues of locusts seriously threatened food supplies, for people could do little to combat them. The Hebrew BIBLE describes plagues of locusts that struck Egypt in the 1200s B.C. Crop failures brought on by other insects or by plant diseases caused by fungus or viruses could also threaten society, as could human disease itself.

These disasters were unpredictable and unavoidable to peoples of the ancient Near East. As a consequence, they depended greatly on the gods' ability to prevent natural disasters. They believed that a disaster could be the result of not worshiping a god properly. For example, Egyptians thought that an unworshiped god would leave Egypt and that disasters would then ensue.

Gradual Disasters. Regions in the ancient Near East also experienced gradual disasters, which occurred because of ENVIRONMENTAL CHANGES. Large tracts of land became useless in Mesopotamia because of the buildup of salt in the soil from heavy irrigation. Ineffective LAND USE hastened erosion and the loss of good soil. Ongoing deforestation all around the Mediterranean turned once-green areas into deserts unable to sustain much life.

Adequate rainfall was critical, and even a little less rain could tip the balance in areas relying on dry farming*. Many rivers and streams dried up as a result of lack of adequate rainfall.

These gradual disasters desolated the land and caused changes to societies just as sudden disasters did. Some societies weakened, enabling conquerors to invade and destroy them. Constant warfare over resources in Mesopotamia grew with the population. Drought and famine in Syria and the Levant* both drew groups together and broke them apart. Other civilizations simply disappeared. Societies that no longer functioned well dissolved again into small groups. This gradual process, called retribalization, occurred repeatedly in areas that saw breakdowns of the societies' ability to maintain themselves. (*See also* **Climate; Economy and Trade; Irrigation; Medicine; Religion; Rituals and Sacrifice; Water.**)

* **dry farming** farming that relies on natural moisture retained in the ground after rainfall

* **Levant** lands bordering the eastern shores of the Mediterranean Sea (present-day Syria, Lebanon, and Israel), the West Bank, and Jordan

Disease

See *Medicine.*

Divination

See *Oracles and Prophecy.*

DIVORCE

All the major cultures of the ancient Near East recognized that marriage is sometimes imperfect and impermanent. Married couples could divorce, or formally end their unions, although generally it was easier for husbands to divorce wives than for wives to divorce husbands.

Laws, customs, and marriage contracts spelled out the conditions under which divorce was permitted and what the rights of each party were. A husband in MESOPOTAMIA, for example, could divorce his wife for any reason. However, he had to give up all claim to her property and might have to pay an additional penalty in silver. According to a law of about 1801 B.C., from the city of ESHNUNNA, a husband who divorced a wife who had borne him sons was driven away from his house and property.

A wife's right to divorce had severe restrictions, though. Many marriage contracts from Babylonia in the 1700s B.C. forbade the wife to divorce the husband on pain of death. Other contracts allowed the wife to divorce the husband but specified that she would sacrifice her dowry*. A few marriage contracts granted the wife the same rights as the husband. In those cases, the women were most likely daughters of rich families or independent widows. While these contracts permitted divorce, it seems that divorce was not often practiced. Marriages were the union of two families, both of whom had interests in the marriage continuing.

Divorce was more common in Egypt, where both husbands and wives had the right to dissolve their marriages and to marry other partners. Reasons for divorce included a partner's adultery*, the failure of the marriage

* **dowry** money or property that a woman brings to the man she marries

* **adultery** sexual relations between a married person and someone other than his or her spouse

to produce children, or simple dislike. A letter from around 1200 B.C. also suggests that men wishing to advance their careers divorced wives to marry women with better positions in society.

When divorce in Egypt occurred, the wife received the household goods she had brought to the marriage, or their value. Some marriage contracts required a husband to support his wife financially throughout her life, even if he divorced her. If the reason for the divorce was her adultery, however, she forfeited this payment. In general, the husband received custody of the children.

The divorce laws of the Hittites of ancient Anatolia (present-day Turkey) dealt with marriages in which one partner was free and the other was a slave or in which both were slaves. If such marriages produced children and ended in divorce, the wife took one child and the husband gained custody of the rest. Hittite laws concerning divorces involving two free people have not been found, but marriage contracts probably regulated the termination of such unions.

Among the ancient Israelites, men could divorce their wives, but women had no such right. A husband probably did not have to get permission from any ruling body in order to divorce his wife, but he was required to take certain measures once he had made his decision. Later divorce laws dating from the Hellenistic* period showed the influence of other legal systems. According to marriage contracts from that period, a Jewish husband could begin divorce proceedings by saying a phrase that had been employed for divorces in Babylonia as well. (*See also* **Family and Social Life; Marriage.**)

See
color plate 5,
vol. 2.

* **Hellenistic** referring to the Greek-influenced culture of the Mediterranean world and western Asia during the three centuries after the death of Alexander the Great in 323 B.C.

DJOSER

ruled ca. 2630–2611 B.C.
Egyptian king

* **funerary** having to do with funerals or with the handling of the dead

* **mud brick** brick made from mud, straw, and water mixed together and baked in the sun

* **artisan** skilled craftsperson

Djoser (ZHOH•suhr) was king of Egypt early in the Third Dynasty. He founded the Old Kingdom (ca. 2675–2130 B.C.), the first long period of peace and prosperity in ancient Egypt. Djoser is best known for his funerary* complex at Saqqara in northern Egypt, which contains the first PYRAMID.

The original plan for the burial site was less elaborate than the final product. Construction took more than two decades, during which time, the plans of Djoser and the royal architect Imhotep changed. In its final form, the tomb became a six-stepped pyramid made of STONE that rose more than 200 feet high and dominated the complex. The pyramid was the first stone building in Egypt and the first example of monumental architecture in the world.

The other structures in the complex were models of important temples and palaces, showing all the settings in which the ruler had acted as the link between the gods and the people. These models, like the king's tomb, were made of stone instead of the reeds and mud brick* used for the originals they imitated. Stone made them durable.

Djoser's project required a complex government administration to coordinate the artisans* and laborers involved. This building project began an era of stone monument building in Egypt and set a precedent for Egypt's later pyramids. (*See also* **Architecture; Building Materials; Burial Sites and Tombs; Egypt and the Egyptians.**)

Doctors

See *Medicine.*

DREAMS

* **divination** art or practice of foretelling the future

* **ecstatic** person who communicates directly with gods through an altered mental state such as a trance, dream, or rapture

* **incubation** practice of inviting or stimulating dreams by sleeping in a temple, shrine, or other holy place

* **epic** long poem about a legendary or historial hero, written in a grand style

Today dreams are regarded as the mind's way of dealing with experiences from one's life. This view, however, is part of modern psychology and is little more than 100 years old. Throughout history, people regarded dreams as signs or warnings about the future. Dreams were also thought to be important messages from the gods.

Many cultures in the ancient Near East took dreams seriously. They devoted much effort, study, and ritual to understanding dreams. Various societies recorded them, interpreted them, and classified them. Dream interpretation was one kind of divination*.

Although important dreams most often came to kings, priests, or other officials, they could also come to ordinary people. Sometimes dreams came through an ecstatic*, who was often associated with a temple. Another practice, called incubation*, involved sleeping in a holy place in the hope of receiving a divine dream. Priests or other seers interpreted such dreams.

Leaders often chose a certain course of action because of dreams they had. For example, GUDEA (ca. 2100s B.C.), governor of LAGASH, followed a dream that instructed him to rebuild a temple. The Assyrian king ASHUR-BANIPAL (ruled 668–627 B.C.) reported that he saw a goddess in a dream who foretold a military victory. A temple priest reported the same dream.

In several versions of an epic* about GILGAMESH, dreams play an important role in the hero's life. Dreams foretell both the arrival and death of Enkidu, and predict several struggles that Gilgamesh undertakes. A HITTITE version of the epic includes a dream of an assembly of gods.

In Egypt, letters from the time of the Middle Kingdom (ca. 1980–1630 B.C.) show family members writing to deceased relatives, expecting to receive their replies in the form of dreams. The Egyptians also kept handbooks of dream interpretations from the time of the New Kingdom (ca. 1539–1075 B.C.). One such interpretation reads: "If a man sees himself looking through a window: good. It means being called by his god. If a man sees himself shod with white sandals: bad. It means roaming the earth." More elaborate dream manuals date from the Ptolemaic dynasty (305–30 B.C.).

The Hebrew BIBLE records many examples of dreams influencing life. The god Yahweh commands Jacob to return to the land of his birth in a dream. He also promises the land to his people in the famous dream of Jacob's ladder. In the book of Genesis, Joseph interprets two of the pharaoh's dreams to be a warning that famine was coming to Egypt. SOLOMON asks for wisdom in a dream, a wish that is granted.

Dreams were an important link to the supernatural world for ancient peoples. The close ties of dreams and prophecy* to religion and leadership made belief in the power of dreams a part of culture for thousands of years. (*See also* **Oracles and Prophecy; Priests and Priestesses; Religion; Rituals and Sacrifice.**)

* **prophecy** message from a deity; also, the prediction of future events

Drought

DROUGHT

* **deforestation** removal of a forest as a result of human activities

* **famine** severe lack of food due to failed crops

* **Levant** lands bordering the eastern shores of the Mediterranean Sea (present-day Syria, Lebanon, and Israel), the West Bank, and Jordan

A drought is an abnormally long period of insufficient rainfall in a region that causes a significant drop in water levels in the ground, lakes, and rivers and hinders the growth of crops. Droughts can be short and last only a few weeks, or they can continue for years. They are caused by variations in normal CLIMATE and weather patterns, such as annual flooding or rainfall, and their impact may be worsened by human activities, such as the misuse of water and land resources. Some droughts in the ancient Near East were made worse by deforestation* and poor irrigation techniques.

Since ancient times, droughts have had far-reaching effects on human societies, causing crop failures, loss of natural vegetation, and depletion of water supplies. Livestock and wildlife, as well as humans, may die of thirst and famine* brought on by drought. Drought can also cause deterioration of the land as fertile topsoils dry out and blow away, leaving land that is not useful for growing crops. When water does fall on deforested land, the ground cannot hold it, so it fails to replenish underground reservoirs. Deforested land becomes dried out and useless for growing crops.

Much of the Near East has a dry climate with sparse rainfall. Drought is an ever present threat, and some ancient societies in the region, such as those in Syria and the Levant*, relied heavily on the small amount of rain, which they collected in cisterns. Other societies, such as those of Egypt and Mesopotamia, relied on rivers fed by rains and snowmelt in sources far away. A drought due to little or no precipitation at the headwaters of a river could result in lack of water in those areas.

Throughout ancient times, droughts periodically ravaged the ancient Near East, causing great hardship to the people and sometimes contributing to the collapse of societies. On occasion, droughts also caused serious political and economic upheaval. Historians believe, for example, that the fall of the empire of the HITTITES in the 1200s B.C. may have been partly caused by a prolonged drought that weakened the Hittites and left them vulnerable to their enemies. When crops failed to grow, it became necessary to import them from somewhere else, thus placing an economic strain on a society. For example, some historians believe that a decline in the levels of flooding of the NILE RIVER may have resulted in a strain on the Egyptian economy of the Old Kingdom.

Droughts also caused the migration of ancient Near Eastern peoples as they sought refuge in places less affected by dry conditions. For example, the migrations of the SEA PEOPLES from the Aegean toward Egypt may have been caused by a combination of drought and famine. Evidence of dried up wells in Greece has suggested that a drought may have caused the Greeks to move elsewhere and colonize in the 700s B.C.

Droughts could destroy or completely change people's lives. As a result, drought became associated with ancient religious beliefs and MYTHOLOGY. The Israelites, for example, believed that their god YAHWEH sometimes caused drought as a punishment for the sins of the people. A story from the Hebrew BIBLE tells of the prophet* Elijah's declaration that a drought was occurring because Yahweh was punishing the cult* that was promoting the worship of the god BAAL in Israel. In the story, Elijah and the Baal worshipers hold a contest to determine the true god. When

* **prophet** one who claims to have received divine messages or insights

* **cult** system of religious beliefs and rituals; group following these beliefs

Yahweh emerges as the true god, the Israelites slay the Baal worshipers, and Yahweh ends the drought with rain.

A number of other ancient myths tell of battles between gods, the results of which were varied. In some Canaanite myths, for example, the gods Baal and Mot struggle for supremacy. A victory for Baal, the god of life and fertility*, resulted in seven years of abundance. A triumph for Mot, the god of death and sterility, led to seven years of drought and famine. For ancient peoples, such myths helped account for periods of drought and abundance.(*See also* **Disasters, Natural; Environmental Change; Famine.**)

* **fertility** ability to become pregnant and bear children or to father children

---

Dumuzi

See *Ishtar.*

DYNASTIES

* **succession** transmission of authority from one ruler to the next

A dynasty is a line of rulers who belong to the same family or group or who trace their descent to a common ancestor. Dynasties exist in kingdoms or empires in which rulership is inherited or passed on from one ruler to the next. Individual dynasties sometimes end because of a lack of heirs. At other times, a ruling family may be overthrown during civil strife. Historically, however, a new dynasty generally rises to replace the old one.

The power of kingship was very strong in the ancient Near East, and many successors came to the throne with little difficulty. Sometimes, however, an appointed successor might meet with opposition from high government officials or other members of the royal family. Such situations could lead to political struggles and even to civil wars. For this reason, succession* and the choice of successors were major concerns of kings and royal officials.

In most Near Eastern societies, kingship was normally passed from father to son. However, brothers, nephews, grandsons, and even brothers-in-law or sons-in-law sometimes assumed the throne after the death of a king. In some cases, women, such as HATSHEPSUT in Egypt, also became rulers. This generally occurred when there were no suitable male heirs or when the successor was too young to assume the throne.

Ancient Near Eastern dynasties ensured their continuity by establishing formal plans for an orderly succession. For example, in the 1500s B.C., King Telipinu of the HITTITES issued an edict, or official order, that established rules and standards concerning succession to the throne. Sons generally had the strongest claims to a throne because of the normal rules of inheritance. However, kings could strengthen the claims of others they chose, such as a nephew or son-in-law, by formally adopting that individual as a son.

In many parts of the ancient Near East, marriage within the family played an important role in the continuation of dynasties. Kings often arranged marriages between royal families to gain loyalty and support, as well as to ensure an adequate supply of potential successors. Within one family, relatives might marry to maintain the purity of the royal bloodline. For example, CLEOPATRA VII coruled Egypt first as the wife of her brother Ptolemy XIII and later as the wife of her brother Ptolemy XIV.

Much of the history of the Near East focuses on the rule of its many kings. KING LISTS—documents listing the succession of rulers—and ancient texts documenting the achievements of rulers have been used to establish chronologies and reconstruct the history of these ancient societies. Historians also use dynasties to divide the history of the ancient Near East into units of time, evaluating each individual dynasty as well as comparing it with other dynastic periods.

Mesopotamian Dynasties. Mesopotamia contained many different city-states*, kingdoms, and empires at various periods in the region's history. Sometimes dynasties ruled individual city-states, while at other times they headed larger territorial states.

* **city-state** independent state consisting of a city and its surrounding territory

Among the most notable early dynasties in Mesopotamia was that established by King SARGON I of Akkad in the 2300s B.C. This dynasty ushered in a new phase of Mesopotamian history where, for the first time, Akkad and Sumer were politically united. NARAM-SIN, Sargon's grandson, expanded his kingdom's boundaries and created the first true empire in the region. Naram-Sin was also the first ruler in the Mesopotamian region to have himself declared a god.

During the period between around 2000 and 1595 B.C., much of Mesopotamia was again divided into separate, independent city-states. The thrones of many of these cities were occupied by dynasties headed by AMORITES, nomadic* peoples who had invaded the region.

* **nomadic** referring to people who travel from place to place to find food and pasture

One of the most notable dynasties in Mesopotamia was that of the KASSITES, who ruled Babylon from about 1595 to 1158 B.C. The longest-ruling dynasty in all of ancient Near Eastern history, the Kassites played a major role in expanding the power of Babylon and bringing about a lasting political unification of Babylonia.

Dynasties in Egypt. The history of Egypt is traditionally divided into 30 dynasties that span a period of nearly 3,000 years, from about 3100 to the year 332 B.C., when Egypt was conquered by ALEXANDER THE GREAT. Historians further organize Egyptian history by dividing these dynasties into several major groups: those of the Early Dynastic period, Old Kingdom, Middle Kingdom, New Kingdom, and Late Period. Three "intermediate periods" containing dynasties fall between these groups. Historians refer to the time after 332 B.C. as the Hellenistic period, during which Egypt was ruled by the Macedonian and Ptolemaic dynasties.

Some Egyptian dynasties are historically more important than others because of the achievements of their kings or the role of Egypt in their periods. The First Dynasty (ca. 3000–2800 B.C.) is best remembered as the time when the city of MEMPHIS was founded. During the New Kingdom (ca. 1539–1075 B.C.), Egypt reached the height of its power and prosperity. The dynasties of this period included the most famous rulers of ancient Egypt, among them Hatshepsut, THUTMOSE III, AKHENATEN, TUTANKHAMEN, RAMSES II, and RAMSES III.

Not all dynasties were ruled by Egyptians, however. At different periods, Egypt was ruled by the HYKSOS—who were invaders from the Levant*—the LIBYANS, the Nubians, and the Persians.

Dynasties in the Levant. According to the Hebrew BIBLE, Saul, the first king of Israel, was deemed unfit to rule by the Israelite god YAHWEH. Thus, the kingship passed to David (ruled ca. 1000–970 B.C.). Following the death of David's son and successor, Solomon, the kingdom was split into the states of ISRAEL AND JUDAH. However, descendants of David continued to rule Judah until its capture by the Babylonians in 586 B.C. Christians believe that Jesus was a member of the Davidic family.

Dynasties in Iran. The most important early dynasties in IRAN were those of Elam. Between about 2350 and 1500 B.C., three dynasties ruled Elam, including the Sukkalmakh dynasty, which ruled for about 400 years. During this dynastic period, Elam became an independent power and had one of the largest territories in the Near East. Perhaps the most famous Iranian dynasty, however, was the Achaemenid dynasty, whose kings founded the PERSIAN EMPIRE, one of the greatest empires of the ancient Near East. (*See also* **Chronicles; Chronology; Government; Marriage; Queens.**)

* **deity** god or goddess

* **epic** long poem about a legendary or historical hero, written in a grand style

* **artisan** skilled craftsperson

A water god and protector of humanity, Ea (AY•uh) was revered by the Akkadians, Assyrians, and Babylonians, as well as the Sumerians, among whom he was known as Enki, which means "lord of the earth." The son of the sky god ANU and Sumerian mother goddess Namma, Ea was the father of MARDUK, the principal deity* of Babylon. Worshiped as part of a trio of gods that included Anu and the earth god ENLIL, Ea played a major role in creation and was associated with wisdom, crafts, music, and MAGIC.

Ancient myths say that Ea helped separate the universe into heaven and earth and then used clay to create humans as helpers to the gods. According to the epics* of Atrakhasis and GILGAMESH, Ea helps humanity escape the great floods sent by an angry Enlil. Aware of Enlil's plan to flood the land, Ea secretly warns a man and instructs him to build a boat and load it with animals, precious metals, "the seed of life of all kinds," his kith and kin, and artisans*, helping humankind survive.

Ea's concern for humans made him beloved by the people of ancient Mesopotamia. Many considered him responsible for bringing culture to humanity. In art, Ea was portrayed as a bearded god wearing a tall headdress studded with several pairs of horns. During the Hellenistic period, this image of Ea became the symbol for the zodiacal sign of Aquarius. Creatures that could represent Ea were the merman (with the upper body and head of a human and the lower body of a fish) and the goat fish (with the fore parts of a goat and the hind parts of a fish). The goat fish became the zodiacal sign of Capricorn. (*See also* **Astrology and Astrologers; Creation Myths; Flood Legends; Religion; Zodiac.**)

* **Levant** lands bordering the eastern shores of the Mediterranean Sea (present-day Syria, Lebanon, and Israel), the West Bank, and Jordan

Earthquakes

* **mud brick** brick made from mud, straw, and water mixed together and baked in the sun

* **tectonic** relating to the structure of the earth's crust

An earthquake is a vibration or shaking of the earth's crust. Earthquakes range in severity from barely noticeable to extremely destructive. The region from Anatolia (present-day Turkey) southward to Mesopotamia and through Iran is part of a highly active earthquake belt, as are the islands of the Aegean and Mediterranean Seas.

Throughout history, earthquakes have devastated property and people, especially those living in structures made of stone and mud brick*. Although few records exist to document ancient earthquakes, evidence suggests that they occasionally occurred in the ancient Near East.

There are two common causes of earthquakes. Tectonic* earthquakes are the result of movements of the plates that make up the earth's crust. The most destructive tectonic earthquakes occur in regions where plates meet near the earth's faults, or fractures. Volcanic earthquakes are associated with eruptions of VOLCANOES. Both are the result of the same underground forces.

Earthquakes appear to be the causes or contributing factors of decline and destruction in the ancient Near East. The island of CRETE suffered from a series of earthquakes in around 1700 B.C. These earthquakes destroyed Crete's first palaces, forcing the Minoans to rebuild. Later earthquakes weakened the Minoan civilization on Crete, and power passed from the Minoans to the Mycenaeans who had come from the Greek mainland.

A volcanic eruption and a resulting earthquake occurred on the island of THERA in about 1500 B.C. The eruption literally blew the island apart. The explosion, quake, and ash fallout ended all life in the Theran city of Akrotiri. The eruption may also have caused some of the later earthquakes on Crete. Some scholars suggest that the destruction of Thera might be one source of the story of Atlantis—a Greek legend of an island continent that sank beneath the sea.

It is probable that the eruption and subsequent earthquake on Thera also caused tsunamis—giant waves of water that can reach 50 feet high and travel 500 miles per hour—in the Aegean Sea. These waves would have caused damage to surrounding lands. As a consequence, shipping and trading on the Aegean were probably disrupted.

Other civilizations may have come to an end or had their progress halted by earthquakes. In Syria, the city of UGARIT was probably destroyed by one severe earthquake or by a series of devastating shocks followed by a fire in the early 1100s B.C. One of the levels excavated in the city of TROY in Anatolia appears to have been destroyed by an earthquake around 1300 B.C. The survivors leveled the ruins and built a new city on top of the old one.

Some societies tried to fix or avert the damage from earthquakes rather than rebuild. For instance, Egyptians built a bracing wall around the pyramid of King Neferkare Pepy II of the Sixth Dynasty (ca. 2350–2170 B.C.) because it had been structurally weakened by an earthquake. Historians also suggest that people in ancient Crete may have attached religious symbols to pillars of their houses so that the gods would protect them from earthquakes or fires.

Earthquakes are mentioned several times in the Hebrew BIBLE. The books of Amos and Zechariah both speak about an earthquake occurring in Israel as a punishment from YAHWEH. Another biblical episode from I Kings tells of the prophet* Elijah waiting on a mountaintop—possibly on the SINAI PENINSULA—for Yahweh to speak to him. As he waits, there is a strong wind, followed by an earthquake and a fire.

* **prophet** one who claims to have received divine messages or insights

EBLA

* **city-state** independent state consisting of a city and its surrounding territory

* **archaeologist** scientist who studies past human cultures, usually by excavating material remains of human activity

* **cuneiform** world's oldest form of writing, which takes its name from the distinctive wedge-shaped signs pressed into clay tablets

* **diplomacy** practice of conducting negotiations among or between kingdoms, states, or nations

* **Semitic** of or relating to people of the Near East or northern Africa, including the Assyrians, Babylonians, Phoenicians, Jews, and Arabs

Ebla (EB•luh) was a city-state* in northwestern SYRIA. The city was known only from references in ancient Akkadian and Sumerian texts until A.D. 1968, when a group of Italian archaeologists* led by Paolo Matthiae identified it with the site called Tell Mardikh.

Among the most important discoveries at Ebla was a collection of more than 17,000 CLAY TABLETS inscribed in cuneiform*. The texts provide much information on the administration of palace affairs. They also contain literary, economic, judicial, and political subject matter.

Ebla experienced several periods of prosperity and importance from around 3500 B.C. until about 1600 B.C. During that time, Ebla became a regional power, with control over several smaller communities. Trade and diplomacy* linked Ebla with Egypt and kingdoms in Mesopotamia. Ebla's fine woolen cloth was a prized trade product.

Around 2350 B.C., the city was destroyed in a fire, probably during an attack by the Akkadians. A rebuilt Ebla flourished again between about 1800 and 1600 B.C., only to fall to another military raid, this one by HITTITES from ANATOLIA. After about 1600 B.C., Ebla survived as a minor village with no political power. Research into Ebla's ruins and texts is providing information on the economic and political life of ancient Syria at a time when city-states were beginning to emerge.

The Eblaites were a Semitic* people whose culture and language were related to those of other West Semitic groups, such as the AMORITES and the ARAMAEANS. Elements of their writing system and literature were borrowed from Sumer. (*See also* **Semitic Languages; Urbanization.**)

ECONOMY AND TRADE

The term *economy* refers to a system in which people obtain and use commodities (articles of trade) they need and want. AGRICULTURE was the foundation of economies in the ancient Near East. The production and distribution of food dominated the economy from earliest times. Although commerce eventually branched out into the management of many goods and services, farming remained the basis of wealth in the ancient Near East. As civilizations in the region grew, their economic systems evolved from small, local economies to large, complex systems in which empires traded and transported resources, finished goods, and labor around the region. Ancient Near Eastern peoples also developed measures of weight and volume to calculate quantities and devised rates of exchange to compare the values of things.

As economies in the ancient Near East developed, they increasingly depended on trade, both within a society and with other groups. TRADE ROUTES

increased communication and awareness of the world. As societies evolved from small communities to great empires, the changes in economies both caused and demonstrated the advance of civilization.

SOURCES OF INFORMATION

Archaeologists* and historians have ample material to draw from, even from the period before writing, to learn about economies and trade. They also examine written materials that were kept to record business transactions in ancient times.

For archaeologists, remains such as stone tools, dwellings, luxury goods buried with the dead, and POTTERY are related to economic activities and give clues to economic life in times when no records were kept. Ancient environments, plants, and animals also yield clues to economic activity, as do studies on disease and nutrition. These indicate what sort of goods were readily available to people and what resources might have been acquired through trade.

Archaeologists study trade patterns by examining the materials found at a site and comparing them to materials usually occurring in that region. By examining trade goods, such as pottery and metals, archaeologists can determine which societies were in touch with each other and the routes they followed to move goods from one place to another. By

* **archaeologist** scientist who studies past human cultures, usually by excavating material remains of human activity

As economies in the ancient Near East depended increasingly on trade, an extensive network of roads was developed. These networks were used for the exchange of goods such as metals, lumber, spices, fragrances, and semiprecious stones. In addition to the exchange of goods, trade also increased communication and cultural exchange among various groups.

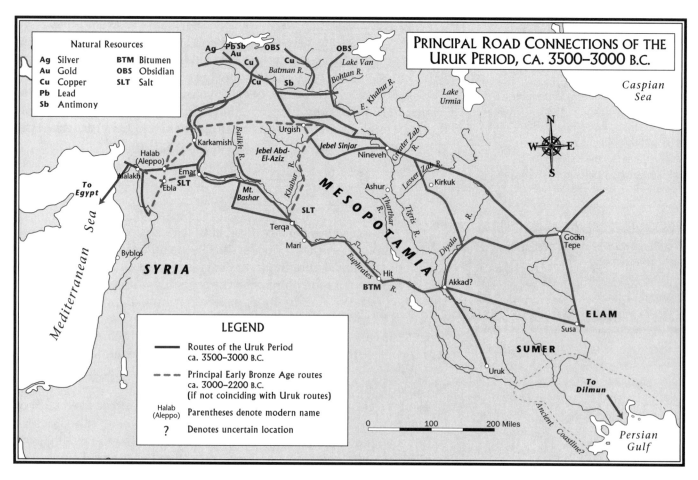

Natural Resources

Ag Silver	**BTM** Bitumen
Au Gold	**OBS** Obsidian
Cu Copper	**SLT** Salt
Pb Lead	
Sb Antimony	

PRINCIPAL ROAD CONNECTIONS OF THE URUK PERIOD, CA. 3500–3000 B.C.

LEGEND

Routes of the Uruk Period
ca. 3500–3000 B.C.

Principal Early Bronze Age routes
ca. 3000–2200 B.C.
(if not coinciding with Uruk routes)

Halab
(Aleppo) Parentheses denote modern name

? Denotes uncertain location

0   100   200 Miles

studying the distribution of goods within a society, they can draw conclusions about how the society was structured and what its people valued.

Around 3100 B.C., when WRITING originated in Mesopotamia, people began to maintain records of economic and business transactions. By that time, cities had been established, societies became organized, and newly formed bureaucracies* began to maintain detailed records of exchanges. These records provide a wealth of information about economy and trade in the ancient Near East.

ECONOMY

An economy is based on the process by which wealth is created, distributed, managed, and used. As civilizations developed in the ancient Near East, new economies emerged and evolved over time. A major change occurred during the Neolithic period*, as people shifted from a nomadic* lifestyle and began to settle in villages and rely on resources found locally. When they began to manage their resources of water, animals, and land, doing so required organization and a greater degree of sharing. Consequently, new economic relationships started to develop among people, and more and different kinds of goods and services became more valuable. Societies that had been based on kinship developed into societies based on rank, privilege, and power based on control of the economy. Soon, when a society produced a surplus of any commodity, that society traded it with other societies and developed relations with them.

Economic historians classify economies into three basic types: reciprocal, redistributive, and commercial. In most economies of the ancient Near East, some mixture of these three methods of exchange may have occurred, at least in some periods.

In a reciprocal economy, goods are transferred between parties who are both consumers and producers. For example, one farmer might supply grain to a craftsperson who makes pottery. In turn, the craftsperson supplies pottery to the grain farmer. Such an exchange of commodities is called barter. Typically, the bartering parties know each other and have some type of social relationship. This relationship develops further because not all transactions happen at the same time and one person may have to wait to receive goods from the other. This leads people to owe and expect things from each other and to trust the other party to fulfill his part of the exchange.

The earliest economies were reciprocal economies. Evidence of barter in the ancient Near East is scarce, however, probably because it existed on a small scale, primarily between individuals or small groups.

In a redistributive economy, commodities are deposited at a common institution that then distributes the wealth to people according to their position in society. This system requires a strong central authority to receive supplies and distribute them. People trust the central authority and depend on it to support, provide for, and defend them. When that trust fails, the system collapses.

Temples often played an important role in redistributive economies of the ancient Near East. An early second millennium B.C.* archive from a temple in the Babylonian city of NIPPUR contains details of goods coming

* **bureaucracy** system consisting of officials and clerks who perform government functions

* **Neolithic period** final phase of the Stone Age, from about 9000 to 4000 B.C.
* **nomadic** referring to people who travel from place to place to find food and pasture

Who Pays the Price?

Merchants from Babylon traveling the far reaches of empires also acted as diplomats. Sometimes they paid ransom for those who had been taken captive by other peoples. The merchants were repaid by the captives, but not if it meant that the captives would lose their property. Babylonian captives were protected by the Code of Hammurabi, which states that if a captive could not pay, the village temple would. The code continues:

[I]f there is not enough in his village temple to ransom him, the palace shall ransom him. His field, orchard or house shall not be sold for his ransom money.

* **second millennium** B.C. years between 2000 and 1001 B.C.

49

into and being distributed from the temple. Redistribution also appears to have been used during the Old, Middle, and New Kingdom periods in Egypt, periods that were characterized by their stability. In Egypt, the responsibility of distributing goods fell to the state treasury.

A third type of economy, one familiar today, is a commercial economy, or one in which goods and services command a price in the market. People accumulate wealth by selling these goods and services at the best possible price. The role of commercial economies in the ancient Near East is unclear, but historians know that they existed in such cities as BABYLON and ASHUR. For example, an edict* published by Babylonian king Ammi-saduqa in the 1600s B.C. discusses how to deal with debts resulting from commercial transactions.

* **edict** pronouncement of the government that has the force of law

Although ancient economies were run and controlled by central institutions, it is not safe to assume that all economic exchanges were directed by them. For example, although merchants in Mesopotamia during the third millennium B.C. (years from 3000 to 2001 B.C.) were partly employed by the temple or the palace, they were probably able to engage in independent trade. In fact, it was often helpful to a merchant in a foreign land if he was not seen as an agent of a governmental institution. A potential trading partner would be less likely to trade with someone who represented a city or city-state* he was in conflict with. Eventually, a more independent business sector did develop. For example, during the Achaemenid period (538-331 B.C.), many citizens of Babylon were involved in private commerce and banking. Maintaining wealth often became a family business, and many of these families left archives that recorded their transactions and dealings.

* **city-state** independent state consisting of a city and its surrounding territory

TRADE

In economic terms, trade is the regular movement of goods from one area to another. As economies grew and trade became more complex, new materials, methods, and ways of living spread throughout the ancient Near East.

Beginnings of Trade. Trade is based on acquiring materials or resources not found locally. Extensive trade for desirable goods existed long before states with a powerful central authority came into being. For example, obsidian* from ANATOLIA (present-day Turkey) circulated widely among Neolithic communities in the Levant*. Likewise, lapis lazuli* from Afghanistan was already being transported to southern Mesopotamia before 3000 B.C.

* **obsidian** black glass, formed from hardened lava, useful for making sharp blades and tools
* **Levant** lands bordering the eastern shores of the Mediterranean Sea (present-day Syria, Lebanon, and Israel), the West Bank, and Jordan
* **lapis lazuli** dark blue semiprecious stone

In Mesopotamia, the unequal distribution of resources between the north and south led to the establishment of trade. Southern Mesopotamia lacked wood, stone, metals, and in early times, animals and plants for agriculture. These items were abundant in the north, but thin soil and fast rivers there made agriculture more difficult than in the south, where soil enriched by the rivers yielded bountiful grain harvests. Consequently, commodities began to flow between the two regions as each supplied the other's needs.

As economies grew, early trade networks were established between societies that demanded raw materials, useful goods, and luxury items. The

This relief from the palace of Assyrian king Sargon II at Khorsabad, dating from the 700s B.C., depicts cedar trunks being transported by water from Lebanon. A prized item throughout the ancient Near East, Lebanese cedar was used for building ships, palaces, and temples. In fact, Babylonian ruler Nebuchadnezzar claimed that he built a road and canal for the sole purpose of carrying the famed Lebanese cedar.

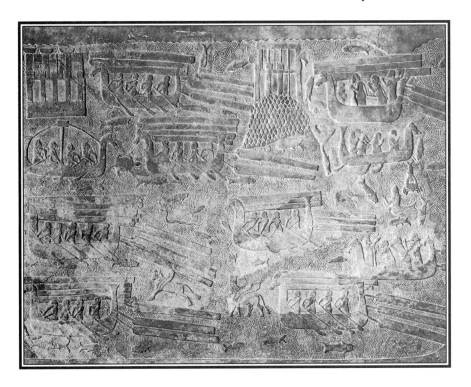

necessities of life were probably available in regions where strong economies developed. However, raw materials for other products and projects were sought beyond the regional boundaries. For example, the Mesopotamian and Egyptian governments could meet the food needs of their population, but they had to import many goods, such as metals, semiprecious stones, wood, and spices, from afar. To meet their needs, the people of the Mesopotamian city-state of URUK set up an active trade network during the Uruk period (ca. 3500–3000 B.C.). The people of Uruk established colonies in Mesopotamia, Syria, and Iran that probably served as places where goods produced in Uruk were traded for those items not locally available. An extensive network of roads was used as trade routes during this period.

Trade Goods. Archaeological evidence from the ancient Near East reveals three groups of trade goods: essentials, staples, and luxuries. Not every type of good was used by all members of a society, however.

Essentials are items necessary for everyday life, such as grain and salt, or for their production, such as grindstones (heavy stone disks used for grinding grain and sharpening tools). Records to prove that ancient Near Eastern peoples traded these goods are scant, although archaeological evidence does exist. For instance, a site in northern Iraq yielded a room filled with more than 300 grindstones that were clearly intended for trade. Vital trade goods such as these were used by everyone and probably account for more of ancient Near Eastern trade than written records reveal.

Staples are items that are used to produce other things, either for direct use or for trade. Most trade in staples involved processed raw materials rather than finished goods. For instance, timber for construction and

51

shipbuilding was plentiful only in the Levant, and most peoples imported what they needed from that region. TEXTILES were commonly traded. Metals such as copper and tin, which were luxuries at first, became essential materials for craft work and military use. For example, during the time of Old Assyrian period (ca. 2000–1750 B.C.), merchants from Ashur established colonies in Anatolia to trade textiles and tin for silver and gold.

Luxury items were important to the government and temple because they reflected the power and prestige of the ruler and his society. In addition, these items were used to adorn, make offerings to, and honor the gods. Shells, lapis lazuli, gold, silver, spices, frankincense and myrrh*, exotic woods such as ebony, or rare materials such as ivory showed the people's and ruler's devotion to the gods who protected them. Consequently, the risk and expense of obtaining luxury goods became the business of rulers and wealthy temples.

* **frankincense and myrrh** fragrant tree resins used to make incense and perfumes

Trade Routes and Centers of Trade. In the ancient Near East, goods were traded overland, sometimes by donkeys and camels, and by water. Geographic barriers, such as mountains and deserts, determined land routes, as did shifting politics and alliances.

The most efficient method of moving large cargoes was by water. Sea traders successfully undertook lengthy voyages on the Red Sea, the Indian Ocean, the Mediterranean Sea, the Arabian Sea, and the Persian Gulf. Traders sailed to many foreign, sometimes distant lands. Dilmun, present-day Bahrain, was the closest and perhaps most important Mesopotamian trading partner in the Persian Gulf. Merchants in Dilmun acted as brokers because goods such as copper and timber from faraway places, such as Magan in present-day Oman, flowed through there. Magan was the source for a decorative black stone that the Sumerian governor GUDEA sought for statues. Mesopotamian city-states also engaged in trade with faraway lands, such as MELUKKHA, probably in India. Whether Melukkha was the source of the wood and ivory used in Mesopotamian boats and temples or was a temporary stopping place for these goods, there was frequent contact between Mesopotamian and Indian societies.

The only distant region to which Egyptians traveled was the land of Punt. Punt, which may have been in present-day Sudan or Ethiopia or in southern Arabia, was a source of exotic animals, spices, gold, and slaves. A number of expeditions, including one sent by Queen HATSHEPSUT, went to Punt.

Kings of Israel also sought riches from afar. The Hebrew BIBLE recounts a trip to Ophir, perhaps in present-day Saudi Arabia, to restock Solomon's treasury with gold from that land. The Phoenicians are well known as both explorers and sea traders, who traded with lands as far away as present-day England and the Atlantic coast of Africa. Such trips indicate the willingness of ancient Near Eastern peoples to explore new sources of wealth for their economies.

Methods of Exchange. For trade to succeed, the merchants involved must be able to exchange items of comparable value. From the Neolithic period, when barter was the chief mode of exchange, ancient Near Eastern

Underwater Discoveries

Advances in underwater archaeology have made it possible to discover and analyze cargoes of lost ships from the ancient Near East, giving a clearer pattern of the quantity and kind of goods traded. No longer forced to rely on only written records and artworks, for example, scholars are now able to get their hands on the actual material remains of trading vessels. For example, a ship from the 1300s B.C. that was excavated near Uluburun, off the coast of southern Turkey, has yielded an inventory of such trade goods as silver, tin, and ivory. Even edibles such as olives, figs, grapes, and almonds have been found, providing information on the diet of the ship's crew.

peoples had developed methods to determine the value of goods. Over time, other methods came into use, eventually resulting in specific objects of exchange, such as coins.

Metals such as copper, bronze, silver, and gold represented values and were items of exchange. Silver, which was more available than gold, was favored. Goods came to be valued in terms of weights of silver. For example, during the late third millenium B.C.*, in the city of LAGASH in southern Mesopotamia, 8.5 bushels of barley were worth 0.3 ounces of silver. Such systems of equivalence allowed for ease of accounting and standardization of values. In Egypt and elsewhere, gold, silver, copper, and grain were used as currency.

Eventually, some metal moneylike objects appeared. Texts from the Old Akkadian period (ca. 2500–2000 B.C.) through the Old Babylonian period (ca. 1900–1600 B.C.) refer to precious metals being cast into rings that may have been used as currency. Silver broken into pieces may also have been used to value goods.

The earliest coins came from Lydia, in Anatolia, in about 650 B.C. Coins were marked to identify the issuing authority and to certify the purity of the metal and perhaps their weight. Nevertheless, people always weighed coins to gauge their values. It took hundreds of years for coins to become established in the Near East, and then only under the rule of foreign powers. ALEXANDER THE GREAT increased the production of coins, and their use spread throughout the Hellenistic* world. (*See also* **Cereal Grains; Government; Labor and Laborers; Metals and Metalworking; Transportation and Travel.**)

See color plate 3, vol. 2.

* **third millenium** B.C. years from 3000 to 2001 B.C.

* **Hellenistic** referring to the Greek-influenced culture of the Mediterranean world and western Asia during the three centuries after the death of Alexander the Great in 323 B.C.

EDICTS

An edict is an official decree or proclamation issued by a ruler, ruling council, or some other governing body. In the ancient Near East, edicts enacted policy, determined succession, or created rules and regulations. They had the force of law and were intended to establish order in society. They reflected the ideas about justice held by the people that issued them. Consequently, edicts were often powerful and dramatic documents, written in simple language and a forceful and energetic style and read aloud before an assembly.

Texts from the ancient Near East frequently refer to edicts, suggesting that such decrees were probably quite common. However, only a few fragments of such edicts have ever been found. One of the best-preserved examples is the *Edict of Ammi-saduqa,* a royal decree issued in about 1646 B.C. by Ammi-saduqa, then king of Babylon. In this edict, the king declared certain types of loans illegal, and he suspended the tax payments owed by some classes in society for a period of several years. Ammi-saduqa probably issued this edict in response to hard economic times in Babylon.

Two edicts survive from the HITTITES of ANATOLIA (present-day Turkey). The *Edict of Khattushili* was issued sometime around 1620 B.C. by king KHATTUSHILI I and dealt with succession to the throne. In this decree, Khattushili disinherited his nephew Labarna and named Murshili, his own grandson, his successor. Probably issued while the king lay on his deathbed, the edict was sent out to important officials and nobles of the kingdom.

The *Edict of Telipinu,* issued by King Telipinu between about 1525 and 1500 B.C., dealt with royal succession as well, but Telipinu went further than Khattushili. His edict established the basic principles for organizing the state and methods for dealing with criminals accused of high crimes, designating an assembly to act as high court. In doing so, Telipinu was probably trying to break age-old patterns of revenge in which entire families were held responsible for the actions of individual family members.

The Hebrew BIBLE tells of an edict issued by CYRUS THE GREAT after he conquered Babylonia and marched into Babylon. In this decree, Cyrus told the Jews, who had been exiled to Babylon, that they should return to Judah and rebuild their temple in Jerusalem. This edict was cause for celebration among the Jews, and it brought Cyrus their support. (*See also* **Government; Law; Rosetta Stone.**)

EDUCATION

* **literacy** ability to read and write

* **apprenticeship** system of training in which an individual learns skills or a profession from an experienced person in that field

* **cuneiform** world's oldest form of writing, which takes its name from the distinctive wedge-shaped signs pressed into clay tablets

* **hieroglyphics** system of writing that uses pictorial characters, or hieroglyphs, to represent words or ideas

* **scribe** person of a learned class who served as a writer, editor, or teacher

* **fourth millennium B.C.** years from 4000 to 3001 B.C.

* **diplomacy** practice of conducting negotiations among or between kingdoms, states, or nations

Education played a vital role in the ancient Near East. The principal goal of education was to develop literacy* and cultural awareness and to train individuals in the skills needed for the administration of government, the economy, and other aspects of society. However, education was not available to all. Children from the upper classes generally had greater access to formal education than those from the poorer segments of society. Moreover, although there are records of educated females, few girls received any formal education. Nevertheless, all children could learn through apprenticeship* training or by observing their parents and elders at work.

Because many ancient Near Eastern societies relied greatly on record keeping and bookkeeping, people who could read and write were needed. Prior to the spread of the alphabet, the complexities of writing in the cuneiform* and hieroglyphic* scripts and the level of mastery required meant that few people could function as scribes*. As a result, reading and WRITING were important skills and became the focus of education.

Mesopotamia. Formal scribal* education existed in Mesopotamia from at least the late fourth millennium B.C.* Scribal training may have taken place in private schools that were separate from temples and palaces. Often located in the homes of individuals, these schools primarily taught reading and writing. Some families hired private tutors who taught the sons of the house in their residence.

With the growth of Mesopotamian civilization, the need for literate people to serve in government led to the development of state-sponsored schools run by experienced scribes. Known as tablet houses, these scribal schools offered an education that was based on producing highly literate students who could function as administrators. The primary focus was on teaching how to read and write Sumerian because it was the language of commerce and diplomacy*. Students also learned other languages, including Akkadian and local dialects.

Education and Religion

The strong link between education and religion among the ancient Israelites developed, in part, from the word of God as revealed in the Torah (part of the Hebrew Bible). In the book of Deuteronomy, for example, God says: "And these words which I command you this day shall be upon your heart; and you shall teach them diligently to your children" (Deuteronomy 6:7). Elsewhere in the Bible, King David of Israel preached that "Wisdom gives strength to the wise man more than the rulers that are in a city" (Ecclesiastes 7:19).

These and other religious texts encouraged the ancient Israelites to make education an everyday experience that would enrich the mind and bring them closer to the word of God.

---

* **divination** art or practice of foretelling the future

* **artisan** skilled craftsperson

During the Old Babylonian period, schools were responsible for preserving Sumerian literature. Consequently, formal education consisted primarily of copying Sumerian texts. By doing so, the students not only mastered the language but also helped preserve literary texts, such as hymns, proverbs, and mythological texts. The round tablet shown here contains a Sumerian proverb inscribed by a student.

Students learned languages by copying and studying standard texts as well as various lists, such as sign lists, vocabularies, and grammatical lists. Beginning students also learned how to prepare the CLAY TABLETS used for writing. Discipline was strict, and students could be punished severely for disobedience, tardiness, and other types of improper behavior. Along with languages, Mesopotamian schools taught LITERATURE, MATHEMATICS, and MUSIC. Music was especially important for individuals who were training for a career in the temples and needed to learn religious songs. Mesopotamians also trained specialists in MEDICINE, ASTROLOGY, divination*, and other fields. Most of these specialists found employment in temples or the government.

Some youngsters learned their father's trade at home, and specialized knowledge was handed down from one generation to the next by artisans*, priests, scribes, and other professionals. Children in Mesopotamia could also learn a profession through apprenticeship training. Surviving contracts show that boys were apprenticed to learn cooking, carpentry, singing, and other skills.

Egypt. Throughout ancient times, literacy was essential to success in Egypt, and scribes were among the most important people in society. During the third millennium B.C., usually only the sons of royalty and high officials received a scribal education, and there was little opportunity for the nonelite population to become literate. A student might learn to become a scribe if his father taught him or if an official was hired to teach him. Princes and sons of high-ranking officials might have also received an education at palace schools.

During the Middle Kingdom period, the government established many state-run scribal schools. This led to an expansion of education among children of diverse backgrounds and also to a more uniform education system. By about the 1500s B.C., education had become quite widespread, and even boys of modest background could attend scribal schools such as those attached to temples, palaces, and other state-run institutions.

Scribal training in Egypt involved a long period of education. Students entered school as early as age 6, and they might continue their education until age 20 or older. Elementary training lasted about four years, after which students began advanced work. The scribal schools aimed at producing competent administrators to serve in the government in a civil or military capacity or to serve at temples. Young men training for the priesthood learned practical matters such as managing temple property and personnel in addition to their normal studies.

Students also studied such subjects as grammar, mathematics, science, and other languages. They generally learned by copying standard texts, writing down materials recited by teachers, and writing lists of words that they had memorized. Students were expected to memorize ancient literature and to be able to recite it. As in Mesopotamia, discipline at schools in Egypt was strict, and students could be severely punished for disobedience or laziness.

Boys could also learn their father's profession by working with him from an early age. Similarly, girls were taught domestic skills by their

Egypt and the Egyptians

mothers or other female relatives. Some children learned skills in architecture, engineering, and sculpture from other adults through a system of apprenticeship. Apprentices were expected to give their teachers the same respect they would give their parents.

Other Parts of the Near East. The need for literate individuals led to the tradition of scribal education being adopted by other cultures in the ancient Near East. However, the simple alphabetic writing system developed in the Levant* at the end of the second millennium B.C.* permitted the gradual spread of literacy across the entire ancient Near East, from Egypt to Persia.

Education was especially important to the ancient Israelites, and it was strongly tied to their religion. It was the scribe's duty to copy the sacred laws of the god YAHWEH and to read them to the people. In this manner, more people—literate and illiterate—could learn and uphold the religious principles the Israelites believed in.

Early education in Persia was based on teaching the Zoroastrian religion and ethics. Later these religious principles were taught along with disciplines such as reading, writing, arithmetic, and fine arts. (*See also* **Books and Manuscripts; Family and Social Life; Libraries and Archives; Schools.**)

* **Levant** lands bordering the eastern shores of the Mediterranean Sea (present-day Syria, Lebanon, and Israel), the West Bank, and Jordan

* **second millenium** B.C. years from 2000 to 1001 B.C.

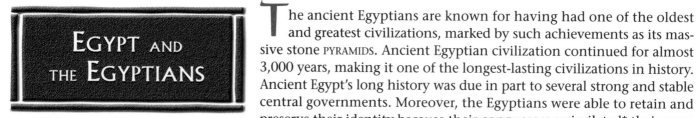

EGYPT AND THE EGYPTIANS

* **assimilate** to adopt the customs of a society

The ancient Egyptians are known for having had one of the oldest and greatest civilizations, marked by such achievements as its massive stone PYRAMIDS. Ancient Egyptian civilization continued for almost 3,000 years, making it one of the longest-lasting civilizations in history. Ancient Egypt's long history was due in part to several strong and stable central governments. Moreover, the Egyptians were able to retain and preserve their identity because their conquerors assimilated* their ways rather than forcing the Egyptians to assimilate.

GEOGRAPHY

Egypt is located along the NILE RIVER in northeastern Africa. It is bordered on the south by Sudan; on the west by Libya; on the east by the SINAI PENINSULA, eastern desert, and the Red Sea; and on the north by the Mediterranean Sea. The borders of ancient Egypt changed through time as it grew more or less powerful and expanded or lost territory. Nonetheless, the populated areas of ancient Egypt generally consisted of three regions: the large Nile River delta*, known as Lower Egypt; the Nile River valley south of the delta, known as Upper Egypt; and the low-lying Faiyum Depression, fed by the Bahr Yusef branch of the Nile River, to the west of the Nile near the delta. The population was concentrated in these three regions because they were the only places where the hot, dry conditions of Egypt's desert were relieved by the floodwaters of the Nile.

* **delta** fan-shaped, lowland plain formed of soil deposited by a river

The Nile River and Delta. The Nile River flows from the central African highlands in the south to the Mediterranean Sea in the north. It was a major transportation route in ancient Egypt, and many individuals made a living transporting goods and people up and down the river. The Nile also provided food for the Egyptians. It was a source of fish, an important component of the ancient Egyptian diet. More significantly, the Nile's annual flooding made the surrounding lands suitable for AGRICULTURE. As a result, the lands could sustain a large population.

The extent of the Nile's annual flooding depended on the amount of rain in central Africa. Some years had much lower floods than usual, causing crop failure, high food prices, and famine*. Other years had much higher floods than usual, causing equally disastrous effects. Years of unusually high or low floods were often marked by social and political instability. This was because Egyptians believed that their rulers were directly responsible for agricultural success and blamed the government when famine occurred.

The many branches of the Nile Delta overflowed their banks each summer, allowing farming in the surrounding floodplain. In fact, the delta had even greater agricultural potential than the Nile Valley, and by 3100 B.C., it had several well-established towns. By 1400 B.C., the delta region dominated Egyptian economy and politics because of its agricultural wealth and closeness to the other civilizations in the Near East.

Faiyum Depression and Other Populated Areas. The Faiyum Depression is a lake and an oasis* west of the Nile River. It was settled by farmers as early as 7000 B.C. and, like the Nile River valley and delta, became more intensively farmed and heavily populated over time. Around 1800 B.C., the water level of the lake was brought under control, and CANALS were built to increase the amount of arable* land. After this, the Faiyum became one of the most prosperous and heavily populated areas of ancient Egypt.

The Egyptian people also settled in several places in the desert west and east of the Nile. To the west, the settlements were centered on oases, many of which were on major trade routes. Sites in the desert east of the Nile were heavily populated because they were important sources of minerals, such as gold and copper, and building materials, such as sandstone and quartzite. Some of these sites may have been worked by local populations under Egyptian control rather than settled by Egyptian people. The eastern desert also was the route to the Red Sea, an important trade destination.

HISTORY

Most modern historians divide ancient Egyptian history into several kingdoms and periods on the basis of the work of the Egyptian priest Manetho, who lived in the 200s B.C. Manetho listed all the kings of ancient Egypt known to him and grouped them into dynasties*. Although historians know that Manetho's list is not completely accurate, much of the information contained on this list does correspond with what they know about the rulers of ancient Egypt. The succession of dynasties reflects the fact that ancient Egypt's history was marked by periods of stability, invasion, and instability.

* **famine** severe lack of food due to failed crops

* **oasis** fertile area in a desert made possible by the presence of a spring or well; *pl.* oases

* **arable** suitable for growing crops

* **dynasty** succession of rulers from the same family or group

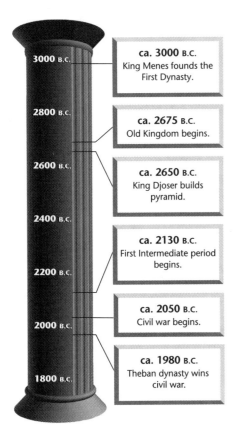

ca. 3000 B.C.
King Menes founds the First Dynasty.

ca. 2675 B.C.
Old Kingdom begins.

ca. 2650 B.C.
King Djoser builds pyramid.

ca. 2130 B.C.
First Intermediate period begins.

ca. 2050 B.C.
Civil war begins.

ca. 1980 B.C.
Theban dynasty wins civil war.

Egypt and the Egyptians

Each of the more than 30 dynasties that ruled ancient Egypt consisted of a succession of related kings. At several points in Egypt's long history, two, or perhaps even three, dynasties ruled in different parts of the country at the same time. The position of king was inherited, and it usually passed to the oldest son of the king's chief wife, although other sons or daughters occasionally took the throne. One dynasty ended and a new one began when a king died without leaving a suitable heir or when outsiders seized power and started their own dynasty. During and after the Eighteenth Dynasty (ca. 1529–1292 B.C.), kings in Egypt were given the title pharaoh, a term that had been used earlier to refer to the palace.

The king was considered the embodiment of the god Horus. In this divine role, the king was the high priest of the Egyptian religion and the sole mediator between the gods and the Egyptian people. After death, many kings were declared gods and worshiped along with the other Egyptian gods.

Predynastic and Early Dynastic Periods. Until about 5500 B.C., Egypt's population consisted of small nomadic* groups who lived by hunting, gathering, and fishing. Around that time, new immigrants from west Asia appear to have moved into Egypt, bringing knowledge of farming and domesticated* crops. The immigrants settled in villages and established more complex societies. Their settlements grew, an eventually,

* **nomadic** referring to people who travel from place to place to find food and pasture

* **domesticated** adapted or tamed for human use

Egypt was one of the longest lasting civilizations in the world, thriving for almost 3,000 years. These years of prosperity brought both innovations and advances in the areas of government, science, writing, and the arts. This map shows the area of ancient Egypt between the Mediterranean Sea and first cataract, and between the Red Sea and Western Desert.

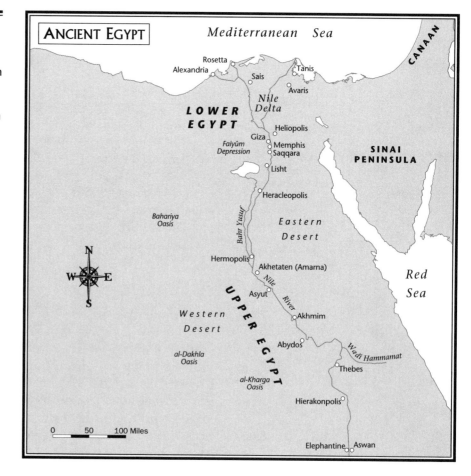

small, local kingdoms emerged in the Nile Valley. Historians refer to this period as the Predynastic* period. Toward the end of this period, the peoples of the Nile Valley came in contact, either directly or indirectly through trade, with the literate* Sumerians of southern Mesopotamia and their neighbors, the Proto-Elamites of southern Iran.

By about 3100 B.C., a few strong kings had come to dominate Upper Egypt. According to Manetho, one of them, King Menes, conquered Lower Egypt and unified the country in about 3000 B.C., founding the first Egyptian dynasty. Menes strategically located the capital of the newly unified Egypt at MEMPHIS, on the border between Lower and Upper Egypt. Menes' successors, the kings of the first two dynasties, reinforced their hold on the country and strengthened the kingdom's central government.

Old Kingdom and First Intermediate Period. By the time of the Third Dynasty, Egypt entered the Old Kingdom period (ca. 2675–2130 B.C.), which was characterized by an era of stability, prosperity, and strong central government. During the Old Kingdom, many of the distinguishing characteristics of Egyptian civilization were established. By then, Egyptians had already invented a paperlike material from PAPYRUS, and their system of writing, called HIEROGLYPHICS. These inventions enabled them to keep the many records needed by the large central government, which had also become very wealthy by this time. The government's wealth and strength are apparent from the massive stone pyramid constructed during the reign of King DJOSER of the Third Dynasty. In fact, the Old Kingdom period is often called the pyramid age because later kings of the period commissioned more and larger pyramids.

By around 2200 B.C., the Old Kingdom had become severely weakened. Several factors may have contributed to this, including the increasing inability of the king to control local leaders and unusually low floods of the Nile that may have led to crop failure and famine. The resulting social unrest was followed by the collapse of the central government around 2130 B.C. Local kings asserted their independence, and Egypt became fragmented. This marked the beginning of the First Intermediate period (ca. 2130–1980 B.C.). During this period, a civil war existed between two rival dynasties, one from Heracleopolis whose members made up the rulers of the Ninth and Tenth Dynasties (ca. 2130–1980 B.C.). The other dynasty was from THEBES, and its members became the Eleventh Dynasty (ca. 2081–1938 B.C.). Whereas Heracleopolis was the capital at the beginning of the First Intermediate period, Thebes became the capital after the victory of the Theban dynasty.

Middle Kingdom and Second Intermediate Period. Around 1980 B.C., King Nebhepetre Mentuhotep II of the Theban Eleventh Dynasty gained control of Lower Egypt and reunited it with Upper Egypt, marking the beginning of the Middle Kingdom. During this period of strong, stable central government and prosperity Egyptian kings built brick pyramids, conquered much of Nubia, and engaged in trade with the Canaanite city-states* in western Asia. Many Canaanites, attracted by Egypt's new prosperity, settled in the eastern Nile Delta. The Middle Kingdom period was also a golden age for Egyptian literature and art.

---

* **predynastic** referring to the period before 3000 B.C., when Egypt's First Dynasty began

* **literate** able to read and write

Stumbling Into History

In the A.D. 1990s, an important discovery was made when the leg of a stumbling donkey went into what turned out to be an opening to a 2,000-year-old tomb. Archaeologists investigating this site at the Bahariya Oasis, 230 miles southwest of Cairo, found a large, apparently undisturbed tomb complex that extends for several square miles and may contain thousands of mummies. The first 105 mummies to be examined date back to the A.D. 100s, when Egypt was ruled by the Roman Empire. The mummies—men, women, and children—range from being plainly wrapped to wearing elaborate, painted masks.

* **city-state** independent state consisting of a city and its surrounding territory

Egypt and the Egyptians

The Palette of Narmer, shown here, dates from Egypt's predynastic period. The two-sided palette, which commemorated the unification of Upper and Lower Egypt, contains carvings of a king's conquests. The king, identified as Narmer from hieroglyphic writing on the panel, is seen viewing his slain enemies in the top panel. The middle panel shows the defeat of mythical animals. The last panel portrays the king, in the form of a bull, attacking a fortified city, represented by a rounded wall. On the other side of the palette, not shown here, Narmer defeats his enemies with the help of Horus, king of the gods.

Amenemhet I, the founder of the Twelfth Dynasty (ca. 1938–1759 B.C.), reinforced Egypt's unity by moving the capital north to Lisht, near Memphis. Kings of this dynasty also expanded Egypt's borders and divided Egypt into four regions. The final ruler of the Twelfth Dynasty was a queen, Nefrusobek, whose reign ended around 1759 B.C. Two dynasties then ruled Egypt. The Thirteenth Dynasty, with some 50 minor kings, ruled from Memphis, while at the same time, the Fourteenth Dynasty held the eastern Nile Delta.

By around 1630 B.C., invaders from western Asia, called Hyksos, took control of the Nile Delta. They then moved south, taking over much of the Nile Valley. This launched the Second Intermediate period (ca. 1630–1523 B.C.), during which several native kings of Upper Egypt ruling from Thebes tried unsuccessfully to overthrow the Hyksos.

New Kingdom and Third Intermediate Period. Around 1530 B.C., Ahmose, the first king of the Eighteenth Dynasty (ca. 1539–1292 B.C.), succeeded in defeating the Hyksos and reunited Egypt. Ahmose's rule ushered in the New Kingdom period, the third and longest period of strong, stable central government in Egyptian history. During this period, Egypt achieved its greatest riches and power, controlling lands as far away as Nubia to the south and northern Syria to the east. The enormous temples and tombs constructed at the capital of Thebes during the times of the New Kingdom reflect Egypt's great wealth at that time.

The New Kingdom lasted almost 500 years and included the reigns of some of the best-known rulers of Egypt, many from the Eighteenth Dynasty, such as Hatshepsut, one of the few women to rule in her own right. Thutmose III, who succeeded Hatshepsut, secured Egypt's empire in western Asia which extended to the Euphrates River in northern Syria. Amenhotep III, who is known for his peaceful reign, built great monuments, such as a temple to Amun at Luxor. Akhenaten was the leader of a short-lived but dramatic cultural and religious revolution. Tutankhamen is famous today for the incredible treasures found buried in his tomb. Another well-known king, Ramses II of the Nineteenth Dynasty (ca. 1292–1190 B.C.), ruled for 67 years and built more monuments—such as the temple at Abu Simbel—than any other Egyptian king.

Ramses II's successors were weak. In about 1200 B.C., the Twentieth Dynasty came to power under circumstances that are not entirely clear. The Twentieth Dynasty's best-known king, Ramses III, did repel a massive invasion of the Nile Delta by the Sea Peoples. However, his successors were also weak, and by around 1075 B.C., Egypt was again split among minor local kings. This was the beginning of a third period of divided rule, called the Third Intermediate period.

This time, no local Egyptian king was able to reunite Egypt and establish another period of strong central government. Egypt's neighbors were stronger than they had been in the past, and trying to resist their invasions drained Egypt economically. Libyans from the west moved into the delta and took over Lower Egypt, ruling there as the Twenty-second through the Twenty-fourth Dynasties (ca. 945–712 B.C.). Nubians from the south took control of Upper Egypt. By around 760 B.C., the Nubians had conquered Lower Egypt as well and reunited Egypt under the Twenty-fifth Dynasty (ca. 760–656 B.C.).

Late and Greco-Roman Periods. The Nubian conquest marked the beginning of the Late Period, a long period with intervals of foreign and native rule in ancient Egypt that lasted until the end of the ancient Egyptian civilization. Beginning around 671 B.C., the Assyrians launched a series of attacks directly against Egypt. The last Nubian king, TAHARQA, fled, and in his place the Assyrian king ASHURBANIPAL, rather than becoming the pharaoh himself, established local rulers throughout the country. When the Assyrians withdrew, the local rulers at Sais in the Nile Delta were able to reunify the country under the Twenty-sixth Dynasty. This last great native dynasty of Egypt lasted for about a century. The Persians held Egypt twice, first from 525 until 404 B.C., when local Egyptian rulers were able to free themselves temporarily, and again between 343 and 332 B.C.

In 332 B.C., ALEXANDER THE GREAT of Macedonia seized Egypt from the Persians and began the Macedonian dynasty. In 331 B.C., Alexander founded the city of Alexandria, which went on to become one of the most important cities of the eastern Mediterranean. Alexander ruled Egypt until his death in 323 B.C., after which his empire, which extended from Macedonia and Greece to the Persian empire and beyond, was divided by his generals. One of his generals, PTOLEMY I, ruled Egypt as governor. In 305 B.C., Ptolemy founded the Ptolemaic dynasty (305–30 B.C.), under which Egypt achieved a new splendor as part of the Hellenistic* world. The Ptolemaic dynasty was the last dynasty to rule ancient Egypt. It ended when CLEOPATRA, last ruler of the dynasty, committed suicide in 30 B.C. after Rome's capture of Egypt. Egypt became a Roman province. It enjoyed prosperity, but most of its wealth was transferred to Rome.

* **Hellenistic** referring to the Greek-influenced culture of the Mediterranean world and western Asia during the three centuries after the death of Alexander the Great in 323 B.C.

* **sluice** human-made channel or passage to direct water flow

* **silt** soil or other sediment carried and deposited by moving water

* **levee** embankment or earthen wall alongside a river that helps prevent flooding

ECONOMY

Throughout all these periods, the economy of ancient Egypt was primarily based on agriculture. Most of the land was divided into large estates owned by the government or major temples. A few large estates were owned by wealthy individuals, including members of the royal family, high-ranking priests, and government officials. Regardless of who owned the land, it was actually worked by hired laborers, who were paid with rations, including a share of the crops. Other sources of wealth included stones for building, precious stones, and minerals, all of which were owned and exploited by the government.

Agriculture. The wealth of ancient Egypt always depended first and foremost on agriculture. Egyptians depended on the floodwaters of the Nile River to provide them with the water necessary to grow crops.

Between July and October each year, the Nile floods because of heavy rains in central Africa. Since A.D. 1830, these floods have been controlled by a series of dams and sluices*. In ancient times, the floodwaters covered most of the land in the Nile Valley. Silt* carried by the floodwaters was deposited on the land, enriching the soil in the surrounding valley and building up natural levees* along the river banks. When the floodwaters subsided, water was trapped in the valley behind the levees. Once the water soaked into the ground, farmers plowed the fields with wooden

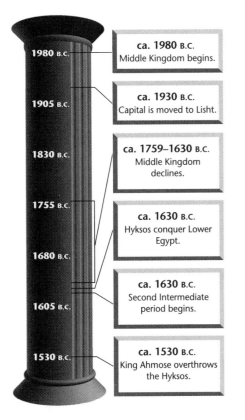

1980 B.C.	ca. 1980 B.C. Middle Kingdom begins.
1905 B.C.	ca. 1930 B.C. Capital is moved to Lisht.
1830 B.C.	ca. 1759–1630 B.C. Middle Kingdom declines.
1755 B.C.	ca. 1630 B.C. Hyksos conquer Lower Egypt.
1680 B.C.	
1605 B.C.	ca. 1630 B.C. Second Intermediate period begins.
1530 B.C.	ca. 1530 B.C. King Ahmose overthrows the Hyksos.

61

In ancient times, Luxor was an important religious center for the Egyptians. It was famous for the Great Temple built by King Amenhotep III around 1375 B.C. About 1,000 years later, King Ramses II added an outer court to the temple, in which he installed several statues of himself. Two of these large sculptures shown here are at the entrance to the temple.

Eating and Entertaining in Egypt

In ancient Egypt, people of all classes washed their hands before meals and ate with the fingers of the right hand. During feasts or banquets, people often sat on the ground next to a small table holding their food. Good table manners were very important, and ancient texts on etiquette warn against appearing greedy or gluttonous. The presentation of food was also important. Meals were often carefully arranged on mats and decorated with flowers. Garlands of flowers were used to adorn jars of wine and beer. Among the upper classes, dinner guests were treated lavishly, with servants to wash and dry their hands, serve their food and drink, and anoint them with scented oils.

plows pulled by oxen and then scattered seeds on the rich, wet soil. Enough moisture was held by the soil to allow crops to grow and mature.

The food crops the Egyptians grew provided them with a relatively healthy diet. The main crops were wheat and barley, which were used to make bread, porridge, and beer, all staples of the diet. Legumes, such as peas, beans, and lentils, provided sources of protein. A variety of fruits and vegetables added vitamins and minerals to the diet.

Papyrus and FLAX crops were also very important in ancient Egypt. Papyrus, which was used to make a paperlike material, could be grown in swampy areas that were not suited for other kinds of crops. Flax had many uses—sails, ropes, and linen for clothing—and was grown in wetland areas.

Trade. Most Egyptians worked as farm laborers, and in exchange for their labor, they received enough grain and other crops to feed their family and to barter for the other goods they needed. The Egyptian economy worked on a system that economists call redistribution. In this type of system, goods are collected by a central authority, such as the government, and are allocated to the people according to their positions and work in society.

The redistribution system worked well as long as the authority of the central government was strong. When the central government collapsed, the system was undermined. The redistribution system probably fell apart after an economic crisis during the Twentieth Dynasty (ca. 1190–1075 B.C.). After this time, the government had less control over the trading system.

How Does It End?

Ancient Egyptian literature has several examples of fairy tales and folktales. Perhaps one of the more mysterious tales is the one known as *The Prince and His Fate* or *The Doomed Prince.* It tells of a prince who is fated at birth to die as the result of a dog, snake, or crocodile attack. The prince goes to seek his fortune in western Asia and marries a princess while trying to avoid his destiny. Although one of the story's themes is the inevitability of meeting one's fate, no one is sure of the ending of the prince's story. Only one copy of the story exists, and its final pages are missing. As a result, the doomed prince has managed to evade his destiny for thousands of years.

* **hieroglyphics** system of writing that uses pictorial characters, or hieroglyphs, to represent words or ideas

* **deity** god or goddess

* **cult** system of religious beliefs and rituals; group following these beliefs

* **mummification** process of embalming and drying a dead body and wrapping it as a mummy

See color plate 1, vol. 3.

Trade, in one form or another, was basic to the ancient Egyptian economy. Almost everything that was grown or made was bartered, or exchanged directly for other goods or services. The direct exchange of goods and services occurred at all levels of ancient Egyptian society. There was private barter between individuals, gifts and tribute from Egyptian citizens to the king and temples, and trade and gift exchanges between the king and the leaders of city-states.

CULTURAL HISTORY

Many aspects of ancient Egyptian life reflected the Egyptians' religious beliefs. These beliefs were not only seen in Egyptian religious practices but in their art, architecture, and literature. The ancient Egyptians used hieroglyphics* to record their view of the world and transmit it to future generations.

Religion. Egyptian religion was based on the belief in a large number of deities*. Some of the most important deities included AMUN, creator god of Thebes, who eventually was merged with Ra to become the great state god of the New Kingdom; ISIS, goddess of nature; SETH, god of storms; and OSIRIS, god of the dead.

Although religion was a part of every level of ancient Egyptian society, historians know most about the official state cult*. They also know about the burial practices of ancient Egypt, because these are preserved in monuments, tombs, and artworks. Far less is known about the everyday religious practices of the ordinary people.

Ancient Egyptians believed that if the gods were not served, they would desert Egypt and great misfortunes would result. It was the king's duty to serve the gods by building and maintaining magnificent temples and by observing the daily rituals of the state cult. In return, the gods assured the Egyptian people peace and prosperity.

The Egyptian religion was the first major religion to adopt the belief in an AFTERLIFE. This belief was reflected in many religious practices, including preserving dead bodies by mummification*, building tombs to house the dead, and worshiping dead ancestors. Egyptians also buried the dead with objects that would be needed in the afterlife, such as the BOOK OF THE DEAD, which contained writings guiding the deceased to Osiris's region of the dead, as well as clothing, furniture, cooking and eating utensils, and food. Painted pictures of these items could be substituted for the actual objects.

In later periods of Egypt's history, animal worship became very popular. Bulls, cats, rams, and many other animals were believed by some people to be sacred, and they were buried in ceremonies along with deceased people.

Art and Architecture. The ancient Egyptians are perhaps best known for their pyramids, the oldest and largest stone structures in the world. Most were built during the Old Kingdom period as tombs or monuments for Egyptian kings.

Egypt and the Egyptians

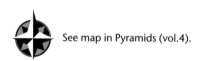

See map in Pyramids (vol.4).

* **bas-relief** kind of sculpture in which material is cut away to leave figures projecting slightly from the background

* **relief** sculpture in which material is cut away to show figures raised from the background

* **Semitic** of or relating to a language family that includes Akkadian, Aramaic, Arabic, Hebrew, and Phoenician

* **indigenous** referring to the original inhabitants of a region

* **scribe** person of a learned class who served as a writer, editor, or teacher

Although the pyramids were built more than 4,000 years ago, it is easy to see why they are considered marvels of architecture and engineering. Building them required knowledge of mathematics, as well as precise measuring and surveying skills. Organizing and overseeing the huge labor force and all the materials needed to build the pyramids was an amazing feat, and it reflected the strength of Egypt's central government.

Remains of many stone temples and other religious buildings from ancient Egypt also exist. The temples built during the New Kingdom were especially magnificent. Many had features that were designed to resemble plants and other natural objects. For example, some temples had columns carved to look like palm trees.

Painting and sculpture were the major forms of official art in ancient Egypt, and both reached a high level of skill and artistry. Most artworks were created to decorate tombs or temples. For example, artists covered the walls of tombs with paintings and bas-reliefs* showing family scenes for the deceased to enjoy in the afterlife.

The best-known sculpture from ancient Egyptian times is the Great Sphinx, a huge statue of a man's head on a lion's body. It is located close to the Great Pyramid at GIZA and probably represents King Khufu of the Fourth Dynasty (ca. 2625–2500 B.C.). The statue is massive, rising 66 feet in height and covering 240 feet in length.

The style of art in ancient Egypt was very distinctive. Figures and objects were not represented as they would appear to an observer. Instead, they were drawn or sculpted following a set of rules that, because of their consistency, were meant to make them easy to recognize. For example, representations of people in reliefs* almost always showed the head, legs, and feet in profile and the rest of the body facing the viewer. Also, artworks showing both the king and ordinary people always showed the king much taller than the others to reflect the king's importance.

Language and Literature. The Egyptian language is a branch of the Afro-Asiatic language family. The language, which was spoken in Egypt since predynastic times, probably started out as a Semitic* language spoken by immigrants to Egypt from western Asia. Then, as the original Semitic language spread throughout Egypt, it picked up features of the North African languages spoken by the indigenous* people.

Around 3000 B.C., Egyptians invented hieroglyphics—picture symbols that represented different ideas as well as sounds—to record their language. Scribes* used hieroglyphics to inscribe monuments and temples. They also used a cursive form of hieroglyphics to keep records and write letters on papyrus scrolls.

During the Old Kingdom period, Egyptians used writing chiefly for record keeping. By the time of the Middle Kingdom, written literature had developed. Literature blossomed in the New Kingdom and flourished even more during the period of the Ptolemaic dynasty.

Scribes produced huge numbers of papyrus scrolls written in cursive hieroglyphics, many of them simply as penmanship exercises. The scrolls included autobiographies, scientific works on subjects such as mathematics and astronomy, religious writings, hymns, poetry, letters, fairy tales, fables, short stories, and essays. A common theme was how to behave well

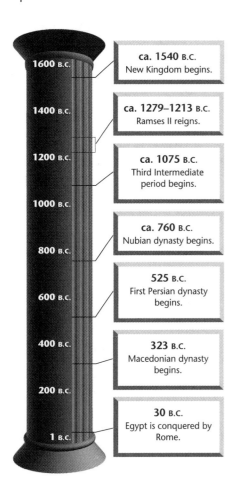

and ensure a happy life after death. Thousands of scrolls accumulated in ancient Egypt's many libraries. The library at Alexandria was the largest, with almost half a million scrolls.

Ancient Egypt also had a very strong oral literature tradition. In fact, much of Egypt's recorded literature came originally from the oral tradition. In addition, many pieces of writing were meant to be read aloud, including letters and texts. As a result, both orators and storytellers were greatly admired and respected in Egyptian society.

FAMILY AND SOCIETY

Ancient Egyptians viewed and portrayed themselves not as individuals but as part of a larger unit—a family or a society. As part of these units, Egyptians lived in communities ranging in size from villages to cities.

Family. The basic social unit in ancient Egypt was the nuclear family, which included a father, a mother, and their children. The father was the head of the family, a reflection of the general male dominance in ancient Egyptian society. When the father died, his oldest son became head of the family.

The main purpose of marriage was to produce children who would provide labor and support their parents when they grew old. Children usually started helping their parents around the house or in the fields as soon as they were old enough to do simple chores. In fact, this is how most children learned their adult occupations. Girls would learn domestic skills from their mothers and boys would learn their fathers' occupations. A few children served as apprentices* to carpenters, pottery makers, or other skilled workers. Some girls may also have been apprenticed in professions such as dancing or weaving. Only boys from wealthy families could afford to go to school, and most schoolchildren studied to be scribes.

Social Classes. The people of ancient Egypt belonged to three main social classes, often referred to as upper, middle, and lower classes. Social class was inherited but not necessarily fixed permanently. Through marriage or hard work, a person could rise to a higher social class.

The tiny upper class included members of the royal family, army officers, doctors, wealthy landowners, and high-ranking government officials and priests. The somewhat larger middle class included merchants, skilled craftspeople, and manufacturers. The largest class, the lower class, consisted of unskilled workers, most of them farm laborers. Prisoners of war formed a separate class of slaves.

Egyptian society gave women many of the same rights as men, such as the right to own and inherit property, file lawsuits, and obtain a divorce. In addition, women served as priestesses in the temples.

Ethnic Diversity. Despite marked class differences, ancient Egyptian society was remarkably uniform in its beliefs and values, especially considering the ethnic diversity of its population. Egypt was first settled

* **apprentice** individual who learns skills or a profession from an experienced person in that field

by people moving into the Nile Valley from virtually every direction, including Libyans from the west, Nubians from the south, and Semitic peoples from the east. People from other cultures who were attracted by Egypt's rich farmland and wealth continued to move into Egypt throughout its history. The ability of ancient Egyptian society to assimilate people of many different ethnic backgrounds without prejudice was one of its characteristic features. (*See also* **Assyria and the Assyrians; Education; Ethnic and Language Groups; Government; Law; Mummies; Nubia and the Nubians; Persian Empire.**)

* **Semitic** of or relating to a language family that includes Akkadian, Aramaic, Arabic, Hebrew, and Phoenician

* **deity** god or goddess

* **pantheon** all the gods of a particular culture

* **second millennium** B.C. years from 2000 to 1001 B.C.

Originally a Semitic* word meaning god, *El* (AYL) later became associated with a specific deity*. El was worshiped in some form by various ancient Semitic peoples, including the Phoenicians and other Canaanites. The god YAHWEH is sometimes called El in the Hebrew BIBLE.

El was the head of the Canaanite pantheon*. He was king of the gods, the creator of the earth, and the father of humanity. Much of what we know about early Canaanite religious beliefs comes from texts found at UGARIT, a Syrian city that flourished in the second half of the second millennium B.C.* Ugaritic texts show that El played an important role in Canaanite mythology. Although El was the chief god, he did not play an active role in the everyday lives of gods or humans. Instead, he was thought of as an aging god, respected but somewhat withdrawn from the forefront of religious activity. In fact, a small stone statue of El found in the ruins of Ugarit portrays him wearing a beard and crown, slouching on his throne in a way that suggests weariness, perhaps even sadness from being overwhelmed by the cares of the world.

Some scholars believe that the early Israelite pantheon included some deities familiar to their Phoenician and other Canaanite neighbors, including BAAL. Over time, the Israelites associated El with Yahweh, a god worshiped only by the Israelites. For this reason and because the word *el* sometimes meant god in Semitic languages, writers of the Hebrew Bible used El as an alternative name for Yahweh. They also created names based on the word *el,* including Elohim (a plural form of El), El-Bethel (god of Bethel), and El-Olam (Eternal god).

* **fourth millennium** B.C. years from 4000 to 3001 B.C.

Established as early as the fourth millennium B.C.*, Elam (EE•luhm) was an ancient kingdom in southwestern IRAN. One of the major powers in the ancient Near East, Elam maintained its independence throughout much of its history despite many invasions.

Geography and Culture. Elam consisted of both highland and lowland regions, and the political balance between these areas fluctuated. The lowland region (present-day Khuzestan) was periodically involved in the affairs of MESOPOTAMIA because of its proximity to that region. The highlands in the Zagros Mountains generally remained more independent.

See map in Persian Empire (vol. 3)

The Most Legitimate Heir

An important and unique title in Elamite civilization was "the son of the sister," which applied to a member of the royal family. Early historians assumed that this meant the king's nephew. In reality, it meant the son whom the king had with his own sister and signified the legitimate heir to the throne. Any children born to women married to the king were considered legitimate heirs. When the king married his own sister, however, the oldest son of their union had a stronger claim to the throne than any of the king's other children—even older ones.

* **cuneiform** world's oldest form of writing, which takes its name from the distinctive wedge-shaped signs pressed into clay tablets

* **deity** god or goddess

* **patron** special guardian, protector, or supporter

* **archaeological** referring to the study of past human cultures, usually by excavating material remains of human activity

* **artifact** ornament, tool, weapon, or other object made by humans

* **city-state** independent state consisting of a city and its surrounding territory

* **dynasty** succession of rulers from the same family or group

Differences in geography contributed to economic diversity within Elam. The lowland areas developed a strong agricultural base dependent on irrigation, and settlements there grew quite large. Susa, the capital of Elam, was located on the edge of a fertile plain. However, the lowland areas were dependent on the highlands for metals, stone, and wood. In the highlands, agriculture was limited to small mountain valleys. River valleys were the main access into the highland regions, and the rugged, mountainous terrain limited the size of settlements.

Geographic diversity also contributed to the development of regional cultures within Elam. Although no single artistic style emerged in the kingdom, the Elamites shared a language that appears to be unrelated to any other regional language. The Elamites eventually adopted the cuneiform* script from the Sumerians and Akkadians.

The Elamites also worshiped many deities*, the most important of whom was Inshushinak, the city god of Susa. They also worshiped many Sumerian and Akkadian gods. Religious activities included rituals, regular public feasts, and OFFERINGS to the gods. The king functioned as the highest priest in the land and was sometimes regarded as divine.

A special feature of Elamite religion was a phenomenon known as the *kiden,* a magical protection associated with a specific god. According to the Elamites, the *kiden* was expressed in talismans (magical objects) symbolizing and linked to particular gods. These talismans had many uses. For example, witnesses often had to take an oath in a room where a talisman was kept, and fear of the talisman's power ensured that the witnesses would tell the truth.

Another unique aspect of Elamite civilization was the importance it accorded to women. Elamite women enjoyed great prestige, and many cities had goddesses instead of gods as patrons*. Priestesses had the same rights and powers as priests. In addition, claims to the throne sometimes passed through the female rather than the male line.

Old Elamite Period. The ancestors of the Elamites who lived in Elam as early as the fourth millennium B.C. are known as the Proto-Elamites. Archaeological* sites have yielded SEALS, tablets, and other artifacts* that have shed some light on their culture. The Proto-Elamites, contemporaries of the Sumerians, were an important part of the period during which literate urban culture first developed and expanded. Because little else is known about the Proto-Elamites, historians date the beginnings of Elamite history at about 2500 B.C., the period when early Elamite rulers adapted Mesopotamian cuneiform to the Elamite language. The first main phase of Elamite history, the years from around 2500 to 1500 B.C., is known as the Old Elamite period.

By the Old Elamite period, conflict already existed between Elam and Mesopotamia. Texts indicate that the Elamites defeated the army of the Sumerian city-state* of UR at least once before this period. During this period, Elam was ruled by the kings of the Awan dynasty*. During much of this dynasty, Elam periodically went to war with Akkad and the Akkadian empire. Around 2300 B.C., Elam was conquered by SARGON I of Akkad. A later Elamite king made a treaty with NARAM-SIN of Akkad, in which he promised to provide the Akkadians with troops. Although the Akkadians

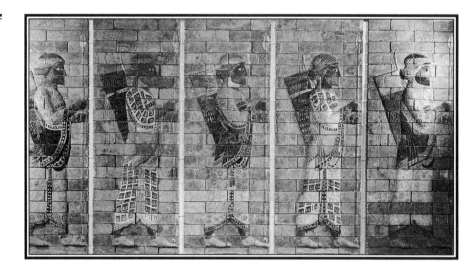

Elam and the Elamites

This is a reconstruction of a wall relief (frieze) from Susa, the capital city of Elam. The archers are Susian guards, recognizable by their twisted headbands, a distinctive Elamite feature. The archers are shown in identical postures, carrying a spear and a bow, and wearing an ankle-length flowing garment.

* **vassal** individual or state that swears loyalty and obedience to a greater power

* **diplomatic** concerning relations with foreign powers

dominated Elam and incorporated much of its territory into the Akkadian state, they allowed the Elamite kings to rule as vassals*. The Awan dynasty collapsed around 2150 B.C., destroyed perhaps by the Gutians, a people who lived in what is present-day Kurdistan. The Gutians also defeated the Akkadians, ending their empire. Then the Shimashki dynasty came to power in Elam, but little is known about them.

Elam faced a new enemy in the 2000s B.C.—the Neo-Sumerian city-state of Ur. King SHULGI of Ur (ruled ca. 2094–2047 B.C.) conquered almost all of Elam. Only the highland regions of Elam kept some degree of independence. Eventually, in about the 1900s B.C., the Elamites rose in rebellion and destroyed Ur, looting the city and carrying away the statues of its gods. The Elamites occupied Ur with a military force for 21 years but later made peace with the dynasties that came to power.

The years between 1900 and 1600 B.C. are the best-documented period in Elamite history. This era was dominated by the Sukkalmakh dynasty, also known as the Ebartids. Elam became a major independent power during this period, with one of the largest territories in the Near East. Its influence, though not political control, extended over city-states in eastern Mesopotamia, and it had diplomatic* and economic contacts with kingdoms as far as away as SYRIA. At that time, the Elamite kingdom may have had a political system in which various members of the royal family—both male and female—shared power.

During the 1700s B.C., Elamite kings became active in military alliances against the Babylonians, whose power was increasing in southern Mesopotamia. Around 1764 B.C., King HAMMURABI of Babylon crushed the Elamites. About 50 years later, however, King Kutir-Nakkhunte of Elam attacked Babylonia and conquered many of its cities. This campaign marked the high point of Elamite military history for centuries.

Over the next few hundred years the Elamites faced a number of new rising powers, including the HURRIANS in the northwest and the KASSITES to the north. When the Kassites conquered Babylon in the 1500s B.C., they seem to have brought the power of the Ebartids in Elam to an end as well, marking the end of the Old Elamite period. The Elamite kingdom entered a period of decline that lasted for about the next 300 years.

The Middle Elamite Period. Elam arose again in the late 1300s B.C., when Elamites from the highlands began to reconquer the lowlands after the Kassites withdrew from Susa. By the 1200s B.C., Elam had reemerged as a major power, with a territory comparable to that of earlier centuries. During this period, Elamite kings undertook major building programs, constructing new cities, temples, and other public works. Elamite literature, art, architecture, and crafts also flourished, and this period became a golden age of Elamite civilization.

In the 1200s B.C., Elam found itself facing a new power—Assyria. Around 1224 B.C., the Assyrians took control of the throne of Babylon. The Elamites invaded Babylonia soon after, destroying and conquering many cities and driving out the Assyrian king. However, about two years later, King Tukulti-Ninurta I of Assyria forced the Elamites out of Babylon and placed a Kassite vassal on the throne. Conflict between Elam and Assyria continued for several years. In the early 1100s B.C., internal conflict in Assyria and struggles between Assyria and Babylonia weakened the Assyrians and provided a period of quiet for the Elamites. During this period, the Elamites reorganized their kingdom. Led by the Shutrukid dynasty, Elam extended its control in southern and eastern Iran and launched new campaigns against Mesopotamia, including a successful and devastating invasion of Babylon in about 1165 B.C.

Despite repeated military victories and destruction of Babylonian cities, the Elamites faced continual threats from the Babylonians. The efforts to subdue Babylonia may have weakened the Elamites, and in the late 1100s B.C., Babylonian king Nebuchadnezzar I launched several attacks against Elam. Around 1100 B.C., the Babylonians attacked and destroyed Susa and overran much of the Elamite kingdom. After this devastating defeat, little is known about Elam during the next 300 years.

The Neo-Elamite Period. Elam reemerged in late 800s B.C., when it became a refuge for Babylonian opponents of Assyria. The kingdom was much weaker than in earlier centuries, and it faced increasing pressures on almost all sides from the Assyrians, MEDES, and Persians.

From 750 to 650 B.C., Elam again became involved in Mesopotamian affairs, often supporting Babylonia in its struggle against the Assyrians. In 720 B.C., the Elamites allied with the Babylonians to defeat SARGON II of Assyria. They joined the Babylonians again in 705 B.C. and defeated the Assyrians at the city of KISH. In spite of these victories, the Assyrians were a formidable enemy. Under King SENNACHERIB, the Assyrians invaded Elam and occupied much of the southern part of the kingdom. They also launched assaults into the highland regions of Elam but were less successful there. While the Elamites struggled against the Assyrians, the Persians began occupying parts of eastern Elam, including Anshan, an ancient Elamite royal city.

Elam experienced a slow decline throughout this period, due in part to the conflicts with Assyria and the threats from the Medes and Persians. Elam also faced internal troubles, as rivals competed for the Elamite throne. Because of these problems, the Elamites were unable to counter the Assyrians. In 647 B.C., King ASHURBANIPAL renewed the Assyrian attacks on Elam and the following year conquered and destroyed Susa. Many of

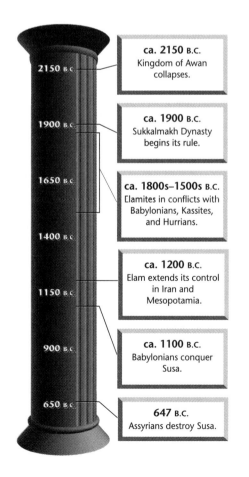

ca. 2150 B.C.
Kingdom of Awan collapses.

ca. 1900 B.C.
Sukkalmakh Dynasty begins its rule.

ca. 1800s–1500s B.C.
Elamites in conflicts with Babylonians, Kassites, and Hurrians.

ca. 1200 B.C.
Elam extends its control in Iran and Mesopotamia.

ca. 1100 B.C.
Babylonians conquer Susa.

647 B.C.
Assyrians destroy Susa.

2150 B.C.
1900 B.C.
1650 B.C.
1400 B.C.
1150 B.C.
900 B.C.
650 B.C.

its leading citizens were sent away to SAMARIA, the former capital of the kingdom of Israel. The Elamite king, Khumban-khaltash III, fled into the mountains, but the people there turned him over to the Assyrians, who soon extended their control over much of Elamite territory.

With the Assyrian victory, the history of Elam as a state ended. For a short time, parts of the highland regions in the north remained under Elamite control, but they soon fell into the hands of the Medes. Meanwhile, the Persians gained control of the eastern portions of Elam. Although references to the Elamites persisted until the 200s B.C., little is known about them after their defeat by the Assyrians. (*See also* **Assyria and the Assyrians; Babylon and the Babylonians, Susa and Susiana.**)

Electrum

See *Metals and Metalworking.*

ENLIL

* **pantheon** all the gods of a particular culture

Sumerians worshiped Enlil (EN•lil), god of the earth and air, who brought both gentle breezes and the winds sweeping storms. Also known as Ellil or Bel (the Lord), Enlil (translated as "Lord Wind") was one of a trio of gods that included ANU—the sky god—and EA—the water god.

Although Anu occupied a higher position in the ancient Near Eastern pantheon*, Enlil played a more significant role. According to Sumerian MYTHOLOGY, he played an important role in creation, separating heaven from earth. Representing energy and force, he was responsible for bringing order and harmony to the universe. Enlil was also the keeper of the Tablet of Destiny, which held the fate of both the gods and humans.

According to tradition, local gods received authority from Enlil. In turn, they passed this authority on to the king, who claimed kingship through Enlil. Enlil could be very hostile and cruel to humans and was often prepared to punish them even for minor offenses. As a god of storms, winds, and war, he could send various calamities—including famine*, fire, hurricane, plague*, drought, and flood—to punish sins and protect Mesopotamia against its enemies.

* **famine** severe lack of food due to failed crops

* **plague** contagious disease that quickly kills large numbers of people

* **second millennium B.C.** years from 2000 to 1001 B.C.

The most important center of worship to Enlil during the Early Dynastic period (ca. 3000–2675 B.C.) was at a temple called Ekur (Mountain House) in the Sumerian city of NIPPUR. By the late second millennium B.C.*, however, the Babylonian deity MARDUK inherited Enlil's role in the pantheon of the gods. (*See also* **Creation Myths; Gods and Goddesses.**)

ENTERTAINMENT

In the ancient Near East, people entertained themselves with a variety of formal and informal activities. Most individuals worked many hours each day just to survive. Once demands for food, shelter, and safety had been met, people developed pastimes, such as music, dance, banquets, sports, games, storytelling, and performances, to amuse themselves.

Music and Dance. Music and dancing were among the most important and earliest forms of entertainment. In Mesopotamia, Sumerians, Akkadians, and Babylonians developed several musical instruments, including flutes, lutes, harps, and drums, which were played at feasts, festivals and celebrations. Evidence from bas-reliefs* and paintings suggests that both men and women might be musicians, singers, and dancers.

Egyptians also enjoyed musical entertainment. During the period of the Old Kingdom (ca. 2675–2130 B.C.), music was organized and included choirs and chamber groups playing pipes and the harp. Female dancers performed at religious celebrations. In the time of the Middle Kingdom (ca. 1980–1630 B.C.), dances were performed at public and private events. Dancers and singers entertained guests at elaborate banquets. In the New Kingdom period (ca. 1539–1075 B.C.), foreigners arriving in Egypt brought new forms of musical instruments and new types of dance.

HITTITES in ANATOLIA (present-day Turkey) developed many forms of music and dance. Most of what is known about their music and dance concerns religious or state rituals. Little is known about the specific role of music and dance in the private lives of the Hittites. However, many documents make references to singers, musicians, dancers, mimes, and actors, who probably depended on the palace for their living.

In ancient Syria and the Levant*, people entertained themselves by singing, dancing, and playing musical instruments. The Hebrew BIBLE

* **bas-relief** kind of sculpture in which material is cut away to leave figures projecting slightly from the background

* **Levant** lands bordering the eastern shores of the Mediterranean Sea (present-day Syria, Lebanon, and Israel), the West Bank, and Jordan

Music was one of the earliest forms of entertainment. Throughout the ancient Near East, feasts, festivals, and state and private celebrations included musical performances, such as those by a lyre or harp player, a piper, and a percussionist. This stone wall relief from Nineveh, dating from the 600s B.C., shows near life-sized Assyrian musicians performing at a feast.

Entertainment

mentions a variety of instruments, including rattles and cymbals, bells and gongs, large and small drums, pipes and horns, and harps and lyres. Jesters, acrobats, and singers were palace servants in UGARIT, an ancient city in present-day north Syria. When King Hezekiah of Judah was forced to pay tribute* to King SENNACHERIB of Assyria, among the prizes he delivered were professional singers and dancers.

* **tribute** payment made by a smaller or weaker party to a more powerful one, often under the threat of force

Banquets. Giving or attending banquets was a form of entertainment in the ancient Near East, as well as the setting for much of the music and dance. Although little is known about such events, it is likely that the guests participated in feasts, music, dance, processions, and other forms of public and private entertainment. Sumerian bas-reliefs from the early 2000s B.C. depict banquets following a battle, a hunt, and the laying of the first brick of a new temple. The Royal Standard of Ur (an inlaid mosaic panel) depicts a victorious battle scene and the ensuing banquet held by the king. In a bas-relief from the Assyrian palace at NINEVEH, King ASHURBANIPAL celebrates with his wife his victory over the Elamites. In a garden, the king reclines on a couch while his wife sits on a throne. They are surrounded by servants who fan them, offer platters of food, and play the harp.

See color plate 2, vol. 2.

Egyptians held banquets to celebrate many events of a person's lifetime, including birth, marriage, and death. Hosting a banquet could be costly, but for those who could afford them, lavish banquets were important. Guests were draped in flowers and served exotic dishes of poultry or beef seasoned with a wide variety of spices. Music and dancing accompanied the feasts. At higher levels of society, men and women dined separately, but this was not the case at all banquets.

Although there are records of feasts in Hittite Anatolia, it is not known whether banqueting for entertainment occurred there. Most of the feasts were seasonal and religious and had a festive atmosphere. The Hittite verb *dusk,* meaning "to rejoice" or "to enjoy," appears often in descriptions of these festivals. It is likely that people did enjoy purely social banquets, especially persons of high social rank.

Banquets were also part of life in Syria and the Levant. In fact, some religious leaders thought ancient Israelites enjoyed feasts too much. The book of Isaiah warns those who "have lyre and harp, timbrel and flute and wine at their feasts" against neglecting their religion.

Sports. Sports and athletic contests provided recreation and entertainment for many peoples in the ancient Near East. However, it is not clear when sports became an organized form of public entertainment. Displays of strength were connected to religious belief because they reflected the might of the society and its gods. Such displays of power in Mesopotamia may have been linked to festivals.

* **pharaoh** king of ancient Egypt

See color plate 15, vol. 2.

In Egypt, sports were a common form of entertainment. Pharaohs* showed their skill in archery and hunting, but they never competed with ordinary people. Other than hunting, sports were not considered an acceptable pastime for elite men or women. Commoners participated in sports such as wrestling, boxing, and jousting in boats. Some ancient ball games and stick fights were similar to those played today in Egypt.

Environmental Change

In Anatolia, Hittite festivals included sports such as juggling, gymnastics, and athletic contests. Mock battles emphasized military power. As with other forms of entertainment, the focus on state and religious ceremonies makes it hard to determine how much sport was a part of daily life. Sports in ancient Syria and the Levant were linked to skills that society valued. Hunting, archery, running, fencing, wrestling, and horseback riding are all mentioned in the Bible.

Storytelling and Performance. Perhaps the oldest form of entertainment is storytelling. All ancient Near Eastern cultures entertained themselves in this way. Egyptians wrote on papyrus* and told stories, poems, hymns, love lyrics, and epics*. Folktales and history passed from generation to generation by word of mouth.

When enacted as performances, these stories were often accompanied by music. Performances of some literary works were part of the cult*. During the Babylonian New Year's festival, the CREATION MYTH (Enuma Elish) was recited, and its battle scenes were reenacted. (See also Dance; Family and Social Life; Feasts and Festivals; Humor; Literature; Music and Musical Instruments; Religion; Rituals and Sacrifice.)

* **papyrus** writing material made by pressing together thin strips of the inner stem of the papyrus plant; *pl.* papyri

* **epic** long poem about a legendary or historical hero, written in a grand style

* **cult** system of religious beliefs and rituals; group following these beliefs

Enuma Elish

See *Creation Myths.*

ENVIRONMENTAL CHANGE

Changes in CLIMATE and landscape affect plants, animals, and humans. This principle is the basis of environmental archaeology. Experts in this field study changes in climate and landscape to understand the relationships between ancient peoples and their environment. They also examine how human activities cause changes in the environment.

Environmental archaeologists believe that changes in the environment create a chain of events that have an impact on economies and society. For example, if a region becomes too dry to support grasses, grazing animals will migrate to other areas. People who depend on these animals have to move or find other ways to live.

Studying Environmental Change. Environmental archaeology includes the work of many specialists. Bioarchaeologists examine the biological remains of ancient plants and animals and analyze the substances found in bone and tissues. Paleobotanists study ancient plant life, often by examining seed grains and other plant remains found at archaeological sites. Paleogeologists study the layers of rock and soil that have built up over the ages. Traditional archaeologists analyze the ruins of ancient dwellings, pottery, and other artifacts*. By comparing their findings with current plants, animals, and climatic conditions, these scientists reconstruct the environment as it was in ancient times.

* **artifact** ornament, tool, weapon, or other object made by humans

Environment of the Prehistoric Period. For most of the early A.D. 1900s, many scientists believed that civilizations emerged in the ancient

73

Environmental Change

* **oasis** fertile area in a desert made possible by the presence of a spring or well; *pl.* oases

* **domesticate** to adapt or tame for human use

 See map in Mesopotamia (vol. 3).

* **Levant** lands bordering the eastern shores of the Mediterranean Sea (present-day Syria, Lebanon, and Israel), the West Bank, and Jordan

* **fifth millennium B.C.** years from 5000 to 4001 B.C.

* **millennium** period of 1,000 years; *pl.* millennia

Near East because of significant changes in the climate there. They suggested that a wet period during the last Ice Age was followed by an increasingly drier climate. This changing climate forced people throughout the Near East to move together into river valleys and oases*, where they began to develop AGRICULTURE and domesticate* animals.

Today some archaeologists do not believe that a major drying period caused the rise of civilization in the Near East. Instead, they believe that it was caused by the melting ice near the earth's polar regions, which raised sea levels, changed coastlines, and brought more rainfall. Between about 9000 and 5000 B.C., the climate of the Near East may have been wetter than it is today, although the general climate of the region is about the same as it was 10,000 years ago.

Small variations in rainfall can make a great difference to agriculture, especially where rainfall and water supplies are scarce. Such variations account for the movements of some early peoples. In much of the region, however, the greatest agent of environmental change was human activity. Peoples' need for farmland, pastureland, and fuel brought about significant changes in the environment, especially in ANATOLIA (present-day Turkey), MESOPOTAMIA, the Levant*, and Egypt.

Changes in Rivers. Ancient Near Eastern civilizations were almost directly affected by the changes in the region's major rivers. In Mesopotamia, periodic flooding of the Tigris and Euphrates Rivers made life unpredictable. Ancient farmers did what they could to control the often violent floodwaters. They constructed CANALS and other earthworks for IRRIGATION, making agriculture possible in regions where rainfall alone would not suffice to support human life and crops.

People in ancient Mesopotamia were also affected by the changing course of the Tigris and Euphrates Rivers, which often forced them to relocate. Moreover, misuse of land and a buildup of salt in the soil as a result of irrigation caused areas to become unusable for farming. The marshlands in southern Mesopotamia, with their surprising diversity of wildlife, changed boundaries as well.

In Egypt, the annual flooding of the Nile River was more predictable and less violent than that of the Tigris and the Euphrates. These floods helped agriculture and contributed to an increase in settlements in the Nile Valley and to the political growth of ancient Egypt. The Nile Valley changed as the human population there increased. As late as the fifth millenium B.C.*, elephants, giraffes, lions, ostriches, hippopotamuses, and antelopes lived in Egypt. However, these animals were later displaced by human settlement. Fields and groves of palm trees also replaced woodlands and various forms of plant life. By about 2650 B.C., the Nile Valley had been dramatically altered by human activities.

Changes in Land. Human activity changed the land in the ancient Near East more than did climate. For example, southern Mesopotamia, initially a grassland, became a desert after several millennia* of irrigation and farming. Many societies in the ancient Near East experienced social and political upheaval around 2200 B.C. Some experts believe that changes in climate further contributed to the strife by weakening agriculture.

However, evidence for such climatic change is inconclusive. What is certain is that humans have had a powerful impact on the environment of the Near East over the last 2,000 years.

Forests throughout the Mediterranean, from Anatolia to Egypt, were once far numerous than they are today. As people cleared forests for agriculture, firewood, and building materials, the tree cover was dramatically reduced and the forests disappeared. For example, Phoenicia (present-day Lebanon) was once home to cedar forests that attracted kings from throughout the ancient Near East for building materials for their palaces and temples. Large-scale tree loss changed wind and moisture patterns, contributing to drier, more desertlike conditions. As trees disappeared, root systems and ground cover were destroyed, allowing rainwater to run off rapidly. As the water rushed downstream in floods, it eroded the land and carried away fertile soil. Consequently, underground water supplies were not replenished, and natural springs dried up. Some streams that had once flowed all the time flowed only occasionally after heavy rainfalls.

Other human activities quickened the process of desertification*. Farmers replaced wooded lands with fields and pastures, eliminating the natural habitats* of wild plants and animals in the process. Subsequent overgrazing by domesticated animals, especially goats, also contributed to desertification. In addition, people drained marshes, destroying the natural resources and filtering action of these wetlands. When people moved or abandoned areas where the environment was damaged, these areas seldom recovered. The result was a drier, bleaker landscape throughout much of the ancient Near East. (*See also* **Drought; Geography; Land Use and Ownership; Migration and Deportation; Rivers; Urbanization; Water.**)

* **desertification** change of useful land into desert through natural processes or human activity

* **habitat** type of environment to which an animal or plant is well adapted

EPIC LITERATURE

* **city-state** independent state consisting of a city and its surrounding territory

An epic is a long poem about a legendary or historical hero, written in a grand style. Such tales of great leaders, warriors, and kings can be found in almost every culture, including those in the ancient Near East. Epics were created as early as 2500 B.C. in Mesopotamia to glorify individual heroes and to honor the values of a warlike class of nobles.

Ancient Mesopotamian epics about the rulers of early city-states* focus on the leadership and cunning of these rulers, as well as their conquests. In the epics, the heroes face national or international threats, which they must turn back with wisdom as well as might. The epics also deal with the relationships between the leaders and their gods. The earliest epics may have been recited aloud by storytellers long before they were written down. Later works were written down to be recited or chanted.

In ancient Sumer, the major epics that have been recovered tell the stories of such legendary rulers as Enmerkar, Lugalbanda, and GILGAMESH. In the epic *Enmerkar and the Lord of Aratta,* Enmerkar of URUK challenges the Lord of Aratta and demands that he recognize Enmerkar as his superior. The Lord of Aratta agrees on the condition that Enmerkar perform many apparently impossible tasks. Enmerkar succeeds and peaceful relations prevail. The plot, albeit very typical, emphasizes cunning over

strength and glorifies the wise ruler. Epics such as this one end in praise of the city's main deity*.

In the epic *Lugalbanda in Khurrumkurra,* the hero is not a ruler but labors in the service of Enmerkar. The youngest of eight brothers, Lugalbanda sets off with his brothers to help Enmerkar fight against the Lord of Aratta. He falls ill along the way, and his brothers leave him to die in a cave. After he recovers, Lugalbanda wisely and skillfully prays to the gods, who help him overcome many dangers. The tale of Lugalbanda continues in *Lugalbanda and Enmerkar,* in which the young man uses his wits to deliver an important message for Enmerkar and helps him conquer the Lord of Aratta.

The most outstanding Sumerian epic hero is Gilgamesh, the king of Uruk, who is featured in five poems, along with his good friend Enkidu. The Babylonians later adopted the legend of Gilgamesh, and he is featured in a very long Babylonian work that is considered one of the world's great literary masterpieces. The Akkadian kings Sargon I and Naram-Sin, who, to subsequent dynasties, represented ideal kings, were also the subjects of numerous epic works written in both the Sumerian and Akkadian languages.

The themes featured in many Mesopotamian epics appear there for the first time in world literature. One of these themes is that of the half divine hero who has a special connection to the gods. Another is the accomplishment of impossible tasks, especially in contests between rulers. A third common theme is that of the cunning hero who achieves his victories against mightier opponents through the use of wit. Related to this is the idea that wisdom or cunning is better than force in achieving goals. These themes were used later in several great epics, including the *Iliad* and the *Odyssey* by the Greek poet Homer. The themes have also been adopted in many works in modern literature. (*See also* **Creation Myths; Literature; Poetry.**)

ERIDU

Considered one of the oldest cities in Mesopotamia, Eridu (ER•i•doo) was a center of Sumerian civilization and of a cult* dedicated to the god Ea (Enki). The city contained various temples, a large ziggurat*, and several other religious buildings.

Sumerian King Lists cite Eridu as the site of the oldest dynasty in Mesopotamia. The myth titled the *Eridu Genesis* also refers to Eridu as the first city created by the gods. Archaeological* evidence supports the city's great antiquity—dating portions of it to about 5000 B.C.—as well as its importance as an administrative, spritual, and economic center. Originally located on the seashore or on an inland lake in southern Mesopotamia near the city of Ur, Eridu was inhabited until the 600s B.C.

Today the site of ancient Eridu is a series of seven mounds, the largest of which is Abu Shahrain. The most extensive excavations at the site took place between A.D. 1946 and 1949. They revealed a remarkable series of temples, religious buildings, palaces, and artifacts* (including a type of dark painted pottery called Eridu ware) spanning a period of several thousand years.

See map in Mesopotamia (vol. 3).

The oldest building found at Eridu was a small, rectangular mud-brick shrine built on sand. This temple was rebuilt several times, and each time, the new temple was larger and more elaborate than the preceding structures. Later temples were constructed on platforms and were structurally more complex. Archaeologists also found large quantities of fish bones in some of the temples and believe that they may be the remains of offerings to the god Ea. They also unearthed a large cemetery containing an estimated 1,000 burial sites. (*See also* **Creation Myths; Cults.**)

ESARHADDON

ruled 680–669 B.C.
King of Assyria

Esarhaddon (ee•sahr•HAD•uhn) was the youngest son of King SENNACHERIB of Assyria and the only son of Queen Naqiya, the king's favorite wife. When Esarhaddon was named his father's heir, his older brothers murdered their father. Esarhaddon then led an army that put down his brothers' revolt. His brothers fled the region, and Esarhaddon marched to NINEVEH—the Assyrian capital—where he was crowned king.

During his reign, Esarhaddon consolidated his power and enlarged the kingdom. His most important act as king was to rebuild the city of Babylon, which was destroyed by Sennacherib in 689 B.C.

To protect himself from death during the lunar eclipses that occurred during his reign, Esarhaddon used the substitute-king ritual at least four times. At these times, he took the place of a farmer while a substitute took his place as king. After ruling for a brief period, the substitute-king was killed, fulfilling the omen, and Esarhaddon resumed his throne.

* **pharaoh** king of ancient Egypt

In 675 B.C., Esarhaddon began the military campaign for which he is most famous—the conquest of Egypt. Four years later, he seized the capital city of MEMPHIS, forcing the pharaoh* TAHARQA to flee. In 669 B.C., Taharqa rebuilt his army and attempted to regain power. Esarhaddon died on his way to Egypt to stop Taharqa.

* **vassal** individual or state that swears loyalty and obedience to a greater power

Because of Esarhaddon's experience with his own succession, he chose his heirs before his death. In 672 B.C., he picked his son Shamash-shum-ukin to rule as governor of Babylonia and gave his son ASHURBANIPAL the throne of Assyria. He made the rulers of his vassal* states pledge their allegiance to these heirs. Consequently, when Esarhaddon died, his sons rose to their thrones without trouble. (*See also* **Assyria and the Assyrians; Astrology and Astrologers.**)

ESHNUNNA

* **tributary** river that flows into another river

* **city-state** independent state consisting of a city and its surrounding territory

The ancient city of Eshnunna (esh•NUN•nuh) was located near the Diyala River, a tributary* of the Tigris River, which flows southward out of the Zagros Mountains of Iran down onto the Babylonian plain. The city was first occupied sometime before 3000 B.C. It became an independent kingdom after the collapse of the city-state* of UR at the beginning of the second millennium B.C.* Over the course of the next 200 years, Eshnunna's military conquered the city of ASHUR and expanded its rule over a large region that extended from the source of the Khabur River to the vicinity of the city-state of MARI in central MESOPOTAMIA. In the 1700s B.C., Eshnunna, which had only recently been captured by the

* **second millennium** B.C. years from 2000 to 1001 B.C.

* **archaeological** referring to the study of past human cultures, usually by excavating material remains of human activity

See map in Mesopotamia (vol. 3).

See color plate 8, vol. 1.

Elamites, fell to the Babylonian king HAMMURABI, and in the following century, it entered a decline.

Archaeological* excavations at the site of ancient Eshnunna, a mound of the remains of successive settlements known as Tell Asmar, began in the A.D. 1930s. The excavations and discoveries at Eshnunna enabled archaeologists to better identify the sequence of events in Mesopotamia in the third and second millennia B.C. Among the most spectacular discoveries were a series of votive statues—figures used as OFFERINGS or dedications to the gods—that had been buried together in a temple beneath the floor near the altar in about 2700 B.C. These statues are among the earliest ones of their type from ancient Mesopotamia that have been found.

A series of public buildings—including several temples and a large palace complex—were also uncovered at Tell Asmar. These buildings, dated to about 2000 B.C., reflect the great wealth and power of Eshnunna and are classic examples of Mesopotamian architecture of that period. They contain the typical Mesopotamian feature of a divided courtyard with inner and outer sections bridged by the throne room, which was used as an audience hall by the ruler. Another building excavated at the site appears to have been a workshop for dyeing cloth, suggesting the presence of a textile industry in Eshnunna.

Also associated with Eshnunna, although not found there, are a series of tablets inscribed with the so-called Laws of Eshnunna. These laws, some of which are based on earlier legal codes, are thought to be decades older than the famous Code of Hammurabi and were possibly written by the Eshnunnan king Dadusha around 1800 B.C. (*See also* **Architecture; Cities and City-States; Palaces and Temples.**)

Ethiopia

See *Nubia and the Nubians.*

ETHNIC AND LANGUAGE GROUPS

Peoples of the ancient Near East belonged to several ethnic and language groups. These groups intermingled with one another, and over time, some merged with others while some disappeared. Although the greatest variety of groups was found in MESOPOTAMIA, even Egypt, which appeared to have a uniform culture, contained several ethnic and language groups during ancient times.

MESOPOTAMIA

Over the centuries, a number of ethnic and language groups lived, fought, and worked together in the various regions of Mesopotamia. Although the Sumerians, Babylonians, and Assyrians are probably the best known of these groups, Mesopotamia was also home to the Akkadians, AMORITES, ARAMAEANS, Chaldeans, HURRIANS, and KASSITES.

Sumerians. The earliest evidence of Sumerian inhabitation of the Mesopotamian Tigris-Euphrates Valley dates to the 4500s B.C. The Sumerians probably included people who migrated to Mesopotamia from various places and had different origins. Their language, which consists of at least two known dialects*, is unrelated to any other known language. The written form of the main dialect may have been an upper-class one rather than a language used by the people as a whole.

Akkadians. Around 2400 B.C., the Akkadians took control of northern Mesopotamia. Soon their influence spread through the region that later became known as Babylonia. By the first millennium B.C.*, the terms *Akkad* and *Babylonia* had become interchangeable in the region's literature. Scholars refer to the specific dialect spoken by the Akkadians as Old Akkadian to distinguish it from other dialects of the Akkadian language spoken in Assyria and Babylonia during the second and first millennia B.C. (the years from 2000 to 1 B.C.).

Babylonians. The Babylonians were a mixture of peoples. Sumerian-speaking groups inhabited Babylonia from as early as 4500 B.C. through 2500 B.C. Thereafter, Akkadians, who spoke a Semitic* language, entered the region. Between 2000 and 800 B.C., other groups arrived in Babylonia. For example, the Amorites had begun arriving from north Syria around 2100s B.C., the Aramaeans from Syria in the 1200s B.C., and the Chaldeans, perhaps from Arabia, in the 800s B.C. These later groups all spoke West Semitic languages.

Assyrians. The Assyrian culture closely resembled that of Babylonia, and the people of Assyria spoke a dialect of the Akkadian language. Shortly before 2000 B.C., the Amorites began to take over parts of Assyria, and the population of the region soon included a large percentage of Amorites. Later migrations into the region by the Aramaeans added another group to the population. Consequently, the Assyrian population included a great mix of groups, most of whom spoke Aramaean by the later period of Assyrian history.

Hurrians. The earliest reference to the Hurrians in northern Mesopotamia dates to about 2000 B.C. From there, they worked their way westward into SYRIA, establishing a number of kingdoms, including the kingdom of Mitanni, which grew into a major power in the ancient Near East during the 1400s and 1300s B.C. The Hurrians spoke a Caucasian language and may have introduced that language into the region known as the CAUCASUS. Hurrian culture was also a major influence on the literature and religion of the HITTITES, people who inhabited north Syria and ANATOLIA (present-day Turkey).

Kassites. A tribal people of unknown origin, the Kassites invaded Babylonia in the 1600s B.C. From about 1595 to 1158 B.C., they ruled over a united Sumer and Babylonia. During this period of political stability and economic prosperity, the Kassites adopted the Babylonian language and culture. Consequently, scholars know very little about the Kassites' own language. However, they do know that it is not related to any of the known languages of the region.

* **dialect** regional form of a spoken language with distinct pronunciation, vocabulary, and grammar

* **first millennium** B.C. years from 1000 to 1 B.C.

* **Semitic** of or relating to a language family that includes Akkadian, Aramaic, Arabic, Hebrew, and Phoenician

EGYPT

Ancient Egyptians believed that humanity was composed of four races: Egyptians, Asiatics, Nubians, and LIBYANS. A painting from the tomb of pharaoh* SETY I shows how the Egyptians saw these so-called races, differentiating each representative by the color of his skin, hairstyle, and dress. Although these figures are just symbolic representations, they reflect Egyptian views on ethnicity.

The three "foreign" groups—Asiatics, Libyans, and Nubians—conquered and ruled portions of Egypt at one time or another. During these periods, Egyptian culture was influenced by the other cultures. The foreign groups also had a significant impact on the diversity of the Egyptian population.

Asiatics. Several Asiatic peoples, including Canaanites, inhabited Egypt, especially the eastern delta* regions, during the Twelfth and Thirteenth Dynasties (ca. 1938–1630 B.C.). Another group, the HYKSOS, entered Egypt between 1720 and 1710 B.C. and ruled that kingdom from about 1630 to 1523 B.C. Although the ethnicity of the Hyksos is debated, it is known that they retained much of their own culture in Egypt. Still, they presented themselves as traditional Egyptian pharaohs. They left an extended empire and important influences on music, religion, and language.

Libyans. Libya is the land to the west of Egypt. As early as the eighth millennium B.C. (years from 8000 to 7001 B.C.), an agricultural culture had been established on its coastal plain, while nomads* flourished on grasslands in the interior to the south. For centuries, the population of Libya remained scattered in various tribal groups throughout the region.

* **pharaoh** king of ancient Egypt

* **delta** fan-shaped, lowland plain formed of soil deposited by a river

* **nomad** person who travels from place to place to find food and pasture

Egyptians believed that humankind was divided into four races—from right to left, Egyptian, Asiatic, Nubian, and Libyan. This painting from the tomb of the pharaoh Sety I shows how Egyptians saw the races. The Egyptian is painted red-brown and has a goatee. The Asiatic and the Libyan are lighter-skinned. The Asiatic has a full beard and the Libyan a long, pointed one. The Nubian is black and clean-shaven. These figures reflect Egyptian views on ethnicity.

Libyan tribes began to migrate into Egypt in the 1200s B.C. Some were captured and placed in fortified camps by the pharaohs. Others were able to settle where they chose. By the early 1100s B.C., Libyans occupied much of the western Nile River delta, and in the centuries that followed, many towns in the delta became power bases for Egyptian rulers of Libyan ancestry. Libyan settlement eventually extended into the northern Nile Valley, and from time to time, Libyans raided farther south. Their numbers remained smaller in the south, however, and they were easily absorbed into the indigenous* populations there.

* **indigenous** referring to the original inhabitants of a region

* **assimilate** to adopt the customs of a society

Most Libyan settlements in Egypt were permanent. They assimilated* Egyptian culture, and rulers of Libyan ancestry considered themselves Egyptian. Between about 945 and 712 B.C., many individuals of Libyan ancestry became members of the Egyptian ruling elite. Their cultural background had a significant impact on the political structure of the period, which reflected the tribal culture of the Libyan homeland.

Nubians. The region of Nubia, which lies south of Egypt, had a settled culture by about 6000 B.C. Still, the first Nubian civilization did not appear until around 3100 B.C. Three Nubian groups appeared between then and about 750 B.C., each with its own distinctive culture.

* **third millennium** B.C. years from 3000 to 2001 B.C.

From at least the early third millenium B.C.*, Egypt had regular contacts with Nubia and controlled much of the region at various times after that. In the mid-700s B.C., Nubian kings conquered Egypt and ruled for about 100 years. They saw themselves as guardians of Egyptian culture and encouraged a revival in art and architecture inspired by Egypt's history. The Nubians lost control of Egypt in 663 B.C. and returned to Nubia. By the end of the first millennium B.C., Nubian culture reflected Egyptian, Greek, Roman, and central African ideas.

IRAN

* **fourth millennium** B.C. years from 4000 to 3000 B.C.

As early as the fourth millenium B.C.*, the Proto-Elamites had established themselves in southwestern IRAN. Beginning in the 1500s B.C., Iran began to be settled by the ARYANS, who migrated from Central Asia. The most important of these Aryan tribes were the MEDES and the Persians. Together, the Elamites, Medes, and Persians influenced the history and culture of Iran.

Elamites. The Elamites inhabited the region north of the Persian Gulf and east of the Tigris River. Their language was unrelated to any other known ancient language. Under the influence of the Sumerians, the Elamites developed a cuneiform* writing system around 3000 B.C. Nonetheless, the Elamites developed unique regional cultures specific to the areas they inhabited.

* **cuneiform** world's oldest form of writing, which takes its name from the distinctive wedge-shaped signs pressed into clay tablets

From time to time, they became involved in the politics of Mesopotamia, often exerting considerable influence on the rulers of Babylonia. The Assyrians conquered much of Elam in the 600s B.C., and other portions of Elamite territory fell to the Medes and Persians in the centuries that followed. The written language of the Elamites remained in use until about the 300s B.C., and the spoken language persisted for several centuries after that.

Ethnic and Language Groups

Medes. Originally village dwellers, the Medes had settled in northwestern Iran by the 800s B.C. Early written records mention the existence of many Median tribes and kings, and evidence suggests that the Medes were a very diverse people culturally, socially, and politically. Nevertheless, by the 600s B.C., the different Median tribes had united into a single state, becoming a major regional power. As allies of the Babylonians, they aided in the conquest of Assyria in 612 B.C. However, the power of the Medes was short-lived. In the 500s B.C., Persian ruler CYRUS THE GREAT overthrew the Medes and went on to establish the PERSIAN EMPIRE. The Medes remained a privileged group within the Persian empire, and many aspects of their language and culture were integrated with Persian culture.

Persians. Evidence suggests that the early Persians may have been tribal nomads. After migrating to the Iranian plateau from lands east of the Caspian Sea, they settled in southern Iran. The Persians were dominated by the Medes until 550 B.C., when Cyrus the Great came to the Persian throne and overthrew the Median rulers. He later conquered Babylonia and parts of Anatolia, making Persia the most powerful empire in the region. Later the Persians conquered Egypt and extended their rule as far as India in the east and Greece in the west. In the late 300s B.C., the Persian empire was conquered by ALEXANDER THE GREAT, but the Persians left a cultural legacy that lasted for centuries.

ANATOLIA

The most important ethnic group in Anatolia during the Bronze Age (ca. 3000–1200 B.C.) was the Hittites. Of unknown origin, the Hittites invaded Anatolia in about 1900 B.C. and imposed their culture and INDO-EUROPEAN LANGUAGE on the indigenous peoples. They challenged the Egyptians, Babylonians, and Assyrians for power throughout the region. During the 1200s B.C., invaders, perhaps the SEA PEOPLES, conquered the Hittites. Nevertheless, Hittite cultural practices continued for many centuries in many of the city-states* in southeastern Anatolia and northern Syria.

The dominant groups in Anatolia during the Iron Age (ca. 1200–500 B.C.) included the Phrygians and the Urartians. The Phrygians were a people of southeast European background. Their language, written with the Greek alphabet, was a member of the Indo-European family and is documented in inscriptions on stone and pottery.

The Urartians dominated eastern Anatolia in the 700s and 600s B.C. They had a distinctive regional culture and spoke a language, written in cuneiform, that was neither Semitic nor Indo-European in origin. Modern linguists believe that the Urartian language is closely related to the language spoken by the Hurrians of northern Mesopotamia.

CANAAN

Ancient CANAAN consisted of the present-day countries of Lebanon and Israel, southern Syria, the West Bank, and western Jordan. Evidence suggests the presence of West Semitic-speaking peoples in Syria early in the second millinnium B.C.* Originally rural pastoralists*, they later began to settle in

* **city-state** independent state consisting of a city and its surrounding territory

* **second millennium B.C.** years from 2000 to 1001 B.C.

* **pastoralist** person who herds livestock to make a living

fortified urban centers. Traces of their language are first seen in the Akkadian-language cuneiform documents written by local Syrian kings of the 1700s B.C. Around 1300 B.C., the dominant language in the region was a Canaanite dialect of Akkadian. During that period, the two most important Canaanite-speaking groups were the Phoenicians and the Israelites. Also present in the region were the Philistines, who spoke an Indo-European language.

Phoenicia. Occupying a narrow strip of land along the Mediterranean coast, Phoenicia consisted of several city-states that shared a single language and culture. Although the Phoenicians called themselves Canaanites, scholars know little about their origin. Their culture developed under the influence of the Akkadians, Amorites, and Egyptians. They Phoenicians became the greatest seafaring people of the ancient world, and they established trading centers throughout much of the Mediterranean region, even venturing out into the Atlantic Ocean.

Israelites. The Israelites were another West Semitic group. According to the Hebrew Bible, patriarchs of the Israelites migrated from Mesopotamia to Canaan during the second millennium B.C. However, some scholars believe that they originally came from the Sinai peninsula. Enslaved in Egypt for generations, they were released from bondage in about 1270 B.C. They returned to Canaan, conquered a large portion of the region, and eventually established the state of Israel with its distinctive religious views.

Philistines. One of the ancient SEA PEOPLES, perhaps of Aegean origin, the Philistines settled along the southern coast of Canaan in the 1100s B.C. Their early history is documented in ancient Egyptian texts and in the Hebrew BIBLE. Very little is known about their native language; only a few words are known, some from inscriptions on SEALS, others preserved in the Bible. A recently discovered inscription from a temple in the Philistine city of Ekron was written in a Canaanite dialect and script, indicating that by 700 B.C., the Philistines had adapted to their Israelite and Phoenician neighbors.

ARABIA

The Arabs were related to several groups from the areas surrounding the Arabian peninsula, including Semitic tribes from northern Mesopotamia. Linguistically, they can be divided into two language groups: North Arabic and South Arabic, both subdivisions of West Semitic languages. Northern Arabian languages consist of several dialects from which grew modern Arabic. These languages were not spoken throughout the peninsula, but scholars do not yet know the extent of their geographical distribution. Southern Arabian languages were spoken for a period spanning about 1,000 years, beginning in the 500s B.C. Archaeologists* have found several inscriptions written in these languages. (*See also* **Akkad and the Akkadians; Arabia and the Arabs; Assyria and the Assyrians; Babylonia and the Babylonians; Caria and the Carians; Chaldea and the**

* **archaeologist** scientist who studies past human cultures, usually by excavating material remains of human activity

Eunuchs

Chaldeans; Egypt and the Egyptians; Elam and the Elamites; Greece and the Greeks; Hebrews and Israelites; Languages; Lycia and the Lycians; Lydia and the Lydians; Nubia and the Nubians; Philistines; Phoenicia and the Phoenicians; Scythia and the Scythians; Semitic Languages; Sumer and the Sumerians.)

EUNUCHS

* **concubine** mistress to a married man

* **second millennium** B.C. years from 2000 to 1001 B.C.

Eunuchs (YOO•nuhks) were men who had been castrated, or had had their testicles removed. In the ancient Near East, eunuchs were often employed as guards for women in the royal household or as government officials. Because eunuchs could not father children, a king could safely employ them to guard and serve his wives and concubines*. Many moved beyond their role as guardians of the royal women to become bodyguards of or advisers to the kings. Among the Assyrians in the second millennium B.C.* and after, eunuchs were highly trusted officials in the government.

Some eunuchs played key roles in government and helped shape the course of history. The eunuch Bagoas commanded the Persian army in Egypt and was an important power in the PERSIAN EMPIRE under ARTAXERXES III. In 338 B.C., Bagoas had Artaxerxes poisoned and placed one of the dead king's sons on the throne. Two years later, he murdered the new king and helped another heir take the throne as King DARIUS III. When Darius resisted the eunuch's control, Bagoas planned to have him poisoned as well. The king learned of the plot and made Bagoas himself drink the poison, ending the manipulative career of one of the most powerful eunuchs of the ancient world.

Nehemiah, governor of Judah in the 400s B.C., was another famous eunuch in the Persian empire. Nehemiah oversaw the rebuilding of Jerusalem's walls, enabling the city's weakening population to flourish. His memoirs are recorded in the Hebrew BIBLE in the book bearing his name.

EUPHRATES RIVER

See map in Mesopotamia (vol. 3).

Running from eastern ANATOLIA (present-day Turkey) to the Persian Gulf, the Euphrates (yoo•FRAY•teez) River played an important role in the history of the ancient Near East. Many of the cities of the ancient Near East—such as BABYLON and UR—were built near the banks of the Euphrates, and these cities depended on both the Euphrates River and the TIGRIS RIVER for their existence and survival. The Euphrates provided water for people, ANIMALS, and AGRICULTURE, as well as a means of transportation.

The Euphrates River, the longest river in western Asia, extends for about 1,700 miles. The character of the river changes dramatically during its long journey to the sea. In its upper reaches, the Euphrates runs through deep gorges and narrow valleys. During most of its middle courses, it flows through broad plains. As the river nears the Persian Gulf, it divides into many channels and travels through a maze of marshes and lakes before making its final journey to the sea.

Throughout history, the Euphrates served as Mesopotamia's main source of IRRIGATION. This was largely because its annual flooding was less severe and more controllable than that of the nearby Tigris and because it was a more reliable water supply. The use of the Euphrates for irrigation helped moisten the soil and provided water for agricultural purposes, thus allowing people to settle along the river.

The Euphrates floods between March and June, when spring rains and melting snows in the mountains of Anatolia feed the river. In the ancient Near East, a network of irrigation canals downstream directed the floodwaters onto farmlands. Since flooding could also cause great damage to buildings, communities such as Sippar built walls around their cities to protect them from rising waters.

Over time, the annual flooding of the river also deposited salt on the land in southern Mesopotamia, which decreased its fertility. This meant that it could not be used for farming, and the people who had settled there had to go elsewhere.

* **millennium** period of 1,000 years; *pl.* millennia

The Euphrates River has also changed its course many times over the millennia* because of changing land formations—both human-made and natural. As a result, some ancient sites that were once next to the Euphrates are now far from it. (*See also* **Floods; Geography; Rivers; Water.**)

FAIENCE

* **amulet** small object thought to have supernatural or magical powers

* **Levant** lands bordering the eastern shores of the Mediterranean Sea (present-day Syria, Lebanon, and Israel), the West Bank, and Jordan

This faience vase in the shape of a woman's head, dating from the 1200s B.C., was excavated in the Levant.

aience (fay•AHNS) is the name used for objects made of shaped quartz that is covered with a glaze. Faience requires the use of high temperatures to harden the object and chemically fuse the glaze to the surface. This process is thought to have been invented in IRAN or northern MESOPOTAMIA around 4500 B.C. Egyptians began using it shortly thereafter. At first, craftspeople made small faience objects such as beads, cylinder SEALS, amulets*, and containers for cosmetics. Later they made faience vases, small statues, architectural decorations, and bricks.

To make faience, artisans first mixed finely ground quartz with water, shaping the material by hand or in molds. Then a glaze was added, either by applying it on the surface of the object or by placing the object in a container filled with the glaze material. The object was then heated to a very high temperature (1,440°F or higher) so that the material hardened and the glaze formed a chemical bond with the surface.

Faience makers used opaque glazes, meaning that the material underneath could not be seen. Such glazes could be used to produce rich colors—and could hide imperfections underneath. Faience produced in Mesopotamia and Egypt was typically blue or green, colors achieved by the use of copper in the glaze material.

During the time of the Middle Kingdom of Egypt (ca. 1980–1630 B.C.), faience began to be produced in the Levant* and Syria. Artisans often imitated Egyptian styles and subjects. During the Late Bronze Age (ca. 1600–1200 B.C.) in the Levant and the New Kingdom period (ca. 1539–1075 B.C.) in Egypt, workshops were producing faience objects in great quantities and distinctive shapes. One popular style in Syria was a goblet in the shape of a woman's head. Artisans used yellow, blue, green, and black glazes, usually in combination. These faience objects were popular in the palaces of local kings and nobles. They were also valuable trade goods and were taken to Assyria, Iran, and Cyprus. After about 1100 B.C., the popularity of faience declined as improvements in glassmaking increased the demand for glass. (*See also* **Glass and Glassmaking**.)

Failaka Island

See *Bahrain*.

FAMILY AND SOCIAL LIFE

The family and household were the basic building blocks of each ancient Near Eastern society. The term *family* refers to people linked by ties of blood, marriage, or adoption. *Household* is a broader term that includes everyone living under one roof, usually under a single authority. A household might include slaves, live-in servants, and other employees as well as family members.

Family had an additional meaning in ancient times. People viewed their families as extending backward and forward in time, and the dead were seen as playing vital roles in the lives of the living. Having children ensured that a person would be properly treated after death.

Mesopotamia. The cultures of ancient MESOPOTAMIA were patriarchal, which means that men dominated private and public life. A person's status depended on that of his or her father's family. Men headed the family unit, made all decisions, and exercised great authority over their wives, children, and grandchildren. The law code of the Babylonian king HAMMURABI states, "If a son strikes his father, they shall cut off his hand." While there is no evidence that this law was ever carried out, the punishment illustrates the respect due to fathers, whose relationship to their families was like a king's relationship to his people. These patriarchs could even give away a family member in payment of a debt. They also had the right—though not the duty—to later buy back the family member.

What we call the nuclear family today—father, mother, and their children—was called a house. A man was supposed to "build a house." If his wife did not provide him with children, he could take a second wife. A couple could also adopt a child, either a newborn who had been abandoned or an older child adopted in return for a sum of money. People also freed slaves and adopted them.

The typical Mesopotamian family had two children. Usually more children than that were born into the family, but many died in infancy. The extended family, called "the house of the father," included all the descendants of the patriarch. These extended families sometimes lived in the same home or in neighboring homes.

Egypt. The basic social unit in ancient Egypt was the nuclear family. Although a young married couple might live with either spouse's parents, ideally a man did not marry until he could afford to establish his own home. One Egyptian text warns that living with in-laws leads to trouble. Men could marry more than one woman at a time, but this practice apparently was rare outside the royal family.

In ancient Mesopotamia, a nuclear family was called a "house," and men were expected to "build a house." To this end, a man married one woman. However, if she did not provide him with children, he could take a second wife. This stone sculpture of a devoted Mesopotamian couple is from the Temple of Innana at Nippur.

Daughters normally lived with their parents until they married or left home to become servants in another house. Sons, on the other hand, might go off to live with other young men of the same age. Women who had no children sometimes raised children fathered by their husbands and born to female slaves or servants. Childless couples or individuals could adopt children or young men to inherit their property and perform funeral rituals for them.

Egyptian households sometimes included more than the nuclear family, but this was not common. Sometimes two related men and their families shared the same household. Widowed, divorced, or unmarried women sometimes lived with their closest male relatives. When several generations or families lived together, the house was often partitioned so that each nuclear group had a private space of its own.

Anatolia. The HITTITES, whose empire covered much of ANATOLIA (present-day Turkey) in the second millennium B.C.*, kept administrative records in which the symbol for "house" referred to a household. The household was a term of economic measurement in which men, women, and children were identified as labor units. If a household's workforce was too small to perform the labor expected of it, the government assigned prisoners of war to the household to make up the shortfall. A "normal working unit" consisted of ten people, suggesting that the average size of a household was about ten: parents, three or four children, and a few servants.

Marriage was expected to result in children. Wives who did not bear children might provide their husbands with slave women for the purpose. Adoption was also practiced, as in other ancient Near Eastern cultures, but details of Hittite adoptions are scanty.

In most cases, a wife went to live in the house of her husband. Occasionally, however, a husband moved into the house of his wife's father. Slaves and indentured servants* were allowed to enter into marriage with free people. In such marriages, the wives and children took on the social status of the husbands and fathers.

Hittite society was also patriarchal, with men generally having unquestioned power over their wives and children. In some cases, though, women had control. Because widows had the right to determine whether their sons would inherit their fathers' estates, sons were encouraged to treat widowed mothers well. On occasion, a husband or father would grant his wife or daughter the right to exercise power equal to his own over the other children. This probably occurred when the man was dying or expecting to be away from home.

Lycia, in southwestern Anatolia, had a matrilineal society, one where the family name was taken from the mother's name. According to a first-century B.C. writer, Lycian women were respected more then men; Lycians made their daughters their heirs, not their sons.

Israel. The people of ancient Israel identified themselves as members of kinship units called tribes. The Hebrew BIBLE usually divides the people of Israel into 12 tribes. Although tribal identification was important in military and territorial organization, the everyday lives of individuals

* **second millennium B.C.** years from 2000 to 1001 B.C.

* **indentured servant** someone bound into service for a set time in repayment of a debt

Family and Social Life

* **clan** group of people descended from a common ancestor or united by a common interest

were more closely governed by subdivisions of the tribe. The unit of kinship below the tribe was the clan*. Men within a clan held different ranks, with the older ones probably being the most honored.

Below the clan was the basic unit of Israelite kinship, the house, sometimes defined as an extended family consisting of a patriarch and up to three generations of his descendants. As in other societies of the ancient Near East, the father was the highest-ranking member of a family. His wife had the next highest rank. The oldest son held the highest status among children. Younger unmarried sons might perform various tasks for their older siblings.

If a wife did not bear children for her husband, she might provide a servant to do so. That servant, however, would not gain any social standing or wifely rights. The father could also adopt a child. When a man without a male heir died, it hindered the inheritance of property. In such cases, it was the duty of the dead man's brother to marry his widowed sister-in-law and to produce an heir with the dead man's widow. In this manner, the property would remain within the family.

Iran. Like the Israelites, the Persians in Iran divided themselves into tribes. The tribes, in turn, were divided into groups called phratries, which were much like the Israelite clans. Within the phratries were patriarchal families, in which men had total control over their children and all the members of their household. Children, in turn, were expected to show respect and obedience to their fathers. So closely were families identified with husbands and fathers that when a man committed a serious crime, his entire family was punished. A father's power was limited by the government, however. Persian boys as young as five years of age were taken from the home and placed in a training program—run by the government—to turn them into soldiers.

Royal men and nobles practiced polygamy, having more than one wife at a time. They sometimes also practiced endogamy, which means marrying female relatives. These practices seem to have occurred among ordinary Persians as well. In Mesopotamia, endogamy kept money within the family. It was also practiced in ancient Israel—for example, when the patriarch Jacob was sent to marry someone from his mother's tribe.

Another Iranian group, the Elamites, may have had a matriarchal society. Kingship may have been based on marrying the king's daughter. Moreover, the fact that Elamite goddesses held places of importance within their societies suggests that women were also regarded more highly than in other societies.

Inheritance. The customs and laws that gave shape to family life in the ancient Near East were concerned largely with transferring ownership of land and other property from one generations to the next. For example, Persian men practiced polygamy to ensure that they would have several descendants and endogamy to ensure that family wealth remained within the family.

In the early third millennium B.C.*, land in Mesopotamia was jointly owned by all the sons of a father. Documents show that when land was sold, brothers were present not because of the need for witnesses but

* **third millennium B.C.** years from 3000 to 2001 B.C.

because they received part of the payment. In cities, property was typically divided among sons or grandsons after a man's death. This division included all property, from land and house to furniture and slaves. A daughter was usually given some property during her father's life. If such a gift had not already been awarded, the sons were obliged to set aside a share as a gift to her when their father died. In some areas, the oldest brother received a double share.

There was also a law in Mesopotamia stating that people could will their goods to anyone of their choice. However, many people died without making a will. In those cases, the law stated that the child who took responsibility for the deceased's burial would inherit his or her property.

Scholars do not know much about inheritance laws among the Hittites, but it appears that women could not inherit property directly from their fathers. There, as in most ancient Near Eastern cultures, sons inherited the family property.

Among the ancient Israelites, a father's land was divided among his sons, but the oldest son received a double portion. If a man had no male heirs, a daughter could receive an inheritance. However, she was obliged to marry within her tribe so that property belonging to that tribe would not pass into the ownership of another.

Social Life. Life in the ancient Near East was not all work and no play. Important family events such as weddings and funerals provided occasions for families to get together and socialize. Families in the ancient Near East also attended community events, such as temple festivals and harvest feasts.

Egyptian art clearly shows that people were viewed not as isolated beings but as members of a community. Even when a person is shown performing a task alone, without the help of an assistant, he or she is typically shown working among other people doing similar tasks. Elite families banquet together. Common folk bake bread, brew beer, and tend fields together. Communal life is a central theme of Egyptian art as well. Sculptures and paintings portray men surrounded by their women folk and children.

The majority of the Hittite population probably lived in the country and engaged in farming. Consequently, many Hittite festivals related to agricultural life. The festivities included banquets, sports competitions, music, and dance. Historians also believe that participants in religious festivals ate, slept, and perhaps performed in taverns.

In Mesopotamia, the temple represented a city's identity as a community. Ancient people in Mesopotamia had several religious holidays a month. During these times, there were games and entertainment events that people could participate in or watch. Music was also a part of temple festivities.

In ancient Israel, poetry had a place in the social lives of the people. Ancient Israelites would attend performances of poets reciting long narrative poems. These events may have taken place during holidays. Such performances were a way of transmitting cultural stories and values to an audience whose members might not be able to read. (*See also* **Children; Divorce; Entertainment; Feasts and Festivals; Houses; Marriage; Property and Property Rights; Women, Role of.**)

Married or Not?

If a man took the daughter of a man without asking her father and her mother, and has not held a feast and made a contract for her father and her mother—even if she lives in his house for a full year, she is not a wife. If he did hold a feast and make a contract for her father and mother, and took her, she is a wife: the day she is caught in the embrace of [another] man, she shall die.

—from a Mesopotamian law code

Famine

FAMINE

* **fourth millennium** B.C. years from 4000 to 3001 B.C.

* **siege** long and persistent effort to force a surrender by surrounding a fortress or city with armed troops, cutting it off from supplies and aid

A famine is an extreme and long-lasting shortage of food that causes widespread hunger and starvation and an increase in the death rate. Famines may affect an entire society or region. Sometimes, however, they affect only certain groups of people, generally the poorer classes of society, who cannot afford to buy foodstuffs that become more expensive during shortages.

Famines are caused by both natural phenomena and human activities. The most common natural causes of food shortages due to famine are DROUGHT, flooding, unseasonably cold weather, plant diseases, and infestations by insects or rodents. All of these natural events can lead to crop failures and food shortages. Among the human factors that contribute to famine are overpopulation, war, and lack of transportation to move food to where it is needed. Overpopulation usually contributes to famine when it is combined with a natural phenomenon, such as drought, that causes crop failures and food shortages. War and lack of transportation contribute to famine when they cause the disruption of the normal production and distribution of foodstuffs, either intentionally or by accident.

Famine posed a periodic threat to societies in the ancient Near East. The earliest recorded famines in this region date to the fourth millennium B.C.* These early famines were primarily the result of natural causes. In Egypt, for instance, decline in water levels of the NILE RIVER caused crop failures as well as a reduction in the area of land that could be farmed. Famine followed relatively quickly under such conditions. A series of disastrous famines may have also caused a period of decline in Egypt between the 2100s and 1900s B.C.

The devastation of famine in ancient Egypt is reflected in ancient Egyptian texts and art. Art in Egyptian king Unas's (ruled ca. 2371–2350 B.C.) burial chamber shows a scene of starving people. It most likely depicts Unas aiding famine-stricken people.

In ancient MESOPOTAMIA, famine was often the result of political disruptions rather than of unfavorable climate conditions. Frequent warfare disrupted AGRICULTURE. For example, cities under siege* by enemies eventually ran out of food supplies, and the people behind the walls would starve. Failure to maintain irrigation systems in times of turmoil contributed to flood damage, which destroyed crops and damaged the land, causing famine. Political conflict also disrupted trade, preventing food from being transported from one place to another. A catastrophic famine in southern Mesopotamia in the 1100s B.C. contributed to a period of decline for the Babylonian empire. Sensing the Babylonians' vulnerability an advantage, Aramaean tribes invaded the already weakened Babylonia.

Some societies tried to protect themselves from famine by stockpiling grains to be used in times of shortages. Other societies imported food from other lands. For example, the Hittites imported food from Egypt and the city of Ugarit during periods of famine. Sometimes famine relief was offered in return for ruling privileges. For example, in the First Intermediate period of ancient Egypt (ca. 2130–1980 B.C.), an official called Ankhtyfy apparently came to the aid of neighboring lands during a famine in exchange for authority over them.

Famine played a role in the MYTHOLOGY of the ancient Near East. Some myths explained famine, as well as other natural events such as drought, as the work of the gods. Sometimes famine was a form of punishment, and at other times, it was the result of struggles among the gods.

According to the Hebrew Bible, a famine caused the patriarchs to migrate to Egypt at an early point in their history. The Bible also mentions famines in Egypt and Canaan. The story of Joseph tells of how he enables the Egyptians to withstand a famine by stockpiling grains. As a result, Joseph becomes highly honored even though he is a slave. Later Joseph aids his brothers who have come from Canaan seeking relief from the same famine. (*See also* **Disasters**, **Natural**; **Floods**.)

Farming

See *Agriculture; Animals, Domestication of.*

FEASTS AND FESTIVALS

See
color plate 8,
vol. 2.

* **city-state** independent state consisting of a city and its surrounding territory

easts and festivals were vitally important to cultures in the ancient Near East. A typical feast involved a shared meal accompanied by entertainment. Festivals varied greatly, but many of them included music, processions of worshipers carrying images of gods and goddesses, and offerings of food and sacrifices at temples.

People have long celebrated feasts to mark the changing of the seasons. The survival of the peoples of the ancient Near East depended on the cycle of planting and harvesting that accompanied each season. Some festivals were dedicated to worshiping the gods, and others celebrated cultural pride or state occasions. These ceremonies helped unify societies and empires. Finally, feasts or festivals marked a rite of passage in a person's life, such as marriage or death. It is not always easy to distinguish between these four types of ceremonies. However, each feast and festival had its own meaning and characteristics.

Seasonal Celebrations. In prehistoric times, people probably observed that seasonal changes affected the animals they hunted and the wild plants they gathered for food. They believed that various gods controlled the forces of nature. Such observations and beliefs led them to develop feasts and festivals, which they thought would please the gods and ensure a continuing food supply. As agriculture developed in the ancient Near East (ca. 9000 B.C.), the most important feasts and festivals were held during planting time and harvest time.

In ancient MESOPOTAMIA, each city-state* or kingdom had its own calendar to guide people toward the proper time for feasts and festivals. Festivals marked the agricultural cycle and celebrated events such as the hitching and unhitching of plows. During certain times of the year, rulers traveled throughout the land to present offerings of crops and meat to the gods. These festivals reflected the Mesopotamian belief that humans were created to serve the gods.

Feasts and Festivals

* **Levant** lands bordering the eastern shores of the Mediterranean Sea (present-day Syria, Lebanon, and Israel), the West Bank, and Jordan

* **exodus** migration by a large group of people, usually to escape something unpleasant

A similar connection between feasts and festivals and seasonal changes existed in ancient Egypt. The annual flooding of the NILE RIVER provided a regular seasonal mark for the month-long festival of Opet, a celebration of the close relationship between the king of Egypt and AMUN, the king of the gods. Because work in the fields was not possible during the flooding, rich and poor alike took part in the festival.

During the festival of Opet, priests bathed, dressed, and adorned the image of Amun with jewelry and brightly colored linen and then placed it in a boat. Led by the king himself, they carried Amun out into the noisy street and then on to the temple of LUXOR at the south end of the city. Along the way, ordinary citizens struggled to catch a glimpse of the god as drums beat and men danced.

In later times, the boat was placed on the Nile and towed to the temple by high officials who vied for the honor. After a ritual at the temple, people asked questions of the god. The questions were phrased so that they could be answered yes or no. If the boat moved forward, the answer was yes; if the boat moved backward, the answer was no. The temple officials also distributed food and drink. During an Opet festival in the 1100s B.C., temple officials handed out 11,341 loaves of bread and 385 jars of beer.

In ancient ANATOLIA (present-day Turkey), the Hittite king and queen participated in a procession on the sixteenth day of the spring festival. The procession went from the palace to the temple and included singers and musicians. Their presence at the temple emphasized the belief that rulers needed the honor of the gods.

In ancient SYRIA and the Levant*, people also worshiped many gods and maintained images of them in temples. Although a wide variety of information about religious practices has been gathered from early sites, such as UGARIT, much of it is unclear. Historians believe that feasts and festivals took place in October and December to mark the plowing and sowing and in the spring to celebrate the harvest.

The ancient Hebrew calendar told the Israelites when to hold their feast and festival days. Several celebrations for particular harvests are mentioned in the Hebrew BIBLE, such as the Pesach and Matsot festivals. The Pesach (Passover) festival involved a pilgrimage in which a yearling sheep or goat was sacrificed and consumed. The Matsot festival (Festival of Unleavened Bread), perhaps originally a holiday associated with the barley harvest, came to be celebrated together with the Pesach festival in remembrance of the Exodus* from Egypt. During these celebrations, families would gather together and eat a special meal of sheep or goat, vegetable (bitter herb), and grain (unleavened bread); drink wine; and instruct children on the meaning of the event. These celebrations demonstrate the importance of seasonal feasts and festivals to the ancient Near Easterners.

Acts of Worship. Some feasts and festivals were acts of religious worship. Although many began as seasonal rites and took place at regular intervals, the intent of these celebrations was to honor the gods rather than mark a particular season.

In Elamite society, in southwestern IRAN, a festival called the Feast of the Pouring Offerings honored Kiririsha, the goddess known as the

State occasions, such as a military victory, were often celebrated with a feast as seen here on the Royal Standard of Ur, a two-sided mosaic panel. Often called the "peace" side, this side of the mosaic shows a feast in progress. In the top panel, the king and his court are seen feasting and enjoying a musical performance. In the panels beneath, attendants bring in captured goods, cattle, goats, and sheep.

mother of the gods by the Elamites. Fattened rams were ritually slaughtered so that their blood flowed down from the altars. Then all the participants received meat from the sacrificed animals.

In Egypt, feasts and festivals honoring the gods were a central part of life. These celebrations of the gods occurred throughout ancient Egyptian history. People were allowed to take time off from work to celebrate festivals of favorite deities. These festivals included processions and sacred dramas, during which performers reenacted the battle between the gods HORUS and SETH. As elsewhere, the number of such festivities increased over time. A temple calendar created during Ptolemaic times (305–30 B.C.) notes more than 40 festivals.

In Anatolia, Hittites and others also held festivals of worship. It was the king's duty to keep the gods content by making annual visits to their shrines during the appropriate festivals. A typical festival involved a purification ritual in which the king dressed in special garments and ate a sacred meal in the temple. Following this, the king made an offering of meat, bread, beer, and wine to the gods. The festival was accompanied by the performance of sacred songs and dances and often included other entertainment, such as juggling, gymnastics, and mock battles. The Hittites believed that if the gods were pleased, they would provide protection from sickness, famine*, and enemies.

In Syria and the Levant, as elsewhere, some acts of worship included feasts and festivals. Thanksgiving for a divine favor or a feast held in payment of a vow to a god were common. Historians believe that monarchs played leading roles in the feasts and festivals as they did elsewhere. An ancient artwork from this region shows a king being presented to a god during a festival ritual.

* **famine** severe lack of food due to failed crops

* **civic** matters relating to citizens or a city

State Occasions. Because the head of state was often the head of religion, it is sometimes difficult to distinguish a feast of worship from one for state purposes. Some ceremonies, however, were clearly civic* celebrations. Feasts or festivals to commemorate historical events or the visit of an important official from another region served political and social purposes. Several documents have been found at UR in Mesopotamia that list rations of bread, beer, oil, fish, and spices given out to foreign rulers and their servants.

Fertile Crescent

The King of Babylon and the *Akītu* Festival

The ancient Babylonians celebrated their New Year's festival—the *Akītu* festival—on the first day of spring. During this 12-day festival, the Babylonians paraded the statue of Marduk, the city god of Babylon. They also recited the Babylonian *Epic of Creation* to explain and assert Marduk's supremacy. The king's role in the cult of Marduk was also renewed at this time. Because the king was central to this festival, it could not be celebrated without him. During the time of the Neo-Babylonian empire, King Nabonidus was absent from the capital for several years, and the *Akītu* festival was not celebrated.

In Egypt, feasts and festivals for state occasions were common. The New Year's festival became the time for giving and receiving diplomatic* gifts. Another state occasion, dating from the beginning of Egyptian history, was the Sed festival. This festival featured a symbolic renewal of the king's powers and rule and took place decades after he first came to the throne. The Sed festival lasted over an extended period of time, during which the king participated in rites that symbolized his taking control of the land anew.

Like the Egyptians, the Hittites held state ceremonies that provided music, dance, and entertainment. One festival included a mock battle between Hittite dancers armed with bronze and their opponents armed with reeds. This dance may have commemorated a specific battle or symbolized Hittite strength.

Rites of Passage. Feasts and festivals also occurred to mark changes in a person's life. In Egypt, feasts and festivals celebrated several rites of passage, especially death. Wealthy Egyptians held a feast every year in memory of their deceased loved ones. At these feasts, guests sat on floor mats and used their fingers to eat their food, which consisted of butter, cheese, fowl, and beef seasoned with cinnamon, parsley, and rosemary and sweetened with honey. Professional dancers whirled and jumped to the music of harps, lutes, flutes, and tambourines as the guests snapped their fingers or clapped along. Guests were encouraged to drink wine until they reached a state of intoxication that made them feel closer to the dead.

Throughout the ancient Near East, feasts and festivals reinforced values and strengthened religious beliefs, the recognition of shared history, and the idea of unity under the power of one ruler. These common bonds forged social and national identities that were important as civilizations developed. (*See also* **Agriculture; Cults; Death and Burial; Family and Social Life; Religion.**)

FERTILE CRESCENT

The Fertile Crescent is a historic, roughly horn-shaped region where the civilizations of the ancient Near East began. The Fertile Crescent starts at the head of the Persian Gulf between Iran and the Arabian peninsula. It stretches up from the valley of the TIGRIS RIVER and EUPHRATES RIVER in lower Mesopotamia, through Syria, and down along the Mediterranean coast of Lebanon, Israel, and Egypt, where it continues down the NILE RIVER valley.

Although the region is bordered by harsh deserts and rugged mountains, the Fertile Crescent itself is watered by a number of rivers and streams fed by seasonal rains. In the past, the climate in this region was probably better suited to productive agriculture than it is today. These conditions made the Fertile Crescent arable* in ancient times, allowing people to settle there. These people were able to establish communities and build towns. As populations grew, they developed systems of government and trade and eventually built cities. As a result, the regions within the Fertile Crescent were home to the earliest civilizations of the ancient Near East. Sumer, Babylonia, Assyria, Phoenicia, and Egypt were all located within the Fertile Crescent, and most settlement was concentrated within the area throughout ancient times.

FISHING

* **artifact** ornament, tool, weapon, or other object made by humans

A long with hunting and gathering, fishing was a basic source of food for the earliest inhabitants of the ancient Near East. Artifacts* from the NILE RIVER valley of Egypt, for example, indicate that people engaged in fishing as early as 9000 B.C. Even after AGRICULTURE was well established in the ancient Near East, by about 4000 B.C., fishing continued to provide people with a nutritious (fish is an excellent source of protein) and tasty addition to their diets, which were based primarily on grains, vegetables, and fruits.

Fishing was a major economic activity in coastal areas as well as along rivers and streams. In other areas, it played a less important role in the economy. Even in those areas, however, people sometimes created artificial fishponds and stocked them with fish. Evidence suggests that people practiced fishing along the banks of waterways and that they also used boats or rafts to fish in the main channels of rivers or offshore in lakes and seas.

Fishing and hunting probably developed at about the same time. The character of these activities, however, differed significantly. Hunting became associated with people from the upper classes, while fishing was linked primarily with the lower classes of society. This is evident in ancient art, where huntsmen generally belonged to royalty and fishermen were usually common folk.

Artifacts, texts, and art have revealed a great deal about the fishing techniques used in the ancient Near East. These techniques were similar throughout much of the region, due largely to cultural exchanges and similarities in CLIMATE. Fishing methods used in the world today are based on techniques that originated in the ancient Near East. Fishermen used spears, fishing poles, lines with hooks, and nets to catch fish. Fishing accessories included stone and lead sinkers and stone net anchors to keep fishing lines and nets submerged.

The earliest fishing nets were made of plant fibers, while later nets consisted of cotton or linen yarn. Nets could be repaired using yarn and netting needles made of bone, metal, or wood. The oldest and most important type of net was the seine, or dragnet. This wall of netting, sometimes as much as 980 feet long, was spread out parallel to the shore. A rope weighted with sinkers at the bottom of the seine kept the net submerged, while wooden floats along its top edge helped keep the wall of netting upright. Fish were surrounded and ensnared when the net was dragged to shore. Seine nets could catch large numbers of fish, and they required the work of several fishermen.

Individual fishermen used cast nets. These circular nets—up to 26 feet in diameter and weighted with sinkers—were thrown into the water by a fisherman standing on the shore, in shallow water, or in a boat. The net landed like a parachute, sank into the water, and was then hauled back with the catch of fish inside. Because of cast nets' smaller size and the method of handling them, they could not catch as many fish as seines.

Fish became an important article of trade in several regions of the ancient Near East. Although they were sometimes transported alive, fish were usually preserved by drying, salting, or pickling. This enabled them to be moved greater distances and remain edible for longer periods. They were also used to pay taxes.

In some areas, such as ancient Sumer, fishermen had to purchase the right to fish in rivers, lakes, and canals from temples, local rulers, and other landholders. Competition for fishing rights sometimes led to conflicts.

Fish and fishing played an important role in the religion and MYTHOLOGY of the ancient Near East. OFFERINGS of fish were often made in temples, and fish and fishing became associated with certain gods such as EA, the Sumerian water god. Fish and fishing also appeared in ancient art. For instance, many ancient Egyptian WALL PAINTINGS and bas-reliefs* show scenes of people fishing. Some of these scenes portray the Egyptian upper classes, who took up fishing for pleasure and relaxation. Fishing also figured prominently in the wall paintings produced by the MINOAN CIVILIZATION on the island of CRETE. (*See also* **Animals; Animals in Art; Food and Drink; Hunting.**)

* **bas-relief** kind of sculpture in which material is cut away to leave figures projecting slightly from the background

FLAX

* **Neolithic period** final phase of the Stone Age, from about 9000 to 4000 B.C.

Flax is a plant that was grown throughout much of the ancient Near East. The people of the region used the fibers of the flax plant to make linen yarn and fabric, and they used its seeds to make oil for cooking. The linen produced from flax was one of the most important TEXTILES of the Near East. In fact, the ancient Egyptians believed that their gods were clothed in linen.

Flax was probably first cultivated in the ancient Near East during the Neolithic period*. It became a commonly grown crop in the region, especially in Egypt, where it was used to make linen as early as about 5000 B.C. Linen remained the predominant fabric in Egypt throughout ancient times.

Flax can be grown in a variety of soils and climates, so it came to be widely cultivated throughout the ancient Near East. After harvesting, the flax stalks were tied in bundles and left to dry. Once dry, the seeds were removed for making oil. The dried stalks were then soaked in water, taken out, and pounded with various tools. The fibers were then removed from the outer bark, divided according to quality and color, and prepared for spinning into yarn.

Flax fibers range in color from golden brown to creamy white, and yarn from flax varies in texture from coarse to very fine and smooth. Depending on the color and quality of the fibers, the people of the ancient Near East could make linen of various colors and textures, from a coarse, canvaslike cloth to fine, smooth fabric. Bleaching the yarn produced pure white cloth, but dyeing it was more difficult because flax fibers are not easily penetrated by dyes. As a result, most linen cloth produced and worn by people in the ancient Near East ranged in color from white to golden brown. (*See also* **Agriculture; Clothing.**)

FLOOD LEGENDS

Legends of a Great Flood can be found in several cultures of the world, including many in the ancient Near East. In many Near Eastern stories, the gods send a great flood to punish the human beings because they have become too numerous, too proud, or too sinful. Typically, a sympathetic god warns one man of the impending disaster. The god instructs him to build a boat and take representatives of all types of animals to ensure continuity of life.

The Old Babylonian *Epic of Atrakhasis* and the Standard Version *Epic of Gilgamesh* (especially the eleventh tablet), contain tales of the Great Flood. The *Sumerian Flood Story,* written down around 1600 B.C., contains another version of the legend. Some Mesopotamian KING LISTS also mention a Great Flood, which often serves as the dividing line between periods in the past. Another flood legend is the story of Noah and his ark. Found in the book of Genesis in the Hebrew BIBLE, this legend was written down between 1000 and 600 B.C. The Greeks also had their own legends, such as the one found in the *Bibliotheca,* the oldest preserved written account of a tale that was retold orally for centuries. Here the god Zeus sends a flood to destroy humankind. However, the god Prometheus instructs his human son Deucalion to build a boat, helping humanity survive.

Flood legends were probably created to explain natural disasters. They also served to impress the power of the gods and expressed the religious ideas of survival and rebirth in a world created anew. (*See also* **Creation Myths; Disasters, Natural; Floods; Mythology.**)

FLOODS

Flooding—the rising and overflowing of a body of water beyond its normal boundaries—may be the most studied and recorded natural phenomenon in human history. The earliest records of the rise and fall of water levels came from the ancient Egyptians who observed the NILE RIVER. As societies established themselves and developed along rivers, the timing and severity of floods became of great importance. Floods could destroy life, property, and agriculture. They could weaken societies by disrupting farming and trade to the point where the society no longer functioned well as a unit. Such societies might then be open to attack or might decide to dissolve and move elsewhere. Floods could also be beneficial; farming in areas of the ancient Near East without sufficient rainfall depended on the water the rivers provided. As a result, one of the great concerns of these early societies was controlling water, and dealing with floods was an important part of social organization. Public works for water and flood control grew with societies, and law and commerce both expanded as a result of such projects.

Floods

* **silt** soil or other sediment carried and deposited by moving water

Archaeology and Floods

A flood leaves behind a layer of mud. Archaeologists look for this layer as they excavate through successive layers of earth. When they find a layer of sediment, they measure its extent and thickness to determine the intensity of the ancient flood. In the 1920s, Sir Charles Leonard Woolley thought that he had proof of Noah's flood when he discovered sediment while excavating the site of the ancient Sumerian city of Ur (in present-day Iraq). The sediment was about ten feet thick, dating from around 4000 B.C. However, the layer did not cover the entire city as it should have if there had been such a large flood. Other evidence showed that society had not been disrupted. Woolley, who contributed greatly to knowledge of early Mesopotamia, had found evidence of a flood, but he had not found Noah's flood.

* **fallow** plowed but not planted, so that moisture and organic processes can replenish the soil's nutrients
* **levee** embankment or earthen wall alongside a river that helps prevent flooding
* **drought** long period of dry weather during which crop yields are lower than usual

Beneficial Flooding. People today usually regard floods as disasters. Floods in the ancient Near East could be disastrous as well, but they were also the basis of life. Not only did seasonal flooding water the land; it also enriched it. Silt* deposited by a flooding river provided essential nutrients to the soil, which promoted crop growth. The lands beside the rivers, called floodplains, were the first and most readily used areas for agriculture.

In Mesopotamia, most civilizations developed close to the TIGRIS RIVER and EUPHRATES RIVER. The "land between the rivers" provided reasonable sites for agriculture. Southern Mesopotamia was more dependent on the seasonal flooding of the rivers for agriculture, while the north relied primarily on rainfall. The Euphrates River was especially useful to early societies, and it was the principal water supply for Sumer, Akkad, and later for Babylonia. The Tigris River was less controllable and therefore not utilized to the same extent as the Euphrates.

In order to use the Euphrates River for agriculture, settlers expanded the floodplain by using channels and CANALS for IRRIGATION. These water management systems were crucial to life in Mesopotamia. In fact, Mesopotamian kings often listed the canal systems they constructed as great achievements of their reigns.

Throughout Mesopotamia, planting took place in autumn, when the water levels in the rivers were at their lowest. At this time of year, the canals were used to bring enough moisture to the land so the plants would grow. Flooding, the result of melting snow and storms in Anatolia (present-day Turkey), occurred in Mesopotamia in April, May, and June—the harvest season. The spring floodwaters would be used to water fields that were lying fallow* in order to prepare them for the next planting season. However, the floodwaters had to be controlled very carefully; otherwise, too much water could spell disaster by ruining crops about to be harvested. To control floodwaters, levees* were used to keep the water from overflowing.

The ancient Egyptians also depended on a river's water. The Nile River made life easier for farmers in Egypt because the great annual flood occurred at exactly the right time. Beginning in June, the waters rose steadily, fed by the torrents of rain that fell in central Africa. The flood crested in September, leaving the soil moist for fall planting. Egyptian farmers learned how to save water from the flood to nourish the young plants. Harvesting took place before the worst of the drought*, which usually began in March. The cycle then repeated itself in June. The silt deposited by the Nile was especially rich, and it refreshed the soil completely each year. As a result, farming did not exhaust the land, and it could be used again each season.

Egyptians developed a practical calendar of three seasons based on the behavior of the Nile: Inundation, or flood; Emergence of the fields from the water; and Drought. Egyptian society developed according to responses to the Nile's condition. During Inundation, when the fields were underwater, the Egyptians worked on building projects. During Emergence, they reserved water for the growing season. During Drought, they harvested and threshed their grain.

The intensity of the Nile's annual flood usually determined the prosperity of Egypt. For example, a large flood sent water farther across the land and meant that more land could be tilled and more food could be grown. When Egyptians were able to grow more grain, which was Egypt's main product, they could export it and increase their wealth.

The Greek historian HERODOTUS, writing in the 400s B.C., called Egyptian civilization "the gift of the [Nile]." The Nile's water gave life to the dry land, and the annual flooding of the Nile determined property values. Consequently, real estate values depended on how regularly land received the benefits of the flood. "Black land" was valuable. "Red land" was almost worthless. Taxes on land varied accordingly and were higher after the annual flood than before it.

The Nile's annual flooding also contributed to the political development of Egyptian society because organization was needed to build and maintain dikes*, catch basins, and canals. The central government could direct the large labor forces necessary for such works, and by the time of the First Dynasty* (ca. 3000–2800 B.C.), water-control projects had been built along the length of the river.

Harmful Flooding. As important as seasonal flooding was, it could not be counted on to be just the right amount of flooding. There was no way of predicting the intensity of a seasonal flood, so if it were too high or too low, it could bring catastrophe to people living near the rivers. Floods also occurred outside of flood season, especially in Anatolia and Mesopotamia, where the rivers are much more affected by local conditions such as heavy winter rainfall.

The water levels and flow of the Tigris and the Euphrates Rivers vary considerably from year to year. They also vary within seasons and with local conditions, such as winter rainfall or the rate and amount of melting snow in eastern Anatolia. The Tigris especially is subject to destructive flooding. In ancient Mesopotamia, the development of sluices* and regulators* helped protect the grain supply from flood. These water-control devices required constant watching and repair, so law codes such as the Code of Hammurabi set penalties for people who ruined crops as a result of the neglect or misuse of water management systems.

Although flooding made life possible in Mesopotamia, it also created risks, the greatest of which was destruction of crops. Annual floods that were too high ruined standing crops in the field. This occurred frequently enough that there are many references to crop loss from flooding in law codes and legal documents. Another problem created by floods was that they could bring too much sediment into the canals and clog them. Clearing them required constant, labor-intensive cleaning.

Seasonal flooding brought yet another problem to the nearly flat land near the Tigris and Euphrates. The land needed water, but it also needed to be drained of water after the floods because the water standing in the fields could draw salt up from the ground below. The salt remained when the water eventually dried, and this buildup of salt, called salinization, was a serious problem. Salinity made soil useless to the farmer, and large tracts of land sometimes had to be abandoned. To slow the salinization process, Mesopotamian farmers tried not to use the same fields over and over again and protected fields from flooding with dikes and levees when they could. Occasionally, the flooding could be so severe, especially if a

* **dike** embankment used to confine or control the flow of water

* **dynasty** succession of rulers from the same family or group

* **sluice** human-made channel or passage to direct water flow

* **regulator** gate or valve to control the amount of water passing through a channel

Food and Drink

* **famine** severe lack of food due to failed crops

* **archaeologist** scientist who studies past human cultures, usually by excavating material remains of human activity

protective levee broke, that cities near the rivers could be buried under many feet of silt.

In Egypt, even the relatively gentle flood of the Nile could bring havoc because there was no way to stop the river's spreading. Although a large flood yielded more grain, whole towns could be ruined if the flood were too high. In fact, Herodotus claimed that during these times, towns looked like islands and ships could sail straight across the country without following the path of the stream. He also said that boats sailed past the pyramids at these times.

A low annual flood could also cause trouble. Less land tilled meant less food, and a famine* could result. To prevent this, Egyptians built dikes and catch basins to trap water. They sank wells and built canals to extend the reach of the river. They invented devices called nilometers to measure the rise of the river. As the boundaries of Egypt grew, the Egyptians set nilometers farther and farther up the river. The earlier they knew what the Nile was likely to do, the better they could prepare for whatever it brought.

The grave consequences of floods or lack of floods made them the subject of intense interest for residents of the ancient Near East. Floods were important cultural and religious events as well. Many of Egypt's religious practices related to the motions of the Nile. Several civilizations had FLOOD LEGENDS that told of great floods, interpreting the tales through the eyes of their religion and philosophy. Archaeologists* have discovered Akkadian, Assyrian, Babylonian, Hurrian, Khatti, Israelite, and Sumerian versions of flood myths. (*See also* **Agriculture; Calendars; Cereal Grains; Law; Religion.**)

FOOD AND DRINK

The diet of the people in the ancient Near East was simpler than that of people today. Their diet consisted primarily of CEREAL GRAINS and a variety of vegetables and fruits. In addition to water and milk, people of the ancient Near East drank both beer and WINE.

Trade in food products took place throughout the ancient Near East, but this type of commerce was rather limited. Instead, each area relied primarily on local products, and many families produced only enough food for their own needs. People also preserved and stored food for later use to ensure that they could feed themselves.

KINDS OF FOOD AND DRINK

Compared to the varied foods and drinks available in many places in the world today, the diet of the people of the ancient Near East was very limited. Breads and cereal grains were the most common food, and these were supplemented with vegetables, fruits, some dairy products, beer, and wine. Meat and fish were rare dishes, eaten usually by the wealthier classes, although other people might eat them on an occasional basis.

Breads and Cereal Grains. Breads and cereal grains were important staples throughout the ancient Near East. Bread was considered the "staff of life" and comprised the most important component of many ancient Near Eastern diets. Bread could be made from the flour of barley, wheat, or other grains, and it was baked in a variety of sizes and shapes. Much of the bread in the ancient Near East was unleavened, or made without yeast. Ingredients such fruit, spices, or herbs might be added to breads before they were baked to provide flavor.

Flour from grains was often enriched with fat, milk, or eggs and mixed with honey or fruits to make sweet cakes and biscuits. Whole grains with the husks removed were mixed with water, milk, or other liquids and eaten like the cereals of today. In Babylon, for example, a common breakfast consisted of a type of porridge made from the grains of emmer wheat mixed with water.

Vegetables and Fruits. The second most important component of the ancient Near Eastern diet consisted of various vegetables and fruits. Consumption of these foods helped balance people's diets by providing important vitamins and other nutrients not found in bread and grains.

The inhabitants of the ancient Near East grew a variety of vegetables. Lentils and peas were widely cultivated in the Levant*, Anatolia, and the Zagros Mountains region by 6000 B.C. Other vegetables included garlic, onions, lettuce, cucumbers, turnips, radishes, and various beans. Common fruits included grapes, figs, dates, and pomegranates. Apples and pears were grown in some areas, such as Mesopotamia.

Fruits and vegetables were often eaten raw, but people also cooked them and used them in soups, stews, and other dishes. Fruits were generally eaten fresh and uncooked, although some—particularly grapes, figs, and dates—were dried for eating out of season. Some fruits were used as the ingredient of more exotic foodstuffs and beverages.

Beer and Wine. Beer was an important drink in ancient Mesopotamia, Egypt, and other areas of the Near East, and it generally was more common than wine. Made from various grains, beer provided a nutritious addition to the daily diet. There were many varieties of beer. The quantity of the grain used in brewing could determine its strength. The cheapest beer was diluted with water. Spices, honey, and dates were added to beer to produce different flavors.

Found primarily in grape-growing regions, such as Egypt, wine was a less common drink in many areas of the ancient Near East. Moreover, wine was generally enjoyed by only the wealthier members of society. Wine was not only made from grapes but also from the juice of other fruits, including dates, figs, and pomegranates. It was generally diluted with water to reduce its strength and increase its volume.

In addition to their consumption as household drinks, both beer and wine played a role in religious rites and ceremonies. They were often served as OFFERINGS to the dead or to the gods.

Dairy Products. The dairy products consumed in the ancient Near East included milk, butter, and cheese. These products came primarily from GOATS and SHEEP, although CATTLE and CAMELS also provided dairy products in Anatolia and Arabia. Milk was usually left to ferment* before it was

Food Rations

Food and drink also made up part of the "pay" for workers in the ancient Near East. The food was rationed and distributed on a daily or monthly basis. Some ancient texts from Babylon, dating from about 2000 B.C., list the typical rations distributed to individuals. Children up to 5 years old received 2.5 gallons of barley per month; those aged 5 to 10 received about 4 gallons; and children aged 10 to 13 were given 5 gallons. Adult men received between 10.5 and 15.5 gallons, while women received about half that amount. Elderly adults generally were given about 5 gallons. Workers also received small amounts of vegetables, fruits, and other foods. Experts believe that most people ate a diet that contained adequate calories to keep them fairly healthy.

* **Levant** lands bordering the eastern shores of the Mediterranean Sea (present-day Syria, Lebanon, and Israel), the West Bank, and Jordan

* **ferment** to undergo gradual chemical change in which yeast and bacteria convert sugars into alcohol

Food and Drink

This sculpture shows an Egyptian woman kneading bread dough. Bread, considered the "staff of life," was made from a variety of flours and in various shapes and sizes. Sometimes yeast was added to the dough, although usually the bread was unleavened. Then, the loaves were shaped by hand and placed in clay pots, which were set on glowing coals until the bread was cooked.

Vintage Wines

Just as wines today are bottled at specific wineries and labeled according to year, some wines in the ancient Near East were labeled in the same way. Certain areas were known as especially good wine-producing regions, and wineries in those areas produced the best-known wines. Jars of wine found in the tomb of King Tutankhamen in Egypt had labels giving the place, date, and year (vintage) of the wine and sometimes information about the wineries. Experts think that some of these wines represent the best vintage years. Wine labels found in other places in Egypt describe the wine in various ways, such as "good," "very good," "genuine," and "sweet."

* **domesticated** adapted or tamed for human use

consumed. A common type of butter used in the Near East was ghee, a liquid butter purified by melting, boiling, and straining. Babylonians also used a round, chalky, very hard cheese that when grated and mixed with water, turned back to sour milk for drinking or other purposes.

Meat and Fish. Meat played a limited role in the diet of most people in the ancient Near East. Domesticated* sheep, goats, and cattle were raised chiefly for their wool and milk, and they were too valuable to slaughter on a regular basis. Moreover, fertile land was too precious to devote to raising livestock primarily for meat. Hunting wild animals was reserved mainly to the upper classes. As a result, meat generally formed a regular part of the diet for only the wealthier members of society, while the poorer classes ate it on rare or festive occasions.

Fish was a more common food among the lower classes, but it formed a part of the diet only in areas near rivers, lakes, or seas. Fowl—including pigeons, geese, ducks, and other wild and domesticated birds—were eaten in many areas, but generally only by the rich.

Oils, Condiments, and Sweeteners. Oils were used throughout the ancient Near East for both cooking and seasoning. Olive oil was among the most common types of oil, and it was an important trade product in many parts of the Near East. Ancient peoples also produced oil from a number of other plants, including the seeds of FLAX, and sesame.

Ancient peoples used a number of food products as condiments and sweeteners. One of the most common seasonings was salt, but people also seasoned food with spices and herbs such as coriander, cumin, mustard seed, marjoram, and rosemary. The chief natural sweetener was honey, but people also used the juice from various fruits as sweeteners.

FOOD PREPARATION AND STORAGE

People in the ancient Near East prepared and stored foods in many ways. Food preparation included the different ways in which foods were cooked and eaten, as well as the processes that made food products suitable for consumption and long-term storage. Food storage was important because it allowed food products to be saved and stored for later use.

Food Preparation. Foods generally were prepared in various ways. Meat, fish, and fowl were roasted, fried, baked, or boiled alone or as part of a stew. Certain foods, however, such as bread and beer, required a specific process for preparation.

The initial step in making bread was to prepare a soft dough by mixing flour with water and a little salt. This dough was shaped by hand and then baked inside a clay oven or cooked on a flat stone placed over a fire. Sometimes yeast was added to the dough, which was then left to rise before it was cooked. Some loaves of bread were baked in molds; others were made in fancy shapes of animal and human figures. Breads were also sometimes topped with seeds or mixed with fruits.

The first stage in preparing beer was to soak grain in water, allowing it to sprout, and then to bake it. It was then dried out, crushed, and mixed with ingredients such as herbs, spices, honey, and dates. The resulting mixture was then combined with fresh grain and warmed in a slow oven. At a certain point, this heated mixture was placed on a large mat to cool. A sweet substance, such as honey or dates, was added to assist fermentation. The last step of the process was to mix the fermented, souplike mash with water in a vat and then to strain, or filter, the finished beer into other containers.

Recipes were probably handed down by word of mouth from generation to generation. Most children undoubtedly learned to cook by simply watching and helping their elders. However, three cuneiform* tablets found in southern Babylonia and written in about 1700 B.C. contain a total of 35 recipes for making soups and meat dishes. These early "cookbooks" could not have been intended for use by the average family because most people could not read. Perhaps these tablets are records of meals prepared for a banquet in the palace or served to the gods in the temple.

Food Preservation and Storage. Unless preserved in some way, all foods last for only a short time before spoiling. Food processing and storage were thus very important to ancient peoples, allowing them to save foods for later use or times of special need. The main techniques for preserving food were drying, salting, and smoking. Meat, fish, and fowl could all be preserved this way, allowing them to be stored for significant periods. Most vegetables were not processed and preserved, so people only ate these foods while they were in season. Certain fruits—including figs, dates, and grapes—could be preserved by drying. The dried fruits were then pressed into cakes or stored in pottery containers.

Certain grains could be preserved by heating, which killed the seeds and prevented them from sprouting. To protect the seeds from spoilage and rodents, the grain was sometimes treated with smoke and fumes and stored in large sealed containers.

Bulgur With Vegetables

Bulgur wheat, which is rich in nutrients, was a staple food throughout the ancient Near East. For an authentic bulgur dish, add **2 tablespoons of butter** and **1 teaspoon of salt** to **3 cups of boiling water.** Next, slowly pour **1 cup of bulgur wheat** into the mix and cover the pot, allowing it to simmer for about 20 minutes or until almost all the water is absorbed. Then place a skillet over low heat on a separate burner. Add **¹/₄ cup of oil** and **1 eggplant peeled and cut into 1-inch squares** to the skillet, stirring frequently. Add **1 chopped onion** and cook until it becomes transparent but not brown. Next, add **¹/₂ head of chopped cabbage, 3 sliced carrots,** and **6 sliced stalks of celery** and cook until they are soft. Finally, add **¹/₂ cup of chopped parsley,** stir in the bulgur, and serve.

* **cuneiform** world's oldest form of writing, which takes its name from the distinctive wedge-shaped signs pressed into clay tablets

See color plate 6, vol. 2.

Fortifications

In individual households, people generally stored foods in clay jars of various sizes and shapes. These might be placed in a certain room, in an area of a courtyard, or in storage areas sunk into the floor. Most communities also set aside special areas for the storage of food. Public storehouses generally were located in areas that were both accessible and easy to guard and defend, such as near a city's main gates or administration buildings. (*See also* **Agriculture; Animals, Domestication of; Feasts and Festivals; Fishing; Hunting.**)

* **city-state** independent state consisting of a city and its surrounding territory

ortifications—structures built to protect against attack—played an important role in the city-states*, kingdoms, and empires of the ancient Near East. This was especially true for cities built on flat plains that had no natural barriers, in regions such as southern Mesopotamia. Most early fortifications consisted of walls built around a city. These walls not only provided protection from enemy attack, but they also marked the limits of the city. Their size and strength symbolized the power and prestige of the state or ruler. In some places, walls also served as barriers against flooding. In addition to city walls, ancient peoples also built fortresses at strategic points within their territory and along its borders to help defend against invaders.

The nature of fortifications varied greatly, depending on a combination of military, political, economic, and geographic factors. These factors influenced the size, shape, and structure of fortifications as well as the materials used to build them. Wealthy, powerful cities could afford to build large and elaborate fortifications. Communities that lacked adequate resources might devise a simple defensive system by arranging an outer ring of houses around the settlement. The rear walls of these houses provided a simple barrier against intruders. As the political and economic fortunes of a city or town changed over time, its fortifications often changed as well.

Basic Elements of Fortifications. The fortification systems of the ancient Near East consisted of several basic elements: a barrier wall or earthen rampart*, GATES, towers, and surrounding ditches and slopes. The earliest and simplest type of barrier was a solid wall of stone or brick. Built to various heights and widths, such walls generally provided an effective barrier against attackers. Sometimes other solid walls were built against the outside of the original wall to make the wall thicker and to provide added defense.

* **rampart** protective barrier

Another type of barrier was the casemate wall, which consisted of two parallel walls with a space between. The space might be filled with soil or stones to provide added strength or left open and used as a storage space. Sometimes the casemate walls were integrated into dwellings and functioned as the rear part of a house. Solid and casemate walls generally had walkways and overhanging balcony-like structures along their tops from which defenders could attack an enemy.

* **archaeologist** scientist who studies past human cultures, usually by excavating material remains of human activity

Some ancient cities had large earthen ramparts, or mounds, rising as high as 295 feet. However, archaeologists* have found no evidence that city walls were built on these ramparts. This suggests that they served to mark city limits or to give inhabitants a feeling of security.

People in the ancient Near East entered and left their WALLED CITIES through gates. There were generally only a few main gates because they represented the weakest line of defense in a wall, the place where the city was most easily accessible to foes. Projecting towers were usually built on each side of a gate, providing a platform from which armed troops could defend it and the city. Rooms within the towers housed guards or served as storage areas. Often towers were spaced apart along other sections of a wall to serve as platforms for defenders. Walls also contained bastions, reinforced corners that enabled defenders to fire at attackers from various angles.

Urban fortifications often included deep ditches called moats, which surrounded the city walls. Constructed at the foot of walls or ramparts to increase their height, moats were especially important on level terrain, where there were no natural slopes or hills to help protect the site. Sometimes moats were filled with water, providing an added level of defense.

Protecting the outer slopes of some walls were inclined layers of soil, bricks, or stone known as a glacis. A retaining wall of brick or stone at the foot of the glacis helped to hold it in place, and the face of the glacis was sometimes covered with paving stone. The glacis served two purposes: it helped protect the foundation of a wall from damage due to erosion, and it created a smooth, slippery slope that was difficult for attackers to climb.

History of Fortifications. Fortifications started to appear in the Near East as early as the eighth millennium B.C.*, when rivalries between neighboring settlements created a need for defensive structures. Among the earliest known examples of a wall and tower are those of the town of JERICHO in the Levant*, which date back to the eighth millennium B.C. In the centuries that followed, fortifications sprang up throughout the Near East, becoming increasingly large and sophisticated.

By the third millennium B.C. (years from 3000 to 2001 B.C.), the rise of large territorial states—often at war with each other—had created a need for extensive fortifications. The most outstanding example of city fortifications in Mesopotamia during this period protected the Sumerian city of URUK. Surrounding Uruk was an enormous wall nearly 6 miles long with about 900 semicircular towers. The best-known fortifications in Anatolia (present-day Turkey) are those of TROY, which consisted of massive city walls, bastions, and towers. Though no remains of fortifications from this period have been found in Egypt, evidence from paintings and other sources reveals that the Egyptians also built impressive urban fortifications.

During the second millennium B.C. (years from 2000 to 1001 B.C.), many cities had begun to incorporate earthen ramparts, glacis, and moats into their fortifications. The most impressive use of these elements was in the Levant, where some cities had massive earthen ramparts up to 130 feet thick at the base and nearly 50 feet high. The steep slopes created by such ramparts and glacis provided better protection against the siege* weapons and techniques of warfare that were used during this time.

The expansion of rival empires in the first millennium B.C. (years from 1000 to 1 B.C.) led to the development of new methods of warfare and more extensive fortifications. NINEVEH and BABYLON had immense

* **eighth millennium** B.C. period from 8000 to 7001 B.C.

* **Levant** lands bordering the eastern shores of the Mediterranean Sea (present-day Syria, Lebanon, and Israel), the West Bank, and Jordan

* **siege** long and persistent effort to force a surrender by surrounding a fortress or city with armed troops, cutting it off from supplies and aid

105

Fruit

Tunneling below walls, using ladders to scale walls, and attacking walls with battering rams were among the methods that ancient Egyptians used to break down a fortification's defenses. This drawing of a painting from a tomb in Egypt shows the earliest-known documentation of the use of a battering ram. Three soldiers are shown here standing under a canopy and attacking a fortress wall with a ram.

* **imperial** pertaining to an emperor or an empire

fortifications that fit their status as capitals of mighty empires. The fortifications of Babylon, included two enormous walls, one inside the other; many towers; and a large moat nearly 330 feet wide. Many large cities built separate defensive systems within such fortifications to provide added protection to palaces and government buildings. Because this was a period of intense rivalry between kingdoms and empires, almost all cities of the ancient Near East constructed strong fortifications for defense.

Toward the end of the first millennium B.C., a new dynamic began to unfold. Fortified cities in conquered territories posed a threat to the conquering imperial* power. This was because the conquered inhabitants might feel that the walls made them secure and that they could therefore revolt. For instance, when the city of Babylon tried to revolt against Persian rule in the 400s B.C., the Persians destroyed the city's walls to deprive the city of defenses. The Persians did the same to other cities in conquered areas to make them defenseless against their imperial forces. At the same time, they established military forts throughout their empire to station troops and secure conquered territories. Such forts had existed throughout the centuries, but they became a standard feature of imperial rule. (*See also* **Archaeology and Archaeologists; Building Materials; Cities and City-States; Wars and Warfare; Weapons and Armor.**)

Fruit

See *Agriculture; Food and Drink.*

FURNISHINGS AND FURNITURE

People in modern Western cultures regard furniture as a necessity. Their homes are furnished with pieces used for sitting, sleeping, eating from, and so on. The people of the ancient Near East, however, were accustomed to sitting, lying, or squatting on the ground. For many, items such as chairs and tables were not necessities but extras, perhaps even luxuries.

Most ancient furniture was made of wood, leather, reeds, and cloth—materials that decay over time. The survival of complete or nearly complete pieces of furniture depends on both local custom and climate. Furniture placed in tombs in an extremely dry climate, such as in Egypt, was most likely to be preserved. Furniture from other areas is known from the parts that have been found, such as bronze hardware or IVORY decorations that were once fastened to furniture pieces. Images and descriptions of furniture in artwork and texts reveal how ancient furniture was used.

ANATOLIA TO MESOPOTAMIA

The archaeological* site ÇATAL HÜYÜK in ancient ANATOLIA (present-day Turkey) contains some of the oldest known furniture in the ancient Near East. Buildings dating from the late seventh millennium B.C.* have platforms made of plaster extending out from the walls. These probably served as benches, tables, and beds. Recesses in the walls probably served as cupboards. The people of Çatal Hüyük may have had movable furniture as well. A small statue found there shows a goddess sitting on a stool supported on both sides by standing cats. This is the earliest known example of a seat with animal supports—a style that was used for the seats of gods, kings, and nobles for the next 6,000 years. While the discoveries at Çatal Hüyük provide valuable glimpses of early furniture, most evidence of furniture from the ancient Near East dates from around 3000 B.C. or later.

Household Furnishings. From very early times, people appear to have kept their clothing and personal possessions in bags, baskets, and boxes rather than in large pieces of furniture designed for storage. A Mesopotamian household would have had many reed chests for storing goods, including inscribed CLAY TABLETS that detailed business or other records. Kitchenware included kettles for boiling water and small jars for oil, liquid butter, and beer, as well as sets of millstones used for grinding grain, spices, and sesame seeds. Household textiles included rugs, carpets, and blankets, made of wool, goat hair, or linen.

Among the HITTITES of Anatolia, household furnishings included baskets and chests to hold blankets, clothing, and other objects. POTTERY pitchers, bowls, cups, jars, and plates were plentiful and were often shaped like animals such as bulls, lions, or birds. These were used in religious rituals and for everyday use.

Household and personal objects of the people who lived in the Levant* included reed mats, which served as rugs. Many people kept their personal possessions in wooden chests, some of which had sliding lids. When these chests were not available, people used reed baskets to store goods. Daylight was supplemented by pottery lamps that held olive oil and wicks made of FLAX.

Furniture. Most people slept and sat on the floor or on platforms or simple benches, with mats, rugs, and cushions for comfort. The wealthy and powerful, however, cherished fine items of furniture.

Tables were in use by 3000 B.C. Some were simply stands to support bowls or pitchers; others appear to have had removable tops that served as trays. Later tables were made with tray tops or tops that had depressions in

* **archaeological** referring to the study of past human cultures, usually by excavating material remains of human activity

* **seventh millennium B.C.** years from 7000 to 6001 B.C.

* **Levant** lands bordering the eastern shores of the Mediterranean Sea (present-day Syria, Lebanon, and Israel), the West Bank, and Jordan

Furnishings and Furniture

See
color plate 1,
vol. 4.

* **stela** stone slab or pillar that has been carved or engraved and serves as a monument; *pl.* stelae

* **sphinx** imaginary creature with a lion's body and a human head

* **booty** riches or property gained through conquest

* **tribute** payment made by a smaller or weaker party to a more powerful one, often under the threat of force

* **artisan** skilled craftsperson

Most furniture in the ancient Near East was made of wood, leather, reeds, or cloth. Many pieces were decorated with fixtures and attachments made of ivory or metal. The bronze furniture attachment shown here has the form of a winged sphinx with a face inlaid with stone. It was made in Urartu in the 600s B.C.

the center to hold food. Some large tables may have been used as serving stands or sideboards. Beds and couches were less common and consisted of wooden frames with resting surfaces of woven rope.

The most common kind of seat in MESOPOTAMIA was the stool. There were many types—boxlike stools of wood or reeds, folding stools with crossed legs, and tall cylinders. Some were elaborately decorated. For instance, stools shown in the Royal Standard of Ur, which dates from around 2500 B.C., include carved bull's legs.

The earliest chairs were simply stools with backs. Chairs were made of many kinds of wood, sometimes painted or covered with copper, bronze, silver, or gold. Seats were sometimes upholstered with leather. The fanciest chairs of all were royal thrones, which were often extensively decorated with ivory, gold, and GEMS. A stela* from about 2100 B.C. shows a god seated on a stool that is decorated with panels that look like the decorations on the outer walls of temples.

In the second millennium B.C. (years from 2000 to 1001 B.C.), furniture became more elaborate. Pieces decorated with ivory carvings have been found in sites from Anatolia, Mesopotamia, and the Levant. These items include finely carved sphinxes* and plaques that decorated wooden boxes. From UGARIT, a city on the Syrian coast, archaeologists have found a round table with a rose design in the center. That rosette, as the design is called, was carved from elephant ivory to show animals and mythological creatures. Thousands of ivory objects, including attachments for furniture, have been found at Assyrian sites dating from the 800s to the 600s B.C. Assyrian kings often commissioned workshops to build pieces for them. They also collected furniture as booty* from their conquests and received it as part of tribute*.

Excavators have found examples of magnificent wooden furniture, together with iron, bronze, and clay objects, in tombs dating from the 700s B.C. at the Phrygian site of Gordion in Anatolia. Some of these pieces have ornate inlays, showing that artisans* had mastered the art of forming patterns by joining together tiny pieces of different colored woods. One table consisted of a walnut top on three curved legs. The legs and framework supporting the top were designed in an intricate geometric pattern made of thousands of pieces of juniper inlaid in boxwood. Even in antiquity, Phrygian furniture was famous. In the 400s B.C., the Greek historian Herodotus recommended to his readers that a wooden throne given by the Phrygian king Midas to the Greek temple at Delphi some three centuries earlier was well worth seeing.

The typical house in the Levant had chairs or stools and tables. Most people slept on reed mats. Beds, which were found only in the homes of the wealthy, were of two types: mud brick with mud-brick pillows or wooden frames that supported leather or rope webbing. Tables were more common. Many had three legs, making them well suited to balance on the uneven dirt floors of most houses. Often the legs were carved in the form of animal legs, paws, or heads. Hollows in the table surfaces may have served as food containers. A typical household owned between three and eight stools or chairs for each table. Seats usually consisted of wooden side rails to which leather or fiber webbing was attached.

EGYPT

Egyptian furniture and home furnishings varied according to wealth and class. The royal family sat on chairs of ebony* or wood with ivory inlays. They stored their clothes in chests decorated with gold paint. The lower classes probably sat and slept on reed mats spread on the floor and kept their belongings in baskets. Examples of furniture and household goods from all classes of society have survived, thanks to the practice of burying goods with the dead and the dry desert air. These grave goods sometimes included furniture used during the person's lifetime. Other pieces were especially made for burial, often in the form of a model or miniature.

Household Furnishings. The interiors of Egyptian houses gained both color and comfort from mats and textiles, including cushions, woven wall hangings, and chair covers. Most houses had lamps, usually small pottery bowls with oil-soaked fiber wicks. Occasionally people placed lamps on tall wooden stands to create a light similar to a modern floor lamp. One such lamp was found among the household goods in the tomb of Kha, an architect who lived sometime around 1400 B.C. It consisted of a stone slab, a tall column carved to resemble a papyrus stem, and a bowl at the top to hold the fuel. Kha's burial goods included a commode—a wooden stool with a hole in the seat, under which a chamber pot was placed.

Marriage documents listing the items a bride brought to her new home are a good source of information about the furnishings of Egyptian households. These items included clothes, textiles, jewelry, metal vessels for washing and cooking, a mirror, and a bed.

The Egyptians used chests and baskets of all shapes and sizes for countless purposes. They stored their clothes in boxes. Rectangular boxes with flat lids, sometimes with four short legs, held linens and household effects. Scribes* kept their writing materials in boxes shaped like shrines; similar boxes also held jewelry and other valuables. Small sturdy wooden chests with legs or boxes made of reeds often held amulets*, strings of beads, metal razors and tweezers for removing facial and body hair, braids of false hair, and cosmetics. Numerous storage containers might be needed, as households often stored large quantities of textiles to provide part of a bride's dowry* or to use as barter for other goods.

Furniture. Stools and small tables were the most common items of household furniture. Wealthy individuals owned chairs and beds. Furniture styles changed over time. Those of the Old Kingdom (from about 2675 to 2130 B.C.) tended to be heavier and more massive. During the times of the Middle Kingdom (from about 1980 to 1630 B.C.) and the New Kingdom (from about 1539 to 1075 B.C.), pieces were lighter. Lion legs were the dominant decoration on furniture. Decorations sometimes reflected the symbols of HIEROGLYPHICS, the Egyptian system of writing. For instance, the posts on a queen's bed from the Old Kingdom were in the form of the hieroglyphic symbol meaning "great." The curved neckpiece on which Egyptians rested their heads when they slept resembled the hieroglyph for horizon.

* **ebony** dark, heavy, and highly prized wood from certain tropical trees

* **scribe** person of a learned class who served as a writer, editor, or teacher

* **amulet** small object thought to have supernatural or magical powers

* **dowry** money or property that a woman brings to the man she marries

See color plate 2, vol. 1.

The stool was by far the most common piece of furniture. Peasants and workers might use rough, three-legged stools, but nobles and kings sat on finely inlaid pieces. Work stools tended to have wooden or leather seats; seats of woven reeds were more likely to be used within the home. There were folding stools, stools made of wicker, and for the poor, stools that were simply small slabs of stone or wood.

Chairs indicated a higher status than stools. A basic type was simply an animal-leg stool with a slanted back added. Some chairs had seats close to the ground and wide enough to hold someone sitting cross-legged. Stools, chairs, and beds sometimes stood on cone-shaped limestone supports, which raised the furniture off the packed-mud floors and helped keep them clean and away from crawling insects. Lavishly decorated chairs served as royal thrones. A spectacular example was found in the tomb of TUTANKHAMEN. The throne is made of wood covered with gold sheeting and decorated with semiprecious stones and colored glass. The legs are carved to resemble lion's paws, and the backrest features a painted scene of the king and his wife.

Those who could afford tables used them for dining. Each diner had his or her own small table—large communal tables are unknown. Those too poor to own tables simply kept their plates beside them on the floor.

Like tables, beds were rarely found in humble households. The early beds slanted downward from head to foot, although later beds were parallel to the ground. Instead of pillows, the Egyptians rested their heads on small wooden or stone headrests or neck rests, sometimes softening these with cushions. Egyptians prized their beds as a mark of elegance and civilization. The hero of *The Story of Sinuhe*, returning to Egypt after long years of travel in less refined lands, rejoices at once more being able to sleep in a bed. Some beds had footboards carved with images of deities* traditionally thought to protect women during pregnancy, childbirth, and nursing. (*See also* **Houses; Wood and Woodworking.**)

Furniture Fit for the Gods

The Egyptians and the Mesopotamians regarded the temples they built as their deities' houses. Like any fine house, a temple needed furniture—and only the finest materials and most exquisite workmanship would do for the gods and goddesses. So important and well known were the beds made for Mesopotamian temples that they were used in the naming of years. For example, a year during the reign of King Shulgi of Ur was "the year in which the bed of Ninlil was constructed." The goddess Ninlil was the wife of Enlil, an important Sumerian god.

* **deity** god or goddess

GAMES

* **Neolithic period** final phase of the Stone Age, from about 9000 to 4000 B.C.

* **archaeological** referring to the study of past human cultures, usually by excavating material remains of human activity

Just as people play games to amuse themselves today, people of the ancient Near East played games to entertain themselves. They played with toys, enjoyed board games and games of chance, and also participated in outdoor games. No one knows exactly how some of these games were played. However, others are familiar to people today.

Much physical evidence of ancient games and toys has not been preserved because most playthings were made of perishable materials such as wood, leather, or unbaked clay. Objects clearly identifiable as things for play appeared in the ancient Near East beginning in the Neolithic period*. It is possible to gain a sense of games and toys and their uses from this time on. Written references, artwork, inscriptions on buildings and pottery, and other archaeological* evidence help create a picture of the games played and enjoyed in the ancient Near East.

In all likelihood, children's outdoor activities were the earliest form of games. Running races, skipping rope, wrestling, and other forms of active play have always been a part of childhood. An Egyptian tomb scene from about 2300 B.C. shows boys engaged in a tug-of-war. Children also played leapfrog and a game in which one child balanced on another's back. They also liked whirling games that made them dizzy, arm wrestling, and swimming. In addition, they probably used swings and seesaws. Boys undoubtedly played war and hunting games with weapons they made themselves. Girls played house with dolls.

Surviving records show that several ball games were played in Egypt, with balls made of leather, fabric, or reeds that might be stuffed with rags. Sometimes balls were made of wood. Scraps of wool served the same purpose in Mesopotamia and the Levant*. These balls rolled but did not bounce. Children used them to play catch and to juggle.

Although almost any object could be used as a toy, ancient Near Eastern peoples had some objects that were clearly intended only for play. Among the earliest play objects were baby rattles, found at numerous sites in the Near East. Other toys, such as miniature dishes, furniture, and animals made of wood and clay, are mentioned in texts that were found at archaeological sites. Archaeologists also believe that many of the small human figures found throughout the ancient Near East may have been dolls.

Tops were also used for play. A toplike toy made of a small disk through which holes were bored for leather straps existed in Mesopotamia and the Levant. When the straps were stretched and relaxed in

See color plate 9, vol. 2.

* **Levant** lands bordering the eastern shores of the Mediterranean Sea (present-day Syria, Lebanon, and Israel), the West Bank, and Jordan

One of the most popular board games in the ancient Near East was a game the Egyptians called *senet*. However, as with many ancient games, we do not know exactly how *senet* was played. This wall painting from the tomb of Queen Nefertari, wife of Ramses II, shows the queen about to make a move on the *senet* game board.

turn, the disk began to spin, jump, and hum. This toy is still in use throughout the world. Other toys with moving parts, often activated by strings, have also been found.

See color plate 4, vol. 2.

Not all games were children's games. Adults also played several games, some of which were taken quite seriously, such as games of chance. Moves on board games were made by throwing dice or animal knucklebones. These knucklebones, called *astrigali,* were among the most widely used gaming pieces in ancient times. With four long sides, they were used as four-sided dice. *Astrigali* were made of stone, metal, and glass, as were other types of dice, including six-sided and pyramid-shaped dice. *Astrigali* were also used in several dice games.

Perhaps the most popular board game was the game the Egyptians called *senet.* This game was known throughout the Near East. It was played on a board of thirty squares, some of them beautifully crafted of rare materials. Dice throws determined the moves. Although the rules of the game are unclear, the object may have been to reenact a quest for eternal life.

Babylonian clay tablets with square fields inscribed with signs of the ZODIAC comprised the board for the "game of princes." Some of the boards were made with precious and semiprecious stones. This game was probably played by throwing *astrigali.* Guessing games, referred to in the Hebrew Bible, and similar games of language or pantomime also amused people in the ancient Near East. (*See also* **Entertainment; Family and Social Life.**)

GARDENS

GARDENS

* fourth millennium B.C. years from 4000 to 3001 B.C.

* pharaoh king of ancient Egypt

Throughout the ancient Near East, gardens were kept as places for growing fruits and vegetables, as places of refuge from the hot and dusty climate, as sanctuaries for rare animals and plants, and as symbols of status and wealth. The ways in which they were planted and cared for depended on the region, the wealth of the owner, and the availability of water.

As early as the fourth millennium B.C.*, the Egyptians began growing gardens in the Nile Valley. Here gardens were cultivated in palaces, houses, and temples, and IRRIGATION was dependent upon the waters of the NILE RIVER. In palaces and houses, the magnificence of a garden depended on the wealth of its owner. Gardens of pharaohs* and wealthy officials sometimes contained zoos, pools, lakes, pavilions, shade trees, and shrines. Conversely, the gardens of less wealthy people usually consisted of only a few trees planted in pots next to their homes. Small gardens were often watered by hand, while large gardens depended on irrigation canals, which brought water from pools and wells.

The rulers of ancient Egypt also collected rare species of plants for their gardens. Queen HATSHEPSUT (ruled ca. 1472–1458 B.C.) sent a plant-collecting expedition to a region south of Egypt known as the land of Punt, while THUTMOSE III (ruled ca. 1479–1425 B.C.) sent an expedition to SYRIA to gather new plants for his garden. RAMSES II (ruled ca. 1279–1213 B.C.) created a garden with fruit trees and flowers from many regions and faraway lands. The walls of some pharaohs' tombs were painted with scenes of garden landscapes because it was believed these paintings gave pleasure and nourishment to the dead.

Egyptian gardens contained a wide variety of fruit trees such as fig, date, and pomegranate, which provided both food and shade. Vegetables and legumes were grown here as well and included such items as lettuce, onions, peas, broad beans, lentils, cucumbers, and radishes.

* **cuneiform** world's oldest form of writing, which takes its name from the distinctive wedge-shaped signs pressed into clay tablets

Cuneiform* texts dating from the third millennium B.C.* provide information about the gardens, parks, and orchards in the cities of MESOPOTAMIA. Here gardens were planted at palaces, estates, and temples. Like the Egyptian rulers, Mesopotamian kings viewed gardens as status symbols and collected rare species of plants and animals to keep in them. Among the Mesopotamian kings who created elaborate gardens were TIGLATH-PILESER I (ruled ca. 1114–1076 B.C.) and NEBUCHADNEZZAR II (ruled 605–562 B.C.). The most famous of the Mesopotamian gardens were the HANGING GARDENS OF BABYLON.

* **third millennium B.C.** years from 3000 to 2001 B.C.

Sumerians developed the technique of shade gardening, in which date palms were planted around the garden to provide protection for the other plants from wind, sun, and sand. Among the crops grown in these gardens were peas, beans, lentils, garlic, leeks, cucumbers, lettuce, melons, cumin, coriander, mustard, watercress, grapes, figs, and apples. These gardens usually were located near rivers and canals.

* **Levant** lands bordering the eastern shores of the Mediterranean Sea (present-day Syria, Lebanon, and Israel), the West Bank, and Jordan

* **satrap** provincial governor in Persian-controlled territory

In Persia, the garden was called *paradeisos,* a name meaning "beautiful garden," which is related to the word *paradise.* The earliest example of a *paradeisos* was the garden in the city of Pasargadae in Persia, where king CYRUS THE GREAT (ca. 559–529 B.C.) planted many trees in even rows alongside his palace. Gardens similar to Cyrus's were created in ANATOLIA, Syria, and the Levant*, and were cultivated by satraps* during the time of the PERSIAN EMPIRE.

GATES

See color plate 12, vol. 3.

Gates played an important role in the FORTIFICATIONS, or defensive structures, of urban settlements in the ancient Near East. They served as entrances and exits to WALLED CITIES, allowing inhabitants to move between their homes in the city and the surrounding countryside. Gates often had a symbolic function as well. Large decorated gates served as symbols of the power and prestige of a city and its rulers.

The earliest gates were probably simple openings in a wall, defended by guards or fitted with wooden doors. Gates needed to be defended because they were openings to the city that could potentially be penetrated by attackers. As such, gates were the weakest points in a wall's defenses. As a result, the peoples of the ancient Near East soon devised ways to protect gates and make a city less vulnerable.

One technique people used to strengthen their defense was to limit the number of gates in a wall, thus providing fewer weak points for an enemy to attack. Large walled cities might have only a few main gates and several smaller ones. To protect the gates themselves, people built towers that projected outward from the wall on either side of a gate. These towers helped protect the approaches to a gate, and their roofs served as platforms from which defenders could fire their weapons at an approaching enemy. The towers flanking a city gate were often very large. Many contained from two to six rooms, which were used to house guards, store supplies, or serve other military or civilian purposes.

The approaches to gates and their towers were sometimes perpendicular to the walls, generally up a sloping ramp or a series of steps. However, sometimes the approach to a gate was angled so that it was parallel to the city walls. This made attackers an easier target for the defenders on the walls above.

In addition to large fortified gates, many cities' walls—such as those in KHATTUSHA in Anatolia (present-day Turkey)—had small, narrow gates with passageways leading through the city walls or under them. Called posterns, these gates provided shortcuts to farmers going to fields in the surrounding countryside. Without them, residents might have had to walk great distances to reach the main gates of the city. Because the posterns were small and narrow, they could be blocked quickly and defended easily from the walls above.

Most large city gates had heavy wooden doors—often clad in bronze or reinforced with metal—that could be locked from the inside by heavy horizontal beams. Sometimes these doors were richly decorated with bas-relief* scenes or designs on the bronze. The scenes on some ancient gates uncovered by archaeologists* depict events from the lives of rulers. For instance, bronze gates erected by Assyrian king Ashurnasirpal II show a battle between Aramaeans and Assyrians.

Some main gates were also decorated with stone bas-relief carvings or colored tiles. Many of the subjects were real or imaginary animals, such as lions, bulls, and sphinxes*, that served as guardian figures to protect the gate. The most highly decorated gates often served a ceremonial function during processions and other important events. One of the most famous of such gates is the Ishtar Gate built by Nebuchadnezzar at BABYLON, a blue-tiled gate with golden images of bulls and dragons. This gate was situated along the approach to the temple of MARDUK, the principle god of the Babylonians. (*See also* **Animals in Art; Architecture; Sculpture.**)

* **bas-relief** kind of sculpture in which material is cut away to leave figures projecting slightly from the background

* **archaeologist** scientist who studies past human cultures, usually by excavating material remains of human activity

* **sphinx** imaginary creature with a lion's body and a human head

See color plate 3, vol. 3.

GEMS

* **tribute** payment made by a smaller or weaker party to a more powerful one, often under the threat of force

* **mosaic** art form in which objects are decorated with small pieces of stone or glass that form an image

* **artisan** skilled craftsperson

* **lapis lazuli** dark blue semiprecious stone

Gems are precious or semiprecious stones, which people value for their color and brilliance as well as for their magical properties. JEWELRY was common in the ancient Near East, but only the richest and most important people—both women and men—could afford jewelry studded with gems. Gemstones added color, protection, and interest—and cost—to the items. Gems were also used as tribute*.

Gemstones are hard enough to last but soft enough to be carved. Most were carved into beads of varying sizes and colors. In some cases, flat pieces of stone were cut into different shapes and set in metal to create mosaics* that depicted, for instance, the feathers of a bird. Gem carvers at first used local stones. However, land and sea trade made gemstones from distant regions available. Consequently, it was possible for artisans* in Egypt or Mesopotamia to work with lapis lazuli* from Afghanistan.

The earliest known use of gems in the area was in ANATOLIA (present-day Turkey), where thousands of malachite beads with holes drilled in them and dating from around 7000 B.C. have been found. In Mesopotamia, the body in a tomb dating from around 3000 B.C. was covered with 25,000 semiprecious stone beads, along with gold jewelry adorned with turquoise and lapis lazuli. At a royal tomb in UR, from around the same time, a queen's body was covered with gold and silver jewelry that contained lapis lazuli, carnelian, and agate.

The living wore gems as a symbol of their wealth and power as well as for protection from evil and illness. Sumerian royalty and the elite wore pins, diadems (headbands), earrings, beaded necklaces, rings, bracelets, and armlets. These pieces of jewelry might contain lapis, carnelian, agate, turquoise, malachite, and other colored gems. Gemstones, in addition to being purely decorative, could also be engraved with a wide variety of images and inscriptions and used as SEALS.

Gems were an important part of Egyptian jewelry making. Although the most prized stones were lapis lazuli (from Afghanistan), turquoise (from the Sinai), and carnelian (from Alexandria and Nubia), Egyptian jewelry makers used many more stones. The colors chosen conveyed symbolic meaning. Red symbolized strength and death. Green referred to the rebirth of life and was thus linked to good harvests.

Egyptians used gems in necklaces, pendants, bracelets and armlets, earrings, diadems, and beltlike girdles. Gems were often used in complex designs and to portray people, animals, and vegetation. One piece from

See color plate 4, vol. 4.

Gems were a symbol of wealth and power in the ancient Near East, especially those studded with the most valued stones—lapis lazuli, turquoise, and carnelian. In addition to their use as a decoration, some gems were thought to have magical properties that could protect the wearer from evil and sickness—red stones symbolized strength and vigor as well as death and sadness; green stones symbolized life.

GEMS OF THE ANCIENT NEAR EAST	
Common Gems	**Colors**
agate	multicolored bands or stripes
amethyst	violet
calcite	white
carnelian	bright red
chalcedony	white, gray, blue, brown
emerald	green
feldspar	colorless; also pink to red
hematite	steel gray
jasper	red; also yellow, green, grayish-blue
lapis lazuli	deep blue or violet
malachite	green
obsidian	black
quartz	white; also colorless
steatite (soapstone)	gray, green
turquoise	bright blue

2000 B.C. shows two birds, two snakes, a scarab beetle, and other religious symbols and is inlaid with amethyst, turquoise, feldspar, lapis lazuli, carnelian, and garnet. The stone inlays are cut into varying shapes and sizes to represent the birds' different feathers. The colors alternate, so each feather is obvious.

A unique use of gems in Egypt was the carved scarab, an image of the dung beetle, which was a popular amulet*. Scarabs were first used in the Old Kingdom (beginning around 2675 B.C.), but their popularity grew during the Middle Kingdom period (ca. 1980-1630 B.C.), when they began to be used as seals. They were worn on pendants, tied to bracelets, or tied with thread or wire to a finger. (*See also* **Amulets and Charms; Economy and Trade; Lapis Lazuli.**)

* **amulet** small object thought to have supernatural or magical powers

GENDER AND SEX

* **archaeologist** scientist who studies past human cultures, usually by excavating material remains of human activity

When archaeologists* and scholars study past human cultures, they focus not only on buildings and artworks but also on the ideas and social structures that determined how people lived. One area of study concerns gender, focusing on the beliefs and customs that determine how a particular culture views men and women. To ancient Near Eastern societies, each gender was believed to have its own rights and responsibilities. Those rights and responsibilities varied considerably.

Social Status. Almost all ancient Near Eastern cultures were patriarchal. That is, men occupied most political positions and dominated decision making. There were exceptions to this principle, however. Some evidence suggests that the Lycians in ANATOLIA and the Elamites in IRAN had matriarchal societies. Moreover, some queens, such as HATSHEPSUT of Egypt, ruled some states, and Assyrian wives acted as the heads of households and businesses when their husbands were away. The very fact that these powerful women stand out in the historical record, however, suggests that they were exceptions to the norm, and society could respond harshly to those who defied gender expectations. The man who followed Hatshepsut on the Egyptian throne took pains to wipe out public memory of her by erasing references to her from monuments.

Images in art and literature offer some clues about a society's attitudes toward gender. However, these images often represent the stereotypical views held by a society. For instance, art of everyday life in the ancient Near East reflects the patriarchal society in which women's roles were seen as distinctly different from and less important than those of men. Mesopotamian art, for example, contains many representations of goddesses but few of earthly women or of everyday activities. When women do appear, they are generally shown as barefoot prisoners, suffering figures in war scenes, or mothers nurturing children.

* **artifact** ornament, tool, weapon, or other object made by humans

Reading artifacts* for clues to ancient social attitudes can be a difficult practice, however. For years, archaeologists suspected that men had active lives outdoors while women did not. There is evidence to support this view. For example, objects of personal adornment found at Hasanlu, a site in northwestern Iran dating from around 800 B.C., include metal belts and armbands for men and hair adornments and dangling earrings for women. Belts, often used to hold weapons, suggest action, and armbands draw attention to the biceps. The men's ornaments, then, are related to action and strength. The women's emphasize the face and beauty and hint at a less active life spent indoors.

On the other hand, further studies suggest that gender distinctions were not so clear-cut. Some of the women whose remains were found at Hasanlu were wearing large, heavy pins in the shape of lions. These symbols of high status and power were normally associated with male pursuits such as hunting. These women apparently wore the decorations because they had high-status positions. Thus, gender may not have been the only factor that determined women's social position. Scholars attempting to interpret the past, then, need to bear these distinctions in mind, as well as to think about gender-related roles.

Evidence from artworks and artifacts does not tell the entire story of status either. In Egyptian art, wives might be shown as smaller figures than their husbands, perhaps reflecting the male-dominated social structure. On the other hand, this might simply reflect the fact that women are generally physically smaller than men. Egyptian law indicates that women were given equal rights to men. Women could own, inherit, and dispose of property and enter into business deals. Unlike women of other cultures, who needed male guardians to speak for them in court, Egyptian women could go to court on an equal footing with men. This equality could work both ways. In one court record, a woman who committed a crime with three men was given the same punishment as the men. Scholars must therefore balance the information gained from artworks and artifacts with what they know from other sources in drawing conclusions about gender roles.

Sexual Behavior. Where sexual behavior was concerned, some men and women lived under what today would be called a double standard. Society and the law had different expectations for men and women—and different punishments when they broke the rules. For example, the ancient Israelites defined the crime of adultery* according to gender and class. A married man who had sexual relations with an unmarried woman was not committing adultery. A married woman who had such relations with anyone but her husband *was* committing adultery and risked execution. Under Hittite law, adultery could be punished by death, but if the act took place in an isolated area, the married woman's life was spared. The assumption under that circumstance was that she could not cry out for help. Egyptian attitudes toward adultery were more lenient. There was no death penalty attached to the act, although participants were open to the disapproval of their neighbors.

Attitudes toward sexual behavior stemmed from the belief that the family was the organizing unit of society. In Mesopotamia, for example, prostitution was considered part of society, yet prostitutes were outsiders, women who had "lost their way." Homosexuals were viewed in the same way by Babylonians, and Assyrians severely punished men for homosexual acts. The Israelites banned homosexuality entirely. Other Near Eastern cultures, such as the Egyptian, may have

Color Codes

A clue to the belief that women were occupied indoors while men worked outdoors is offered by Egyptian art. Typically, women are shown with light, yellowish-brown skin. Men's skin is a darker reddish-brown. The lighter color for women may indicate that they were less exposed to sunlight. Male high officials are also shown with light skin. This suggests that they may have reached a point in their careers where they could spend most of their time working indoors.

* **adultery** sexual relationship between a married person and someone other than his or her spouse

117

tolerated homosexuality but regarded anyone who did not marry and have children as abnormal. (*See also* **Family and Social Life; Marriage; Women, Role of.**)

The geography, or the physical and biological features, of a region determines many aspects of life for the people who live there. A region's geographical features can isolate it or can attract people from other lands. The geographical features of the Near East range from coastal plains to barren deserts, from rugged mountains to fertile plateaus.

Mesopotamia. The Greeks gave MESOPOTAMIA (present-day Iraq and eastern Syria) its name, which means "land between the rivers" to mark its geographical location. Mesopotamia, a plain bordered by the EUPHRATES RIVER on the west and the TIGRIS RIVER on the east, lies in the eastern third of the horn-shaped region of the Near East known as the FERTILE CRESCENT.

The Tigris and Euphrates are 250 miles apart as they flow out of ANATOLIA (present-day Turkey). The Euphrates takes an 800-mile southeasterly course, the Tigris a more southerly course for about 550 miles before the two rivers join to form the Shatt al Arab River in southern Mesopotamia. In northern Mesopotamia, the Euphrates and Tigris flow through plains, but the Tigris cuts so deeply into the plains that it is surrounded by cliffs and hills.

South of the great eastward bend in the Euphrates, in the central part of Mesopotamia, the rivers enter the southern alluvial* plain. There, after centuries of carrying and depositing silt, the rivers have created a fairly flat plain. This flat landscape makes it easy for the floodwaters to reach the land in spring and makes it possible for the rivers to change their courses. One advantage of the flat land is that it facilitates IRRIGATION, so early peoples did not have to rely on the irregular and sparse rainfall to provide water to the land. When adequately watered, the soil yields abundant crops. The Tigris, however, is not as suitable for irrigation as the Euphrates because it tends to flood destructively.

Mesopotamia's climate varies according to region. The southern part is an arid region, where some of the world's highest temperatures have been recorded. Winters in the south are generally mild. The northern part of Mesopotamia is cool, and it is subject to cold winters. Summers in the north are hot and dry, but they are cooler than in the south. Mesopotamia receives very little rainfall in the summer, but the northern part receives a fair amount of rain in the winter.

Egypt. Located along the northeastern edge of the African continent, Egypt is bordered on the south by Sudan; on the west by Libya; on the east by the SINAI PENINSULA, eastern desert, and the Red Sea; and on the north by the Mediterranean Sea. Huge, sandy deserts lie south of Egypt as well as to the west and east of the NILE RIVER valley, isolating the region.

Settlements in ancient Egypt were established along the Nile River, which provided the water necessary to sustain life. The Nile flows northward,

* **alluvial** composed of clay, silt, sand, gravel, or similar material deposited by running water

out of Sudan. The river floods annually, between June and October, when the flow of its tributaries is increased by melting snows and rains in Ethiopia. However, since A.D. 1830, the floods have been controlled by a series of dams and sluices*.

Egypt's climate consists of a hot season and a cool season. There is some rainfall in the coastal area, but it is rarer in the south. Few places in Egypt receive more than one inch of rain per year. Temperatures can range from freezing to hot, depending on the location.

Anatolia. Situated in the westernmost part of Asia, Anatolia (present-day Turkey) is dominated by mountains surrounding a central plain known as the central Anatolian plateau. Anatolia's highest peak, Mount Ararat, rising to 16,854 feet above sea level, lies in far eastern Anatolia, the most rugged and mountainous part of the region. Out of these mountains, both the Tigris and Euphrates Rivers flow south. In the extreme southeastern part of Anatolia is rolling, fertile land. This area is the northern extent of the Fertile Crescent.

The Taurus Mountains, which lie to the south of the central plateau, run the length of the Mediterranean coast. In western Anatolia, alternating mountain peaks and valleys serve as a barrier between the narrow coastline along the Aegean and Mediterranean Seas and the central Anatolian plateau.

* **sluice** human-made channel or passage to direct water flow

This map shows some of the important physical features of the ancient Near East around 1500 B.C. The woodland and forest areas, which included the Nile, Tigris, and Euphrates River valleys, as well as parts of Anatolia and Iran, contained the most fertile and populated land in the region. The grasslands and steppes, which provided pasture for grazing animals and open habitats where wild wheat and barley thrived, were attractive to hunter-gatherer populations. The desert regions were mostly barren, intermittently forcing peoples to migrate to the fertile river valleys.

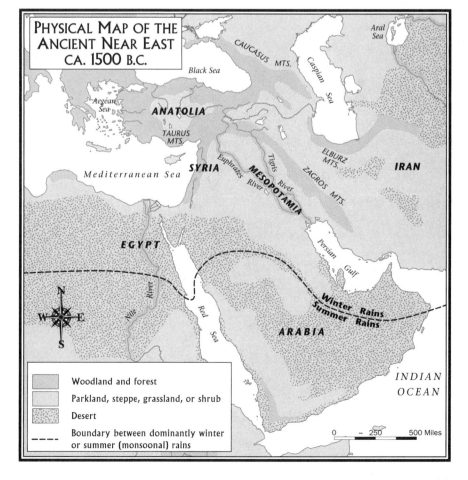

The Anatolian climate varies widely, depending on geographic factors such as altitude and nearness to the coast. In general, coastal areas are humid and experience warm summers and mild, rainy winters. Interior areas are semiarid, with greater seasonal variation in temperature.

Anatolia's rivers are fed by irregular rainfall in most areas and by seasonal snowmelt. The irregularity of the water level and the shallowness of the riverbeds make navigation nearly impossible on almost all of the region's rivers. In spite of its irregularity, rainfall is generally plentiful enough to sustain grasslands in valleys and on plateaus as well as deciduous forests (forests in which trees shed their leaves annually) on the mountain slopes.

Iran. The majority of IRAN is made up of the huge central plateau and its surrounding rugged mountain ranges. In the west, the Zagros Mountains run southeast all the way to the Persian Gulf. These mountains form a barrier between Mesopotamia and Iran. In the north, the Elburz Mountains lie along the southern shore of the Caspian Sea. East of the central plateau are smaller mountain ranges. The central plateau also contains two large deserts. To the north is Dasht-i-Kavir, a harsh, salt-covered land in which neither plants nor animals live. To the east lies Dasht-i-Lut, a barren, rocky desert that is equally uninviting.

Iran consists of three main climatic regions. The Elburz Mountains in the north are extremely cold. The northern slopes of the mountains, however, benefit from warmer, moist air from the Caspian Sea. The central plateau is temperate, experiencing moderate temperatures and distinct seasons. Along the southern shores of Iran, the climate is quite hot. It is rare for the temperature to go below freezing, even in January, the coolest month.

Most of Iran receives very little rain. Average annual rainfall ranges from about eight to ten inches. The rivers run dry in the summer, and the water in many lakes evaporates significantly, leaving behind water with a high salt content.

The Levant. The lands bordering the eastern shores of the Mediterranean Sea, including present-day Syria, Lebanon, Israel, the West Bank, and Jordan, are known as the Levant. The climate in this region is affected by its proximity to the Mediterranean Sea. Near the coast, the summers are hot and dry and the winters are mild. Further inland, the weather varies more depending on the geographical features.

Syria has a narrow, flat coastal plain—only about 20 miles wide—along the Mediterranean Sea. Beyond the coast, a narrow mountain range, called the Jebel an-Nusayririyah runs north and south. To the south of this range, along the Syria-Lebanon border, lie the Anti-Lebanon Mountains. Syria's highest peak, Mount Hermon, at more than 9,000 feet above sea level, is located in this range. To the east, stretching from the coastline and mountains is a plain that extends all the way to the Euphrates River. Known as the Syrian Desert, the plain extends through several countries. The land is not shifting sand but a rock and gravel steppe*. The treeless steppe supports only sparse, bushy growth, except along rivers, where trees grow naturally or can be cultivated.

Oases: Islands of Life

West of the Nile River lies the Libyan Desert, also known as the Western Desert. Its sandy expanse is broken only occasionally by slight depressions, or hollows. In some of these hollows, natural springs provide enough water for both domestic and agricultural use. These oases, with their striking fertility amid the vast desert, have served as resting places for trade caravans. They also sustain small communities and have done so since ancient times. Signs of very early agriculture have been found at many oases, although oases were valued more for their location and water than for their agricultural uses. The oases range in size from 2 acres to more than 896,000 acres.

* **steppe** large semiarid grassy plain with few trees

Away from the Mediterranean coast the seasons are more marked. Temperature extremes are more distinct in the arid climate of the Syrian Desert. The summers are hot and winters are cold and snowy on the steppe. Moving eastward from the coast, the average annual rainfall decreases from a maximum of 40 inches to approximately 5 inches in the far reaches of the steppe.

Variety marks Israel's landscape, which shares features with the Palestinian Gaza Strip and the West Bank. The region contains several mountain ranges, including the mountains of Galilee in the north and the Mount Carmel range in the northwest. At the southern end of Israel lies the harsh Negev Desert. Bordered by Israel, the West Bank and Jordan and fed by the Jordan River is the Dead Sea, which, at 1,300 feet below sea level, is the lowest point on the earth's surface.

The Jordan River in the east forms a boundary between Israel and Jordan. In ancient times, the Jordan River was the largest and most dependable source of freshwater for this part of the Levant, but it was not navigable*. Because its riverbed was deep, it was impossible to use the river's waters for irrigation.

* **navigable** deep and wide enough to provide passage for ships

Israel receives only modest rainfall, and most of that falls during the winter months. Rainfall is significantly lower in the south than in the north. The modest rainfall and mountainous terrain limit Israel's fertility.

Lebanon lies on the Mediterranean coast, to the north of Israel and east of Syria. The Lebanon Mountains are Lebanon's most distinctive land feature at approximately 100 miles long and 6 to 35 miles wide. Fertile lands for agriculture are found on the coastal plain and in the northern mountains. Rivers in Lebanon tend to run only in the winter as they drain the slopes of the Lebanon Mountains. The climate in Lebanon is hot and dry in the summer and mild and humid in the winter.

The Arabian Peninsula. The vast peninsula of Arabia is bordered on the west and in the extreme southwest, along the RED SEA, by mountains. The rest of the peninsula is a plateau that slopes somewhat to the east, toward the Persian Gulf. On the plateau are several large, sandy deserts, some of them the largest in the world. Arabia's extreme dryness causes the region's rivers to run dry during the hot, dry summer months. (*See also* **Agriculture; Building Materials; Environmental Change; Water.**)

GILGAMESH

Gilgamesh (GIL•guh•mesh) was one of the earliest and most important heroes in ancient Near Eastern LITERATURE. Many scholars believe that Gilgamesh, who is listed in Sumerian KING LISTS, was the ruler of the city of URUK around 2700 B.C. Others believe that the character of Gilgamesh is based on a Sumerian god called Gilgames (or Bilgames). All scholars agree that the fantastic adventures of this legendary character are purely fictional.

Tales About Gilgamesh. Among the earliest tales known about Gilgamesh are several Sumerian poems that were probably composed around 2100 B.C. The surviving fragments are of copies made around

Gilgamesh

When Gilgamesh refused the goddess Ishtar's offer of marriage, she became enraged and sent the Bull of Heaven to destroy him. This cylinder seal impression from the Neo-Babylonian period shows Ishtar (on the right) as she tries to prevent Gilgamesh (second from left) and his friend Enkidu from slaying the bull.

* **epic** long poem about a legendary or historical hero, written in a grand style

* **second millennium B.C.** years from 2000 to 1001 B.C.

* **archaeologist** scientist who studies past human cultures, usually by excavating material remains of human activity

1700 B.C. These works include *Gilgamesh and Khuwawa; Gilgamesh and the Bull of Heaven; Gilgamesh and King Agga of Kish; Gilgamesh, Enkidu, and the Nether World;* and *The Death of Gilgamesh.* They relate the incidents and adventures in the life of the hero.

The most famous and complete record of the adventures of Gilgamesh appears in the *Epic of Gilgamesh,* a long epic* poem, a version of which was composed in the Akkadian language in the first half of the second millennium B.C.* This work was later rewritten, and copies of that version were made during the 600s B.C. Several of these copies have survived, but the most complete one was found by archaeologists* at the site of the ancient city of NINEVEH. This surviving version, known as the Standard Version of the *Epic of Gilgamesh,* marks an important step in the development of Mesopotamian literature. In it, many of the stories of Gilgamesh are woven into a single narrative. A major theme of the epic is Gilgamesh's acceptance of his mortality. He seeks fame and glory through heroic deeds but finally realizes that he cannot achieve the impossible, and he accepts the fact that he, like all humans, must die.

The Epic. The version of the story found at Nineveh was inscribed on 12 tablets in the 600s B.C. The first tablet contains a prologue in which Gilgamesh is described as part human and part divine, the son of King Lugalbanda of Uruk and the goddess Ninsun. Gilgamesh is praised as a wise man and mighty warrior, and his great achievement of building the walls of Uruk is noted. However, he is also described as a tyrant who mistreats the young people of his city. The god ANU had the mother goddess Aruru create a man named Enkidu to fight Gilgamesh in the hope that this will cure the king of his harshness toward the people.

The second tablet narrates the confrontations between Gilgamesh and Enkidu at Uruk. Gilgamesh wins the struggle, but he is so impressed by his opponent's skill and courage that the two become friends. (In the earlier Sumerian poems about Gilgamesh, Enkidu was his slave.) The third, fourth, and fifth tablets describe Gilgamesh's quest for eternal fame. They relate the story of how he travels with Enkidu to a distant cedar forest to battle the monster Khumbaba (or Khuwawa), the guardian of the forest. Gilgamesh kills the monster, believing that that heroic deed will help him win the favor of the gods.

In the sixth tablet, Gilgamesh returns to Uruk, where ISHTAR, the goddess of love, proposes marriage. However, Gilgamesh refuses the offer, insulting the goddess. Enraged, Ishtar sends the divine Bull of Heaven to destroy Gilgamesh. Enkidu and Gilgamesh kill the bull in another heroic adventure.

In the next two tablets, Gilgamesh's views on life, death, and immortality change. Enkidu has a dream in which the gods Anu, EA, and Shamash decide that he must die for killing the Bull of Heaven. Shortly thereafter, Enkidu falls ill and dies. Gilgamesh grieves over the death of his friend. He then becomes determined to gain immortality and possibly become a god.

The ninth, tenth, and eleventh tablets describe Gilgamesh's travels to find Ut-napishtim, the survivor of the Great Flood who had gained immortality. He journeys through strange lands and meets creatures who try to talk him out of his pursuit. Finally, he finds Ut-napishtim, who offers a challenge: if Gilgamesh can stay awake for seven days, he will get the immortality he desires. Gilgamesh accepts the challenge but falls asleep. Pitying him, Ut-napishtim tells him the location of the Plant of Life, which can restore youth. Gilgamesh finds the plant and proceeds on his way home, where he plans to test it on an old man first. On the way, Gilgamesh puts the plant down when he stops to bathe in a spring, only to find that a snake had taken the plant and shed its skin (rejuvenated itself) as it slithered away. Betrayed by his humanity, its frailty and its limitations, Gilgamesh returns home, disappointed and tired but wiser and at peace. Weeping, he says simply, "I should have turned back." He sees that he should not have attempted to escape death or cheat it. Then Gilgamesh repeats the words from the epic's prologue about building the walls of Uruk, indicating that he has come full circle, giving the reader a sense of finality and completeness.

The twelfth tablet of the epic, which some scholars consider a later addition to the poem, relates how the spirit of Enkidu returns from the dead and describes the underworld* and AFTERLIFE to Gilgamesh. The complete work remains one of the world's greatest epics. Rich in timeless themes, it provides a unique look into the hearts and minds of the people of the ancient Near East. (*See also* **Epic Literature; Flood Legends.**)

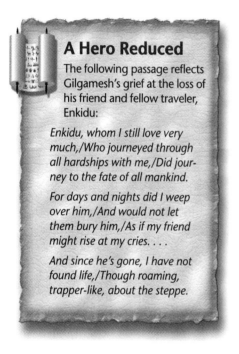

A Hero Reduced

The following passage reflects Gilgamesh's grief at the loss of his friend and fellow traveler, Enkidu:

Enkidu, whom I still love very much,/Who journeyed through all hardships with me,/Did journey to the fate of all mankind.

For days and nights did I weep over him,/And would not let them bury him,/As if my friend might rise at my cries. . . .

And since he's gone, I have not found life,/Though roaming, trapper-like, about the steppe.

* **underworld** world of the dead

GIZA

Giza (GEE•zuh) is a modern-day city in northern Egypt located in the desert west of the NILE RIVER. It is famous as the site of Egypt's largest and best-known PYRAMIDS and of the statue known as the Great Sphinx. These monuments date from the Old Kingdom period (ca. 267–2130 B.C.). The site was ignored for several centuries but became a popular religious destination during the time of the New Kingdom (ca. 1539–1075 B.C.).

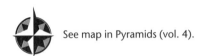

Glass and Glassmaking

See map in Pyramids (vol. 4).

* **mastaba** ancient Egyptian burial
  structure with long rectangular sides
  and a flat roof over a burial pit or
  chamber

* **Egyptologist** person who studies
  ancient Egypt

* **sphinx** imaginary creature with a lion's
  body and a human head

* **pilgrimage** journey to a sacred place as
  an act of religious devotion

* **first millennium** B.C. years from 1000
  to 1 B.C.

Three kings of the Fourth Dynasty had huge pyramids built at Giza as their tombs. The largest, called the Great Pyramid, was built by king KHUFU (ruled ca. 2585–2560 B.C.). More than 480 feet high, it is the largest stone structure in the world. Two other large pyramids were built by Khufu's son and grandson. Together these three pyramids were considered one of the Seven Wonders of the Ancient World. There were also a number of smaller pyramids built to house the remains of royal wives and mastabas* for top government officials and others of the royal family.

In the quarry near the pyramids that provided much of the stone for their construction, there remained a large outcropping of rock that artisans sculpted into the Great Sphinx, a seated lion with a human head wearing a king's headcloth. Most Egyptologists* believe the face of the sphinx* is that of Chephren, Khufu's son, although it has been suggested that the face is that of Khufu himself.

At the end of the Old Kingdom, Giza was abandoned. The pyramids suffered in the chaos that followed the collapse of the Old Kingdom, when the tombs were probably robbed of their contents. During the New Kingdom period, however, Giza regained prominence. Thutmose IV (ruled ca. 1400–1390 B.C.) employed workers to remove the sand that had covered the Great Sphinx. People began making pilgrimages* to Giza to worship the sphinx, which was then thought to represent a form of the god HORUS. People also came to Giza to worship the goddess ISIS, who had a temple in the complex. During the first millennium B.C.*, the area was once again favored as a burial site. (*See also* **Egypt and the Egyptians; Sphinx.**)

GLASS AND GLASSMAKING

* **artisan** skilled craftsperson

See
color plate 15,
vol. 4.

Glass is made by mixing fine sand or ground sandstone and an alkali such as potash, made from the ashes of burned plants, and ground limestone. The mixture is heated to a very high temperature in an oven so that the ingredients completely melt and fuse together. Then the liquid is poured into molds, blown, or rolled into sheets and allowed to cool. The shaping must be done quickly because the glass cools to a solid in only a few minutes. Glass can be colored by adding minerals to the mixture. This method of glassmaking, invented almost 4,000 years ago, is fundamentally the same method used today.

Some glasslike objects that have been found were made as early as 4000 B.C., but these are thought to be accidents that were created when artisans* were making FAIENCE, which is similar to glass. The Mesopotamians are credited with the invention of glass in about 1600 B.C. Glassmaking quickly spread to Egypt.

CUNEIFORM texts from around 1500 B.C. indicate that the principal use for colored glass was to imitate rare and precious GEMS used for JEWELRY and SEALS. Glass, often of brilliant colors, could also be made into hollow vessels. Glass vessels were shaped in several ways. Molten glass was gently sloshed around the inside of a clay bowl (or other shape) to form an even layer. After the glass hardened, the clay was carefully chipped away. Similarly, a layer of softened glass could be formed around a solid clay shape with an opening. After the glass hardened, the clay inside was removed to leave the formed glass. Finally, a snakelike ribbon of molten glass could be wound around and around the same sort of core shape, resulting in textured glass.

The first glass vessels were small, used as containers for perfume and cosmetics. The colors of the glass included red, green, yellow, white, and blue. Egyptian glassmakers favored red and blue. Early glass was not transparent.

Glass was decorated in several ways. Designs could be gently carved into it, or glass threads of different colors could be applied to the surface. There was a special technique for making mosaic* glass vessels. Pieces of colored glass were cut into the desired shapes and sizes, then fitted together over a solid clay or packed sand core. Over this was placed a mold. The mold was heated just enough to fuse together the glass pieces underneath. Then the mold and core were removed.

Amassing the materials for glassmaking was labor-intensive. In the 600s B.C., Egyptians discovered that they could slightly vary the formula for glass to make use of plentiful and easily quarried local materials. At that point, glassmaking became an industry, including an export trade.

Glassmaking became an important industry in the Levant*, eventually replacing faience as a luxury good produced for trade. Syrian glassmakers showed great skill. In the 700s B.C., they began producing cut glass—glass that is scored to produce interesting shapes. After the 100s B.C., they were producing objects by glassblowing. In this process, a lump of molten glass is put on one end of a hollow tube. The glassblower blows through the tube, as if blowing up a balloon. This produces thin-walled objects in round, oval, and any other desired shapes. The process may have been adopted from IRAN, another leading center of glassmaking.

Glassmakers in Iran produced cut and polished glass vessels and combined glass and gold to make bowls fit for—and used by—kings. They also perfected the manufacture of almost colorless glass.

* **mosaic** art form in which objects are decorated with small pieces of stone or glass that form an image

* **Levant** lands bordering the eastern shores of the Mediterranean Sea (present-day Syria, Lebanon, and Israel), the West Bank, and Jordan

These beaded head pendants, made of sand-core glass, date from the 300s B.C. They were excavated at Carthage, in present-day Tunisia, on the coast of North Africa. At the time, Carthage was controlled by the Phoenicians, who were skilled at producing colorful glass beads in the form of human and animal heads.

Goats

* **domesticated** adapted or tamed for human use

* **third millennium B.C.** years from 3000 to 2001 B.C.

G oats and SHEEP were the earliest and most important domesticated* animals in the ancient Near East. Combined with the development of AGRICULTURE, the domestication of these animals led to the establishment of settled communities based on farming and the herding of livestock.

In very early times, people in some parts of the ancient Near East hunted wild goats for food. Evidence suggests that goats were first domesticated in the Zagros Mountains of western IRAN sometime between 7500 and 7000 B.C. The earliest domesticated goats may have originated from a wild species with long curved horns known as the Bezoar goat, found in mountainous regions throughout western Asia. By the third millennium B.C.*, goats of several species had been domesticated throughout the ancient Near East. Some of the species could thrive in areas far beyond their normal environments.

People in the ancient Near East valued goats for their milk, meat, and hides and for their ability to lead flocks, which often included sheep. Herding goats and sheep was an important economic activity, and herders moved flocks continually from one pastureland to another. Temples also maintained large flocks of goats, not only for their milk, meat, and hides but also for use in ritual sacrifices and OFFERINGS. These flocks sometimes consisted of as many as 350,000 animals. Temple goats also played a role in divination. Priests examined the internal organs of sacrificed animals to foretell a god's will on various subjects. (*See also* **Animals; Animals, Domestication of.**)

GODS AND GODDESSES

* **oracle** priest or priestess through whom a god is believed to speak; also, the location (such as a shrine) where such utterances are made
* **deity** god or goddess
* **piety** faithfulness to beliefs

F or the people of the ancient Near East, gods and goddesses played an important role in everyday life. People frequently consulted the oracles*, asking the gods for advice, help, and protection. They thanked the gods for providing good harvests and other blessings and prayed for pardon when they believed the deities* had been angered.

People considered the gods and goddesses to be the ultimate rulers of heaven and earth. Human beings were considered the servants of the gods and had a responsibility to worship them, maintain their temples, and provide nourishment to them through OFFERINGS, rituals, and sacrifices. Ancient Near Eastern peoples believed that human behavior was closely watched by them, who handed out both rewards and punishments. It was the role of priests to determine what would make the gods happy, and it was up to the people to express their piety* by providing the necessary offerings and praise.

Ancient Near Eastern mythology is filled with stories about gods and goddesses. CREATION MYTHS recount how the gods created heaven, earth, and living things. All the myths about the gods reveal the gods' characteristics, including their strengths and weaknesses. The gods could be kind or cruel, fair or unjust. In many ways, the deities were anthropomorphic; that is, many looked like humans and had similar traits and characteristics. They displayed anger, jealousy, and hatred, as well as kindness, understanding, and love. Unlike humans, however, the gods were larger than life and had supernatural powers. Many were immortal.

* **city-state** independent state consisting of a city and its surrounding territory

* **fourth millennium B.C.** years from 4000 to 3001 B.C.

* **patron** special guardian, protector, or supporter

* **cult** system of religious beliefs and rituals; group following these beliefs

* **Semitic** of or relating to people of the Near East or northern Africa, including the Assyrians, Babylonians, Phoenicians, Jews, and Arabs

This stela from the mid-700s B.C. shows an Aramaean storm god. Standing on the back of a bull, the deity holds a three-pronged fork representing lightning in his right hand. Because rain was essential for agriculture, storm and weather gods and goddesses were among the most important deities in Near Eastern pantheons.

Each of the ancient Near Eastern cultures had many deities. Some were major deities, while others were of only minor importance. Together, all the gods and goddesses of a culture formed its pantheon. Each of the ancient Near Eastern city-states* had its own pantheon but was especially dedicated to the worship of a particular god or goddess. Many of these gods and goddesses had counterparts in other cultures. While the names of the gods often differed, their power and characteristics were quite similar.

Mesopotamia. The earliest Mesopotamians were animists, concerned with nature spirits. By the late fourth millennium B.C.*, these spirits were perceived as having human forms and emotions. Each city, town, and village in MESOPOTAMIA had its own patron* deity, whom the people considered a king. The local deity, along with the god's family and servants, was thought to live in a temple, the palace of the god. A statue of the deity in the temple allowed the god to be accessible to worshipers. The temple was the center for the god's cult*, the members of which were responsible for providing the god with shelter and food.

During the third millennium B.C.—the years from 3000 to 2001 B.C.—the Mesopotamians established linkages among their gods and goddesses. For example, the god of one town might be the son of a goddess worshiped in another town. The gods of the largest cities eventually became the most important deities in the pantheon, and these major gods were worshiped throughout Mesopotamia. Over time, the gender and family ties among deities sometimes changed, and their names might change as well. For example, as the influence of Semitic* peoples increased in ancient Sumer, many Sumerian gods received Semitic names.

Ancient Mesopotamian myths explained how the major deities organized the world after the separation of heaven and earth. Lesser gods labored for the major gods, digging rivers and canals and building homes. Burdened by such tasks, the lesser gods eventually rebelled, and the major gods agreed to create humans to act as servants instead. EA, the god of wisdom, then created humans. His mother, Namma, a goddess who represented the primal waters*, helped him in this task.

According to early Mesopotamian myths, the responsibilities for heaven and earth were divided among the gods. ANU, the god of heaven, presided over the divine assembly of gods and goddesses. His son Ishkur, the storm god, was responsible for rain and thunder. ENLIL, the city god of NIPPUR, organized the world after creation. His son Ninurta, the war god, defeated the forces of evil that threatened divine rule.

Enlil's son Nanna, the moon god, resided in the city of UR and was responsible for the division of time. Nanna had a son, Utu, and a daughter, Inanna. Utu, the sun god, lived in the cities of Larsa and Sippar and was responsible for justice. Inanna, the goddess of the morning and evening star (Venus), resided in URUK. Responsible for love and war, she later became known as ISHTAR.

Besides these major deities, there were hundreds of minor gods and goddesses associated with Mesopotamian cities and towns. There were also thousands of unnamed deities, who served as the personal gods of individuals, as well as many DEMONS, who served the gods.

Gods and Goddesses

* **primal waters** in mythology, the original oceans that covered everything in earliest times

* **second millennium B.C.** years from 2000 to 1001 B.C.

This Egyptian wall painting shows the pharaoh Sety I with the goddess Hathor. Daughter of the sun god Amun, Hathor was worshiped throughout ancient Egypt. She is depicted here in her most common form—a woman wearing cow's horns with a sun disk in between. A benevolent goddess, Hathor was associated with women, music, dancing, and sexuality.

In the second millennium B.C.*, alliances and military conquests united the cities and towns of Mesopotamia into nations and empires. As the region united, some city gods became national gods, worshiped by people throughout all of Mesopotamia. Two of the most important of these national gods were ASHUR in Assyria and MARDUK in Babylonia.

When illustrated in art, Mesopotamian deities were distinguished from humans by their size, costumes, crowns (often with several pairs of horns), and symbols. The depictions illustrate the deities' power or the myths and stories about them. The storm god Ishkur, for instance, is often shown holding forked lightning in his hands.

Egypt. As in Mesopotamia, the people of ancient Egypt also worshiped many gods and goddesses. Egyptian temple worship focused on the main deity of the temple, but it included other divine beings as well. Many of the gods were related to one another in some way. Although Egyptian deities lived in heaven, they also appeared on earth, where they resided in temples with their divine families. Cult statues of deities, made by the temple priests in secrecy, were kept in the innermost section of the temple. The image of the principal god of the temple was placed in a special shrine within the temple.

Egyptian myths described the powers of the gods and explained the relationships among them. Creation myths are particularly revealing, explaining how the gods created heaven, earth, and humans and describing the responsibilities of the pantheon of gods. Throughout Egypt's long history several different views arose at different times in different religious centers. According to the mythology of priests at Heliopolis during the Old Kingdom period (ca. 2675–2130 B.C.), only the primal waters existed at first, and in them was Atum, the creator. A pantheon of great gods emerged from Atum as manifestations of him. The first deities to emerge from Atum were Shu, god of the space between heaven and earth, and his sister, Tefnut, the goddess of moisture. They represented the male and female forces of the universe. The next generation of gods was Geb and Nut. Geb, the god of the earth, was also known as father of the gods. Nut was the goddess of the sky. Together, they formed a permanent boundary between the newly created world and the primal waters that surrounded it.

The next god to appear was Ra, the sun god, who divided day and night and brought order to the universe. Worshiped in Egypt, Ra was often combined with other gods. After the 1500s B.C., Ra was combined with AMUN, a local god of the city of THEBES, to become Amun-Ra. One of the most important Egyptian deities, Amun-Ra was considered the king of gods, creator of the universe, and father of Egyptian monarchs.

Geb and Nut had four children—two sons, OSIRIS and SETH, and two daughters, ISIS and Nephthys. Organized in pairs, Osiris and Isis represented order and the fertility of the earth and humankind, and Seth and Nephthys represented disorder, confusion, conflict, and infertility. Seth brought death into the world by killing Osiris, but Isis raised Osiris from the dead, and he became the lord of the underworld, where he judged the souls of the dead. HORUS, considered the son of Isis and Osiris as well as Osiris reborn, defeated Seth in battle and became god of the sky and of

* **pharaoh** king of ancient Egypt

* **scribe** person of a learned class who served as a writer, editor, or teacher

* **embalming** treating a corpse with oils or chemicals to preserve it or slow down the process of decay, usually after body fluids have been removed

A God's Best Friend

Many Mesopotamian gods were associated with particular real animals or fantastic beasts, and the deities were often depicted with these creatures. A god might be linked to an ordinary animal, such as a lion, a snake, or a bull. However, the beasts associated with gods could also be fantastic creatures that combined different animals, such as a lion dragon or a goat fish. Some of these beasts combined the parts of several creatures. For example, the snake dragon associated with the gods Marduk, Nabu, and Ashur, had a snakelike body, horns, the forelegs of a lion, and the hindlegs of a bird. Statues of these beasts often stood at the entrances to temples and shrines to guard as watch beasts. Statues of beasts also were used inside temples and shrines as altars.

* **indigenous** referring to the original inhabitants of a region

See color plate 5, vol. 1.

earthly kingship. Horus represented the final form of the creator god Atum, and each pharaoh* was considered a manifestation of the god.

Egyptians worshiped many other local and national deities. Among the most important were Thoth, Anubis, Ptah, HATHOR, and ATEN. Thoth, the moon god, was a scribe* for the gods. His responsibilities included learning, writing, and good government. Anubis was the god of death and embalming*. The god Ptah, worshiped primarily at the city of Memphis, was a creator god. Hathor was the goddess of women and of music and dancing; she could also be the source of drunkenness and sexual arousal. For a short time, the god Aten became a major deity during the reign of AKHENATEN (ca. 1353–1336 B.C.), who attempted to make him the sole and exclusive god of Egypt.

When illustrated in art, Egyptian deities were shown as composite in form, combining human and animal characteristics. In the later periods of Egyptian history, they were represented as the animal itself or as a human with the head of the animal. For instance, Horus appeared as a hawk or falcon, Thoth as a baboon or ibis, Hathor as a cow, Amun as a ram or goose, and Anubis as a jackal. Just as in Mesopotamia, the artworks depict the deities' power or the myths and stories about them.

Anatolia. The region of ANATOLIA (present-day Turkey) was occupied by different peoples in ancient times, including the Hattians, HITTITES, and HURRIANS. Each group had its own deities. In their traits and powers, the deities resembled those elsewhere in the ancient Near East.

The Hittites were among the most important peoples to occupy Anatolia. They had a remarkably complex pantheon of deities, which they called the thousand gods. This pantheon included Hittite gods as well as deities borrowed from the Hurrians, Hattians (indigenous* people who lived in Anatolia before the Hittites), and others. The Hittites often adopted deities directly from other cultures, merely changing the names. Thus, the Hattic goddess Inar became the Hittite Inara. Consequently, gods in the Hittite pantheon often had many manifestations, or forms, that included different names and genders.

Hittite religious texts dating from between 1600 and 1400 B.C. mention several Hattian gods. Among these were a storm god who went by different names and several deities of the sun, including the sun goddess of Arinna. The children of the storm god and sun goddess included two sons, the storm gods of Nerik and of Zippalanda. Other deities of Hattic origin were Telipinu, a god of vegetation, and the sun god of Eshtan.

Between 1350 and 1200 B.C., the Hittites adopted several Hurrian deities, including the storm god TESHUB, the sun god of Shimegi, the vegetation god KUMARBI, and the moon god Kushukh. Teshub's mate was the sun goddess KHEPAT, who had been combined with the Hattic goddess of Arinna. As in other religions of the ancient Near East, the storm god always held a prominent place in Hittite religion because of the importance of rain for AGRICULTURE. The Hittite pantheon also included several Aryan deities, including Indra, Mithra, Varuna, and the Natwatwa twins, as well as a Syrian goddess named Kubaba. Later worshiped by the Phrygians as their primary goddess, Kubaba was eventually adopted by the ancient Romans as the goddess Cybele.

See
color plate 13,
vol. 1.

From Architect to God

A man known as Imhotep worked in the court of King Djoser in Egypt during the 2600s B.C. What scholars know of Imhotep makes it clear that he was a multitalented person. He explored many different areas of human endeavor. He held the offices of chief executive and master sculptor. Credited with inventing the technique of building with cut stone, Imhotep probably was the architect who planned Egypt's first pyramid, the Step Pyramid at Saqqara. An author of a book of instruction, Imhotep was also a healer and a priest. After his death, in honor of his extraordinary gifts, Imhotep was considered a god, the son of the god Ptah. A shrine to Imhotep was built at a temple in Thebes, and Egyptians also worshiped him at a chapel on the island of Philae in the Nile River.

* **Levant** lands bordering the eastern shores of the Mediterranean Sea (present-day Syria, Lebanon, and Israel), the West Bank, and Jordan

Many Hittite deities served as protectors of certain places or groups. The Hittites also recognized other divine spirits. Mountains, rivers, springs, and other natural features were considered holy and received offerings just like other gods.

Iran. As in Anatolia, several groups lived in IRAN at different periods in history, including the Elamites and Persians. Among the earliest Elamite deities was Simut, the "god of Elam" and "powerful herald of the gods." Other Elamite deities included Narunde, the goddess of victory; the sky goddess Pinengir; the Seven Wise Men; and Khumban, who was associated with the Sumerian god Enlil. Ruler of the atmosphere, he sometimes caused disastrous storms. The most important and powerful Elamite god was Inshushinak, the "King of the Gods."

The most important god of the Persians was AHURA MAZDA, the "Wise Lord." His evil counterpart was his twin brother, AHRIMAN. In the 600s B.C., the Persian prophet Zoroaster proclaimed that there was only one god—Ahura Mazda. Many Persians continued to worship other deities, including Mithra, the sun god and god of war, a popular Aryan god.

Syria and the Levant. For most of ancient history, the region comprising present-day Syria and the Levant* consisted of many fortified city-states, each with its own deities. As in Mesopotamia, these city gods were related to each other, and they had specific responsibilities. The gods were present in all phenomena, including rain and thunder, birth and death, drought and fertility, beauty and terror. At the same time, worshipers had a very personal relationship with their gods because the gods possessed human characteristics and resembled humans.

The oldest known pantheon is that of EBLA. Its principal god, Dagan, became one of the most popular deities of this region. Next in rank to Dagan was ADAD, the god of storms and weather. Among later Syrian gods, the most important seems to have been EL. However, El's importance later declined in favor of BAAL, a storm god. Baal's wife and sister ANAT was a goddess of war and fertility. She was eventually displaced by the Phoenician goddess Astarte. Two other important Syrian gods were Mot—the god of death—and Reshef—the god of the underworld.

Unlike their neighbors, the Israelites strived to abandon the worship of all other deities in favor of just one god—YAHWEH. Yahweh's dominant place in ancient Israel evolved gradually, and at times, he was associated with other gods such as El. Nonetheless, at many points throughout their history, the peoples of ISRAEL AND JUDAH turned to the worship of the gods of their Canaanite neighbors, especially BAAL. Eventually, however, the Israelites rejected all other gods and worshiped only Yahweh, the god of the Hebrew BIBLE. (*See also* **Animals in Art; Birds in Art; Cults; Egypt and the Egyptians; Mythology; Palaces and Temples; Priests and Priestesses; Religion; Rituals and Sacrifice; Theology.**)

Gold   *See Metals and Metalworking.*

Gordium

See *Alexander the Great.*

GOVERNMENT

* **city-state** independent state consisting of a city and its surrounding territory

* **patron** special guardian, protector, or supporter

* **secular** nonreligious; connected with everyday life

* **fourth millennium** B.C. years from 4000 to 3001 B.C.

The peoples of the ancient Near East developed various institutions of government to maintain order, administer the law, defend against enemies, and provide services that supported the economy and society. Before the rise of cities and city-states*, governing was the concern of tribal chieftains and village councils. As settlements grew, local leaders assumed more power, and kingships arose. Kingship became the main form of government in the ancient Near East, and other institutions existed mainly to help the king with the administration of the state.

GOVERNMENT IN MESOPOTAMIA

The ancient lands of Sumer and Akkad consisted of several city-states. Although every city was protected by a patron* god or goddess, it also needed a form of secular* power. This power was always held by a ruler and his representatives.

Early Rulers. The rulers of early Mesopotamian city-states had different titles, depending on the role they played in their societies. At the end of the fourth millennium B.C.*, the period of the earliest written texts, each city's ruler was connected in some way with the temple—the center of the economic and societal systems through which all goods and services circulated. At URUK, the ruler was called an *en;* at LAGASH, an *ensi;* and at Isin, a *sanga.* Beginning in the early third millennium B.C. (years from 3000 to 2001 B.C.), the palace, headed by a *lugal,* or king, whose principle functions were military, began to replace the temple as the center of economic and governmental power. Whether secular or religious, all rulers were believed to hold power only by the authority of the gods. Mesopotamian rulers were seen as representatives of the city god.

No matter what title a ruler held, his religious responsibilities included building and maintaining the city's temples and satisfying the gods through rituals, OFFERINGS, and religious festivals. A community's favor with the gods and its prosperity depended on how well its ruler fulfilled these duties. Consequently, it was in the ruler's best interest to honor his religious obligations. Another duty of Mesopotamian rulers was to administer the laws that the gods had entrusted to him. Justice and the protection of the poor and weak were inseparable parts of social order and peace. Thus, while a ruler's power as an enforcer and lawmaker came from the gods, it served an important secular role as well.

City Governments and Institutions. Cities were often divided into districts, which were generally governed by an assembly, often known as the Elders. Membership in this assembly, which included the heads of powerful local families, was based almost solely on heredity. Elders were responsible for enforcing laws, maintaining order, and resolving disputes

131

Government

* **dynasty** succession of rulers from the same family or group

* **provincial** having to do with the provinces, outlying districts, administrative divisions, or conquered territories of a country or empire

* **bureaucracy** system consisting of officials and clerks who perform government functions

* **deity** god or goddess

* **divinity** state or quality of being a god

* **second millennium B.C.** years from 2000 to 1001 B.C.

* **vassal** individual or state that swears loyalty and obedience to a greater power

and other local issues. They also helped select citizens to provide labor or military service to the state. In some cases, the district governments were completely controlled by the ruler of the city-state. However, many local governments were able to maintain a significant degree of independence.

Changing Patterns of Government. With the rise of the Akkadian empire in the late third millinnium B.C., governments changed to accommodate the demands of a large territorial state. The founder of the dynasty* of Akkad, SARGON I (ruled ca. 2334–2278 B.C.), made several changes during his rule that centralized power within the kingship.

To gain greater control over his growing empire, Sargon replaced local rulers with loyal provincial* governors. There was a civilian governor, who performed religious and judicial duties, and a military governor, who was supported by troops sent by the central government. Sargon also built military posts in many cities and sought to ensure the loyalty of his armies by awarding soldiers large grants of land. A large bureaucracy* was established to keep all sorts of administrative records, such as shipments of goods, offerings to temples, and the collection of taxes.

Despite these changes, Sargon and his successors did not break completely with the traditions of previous governments. They adapted to local politics and assumed roles with traditional structures. For example, at the city of UR, Sargon installed his daughter as the high priestess of Ur's patron deity*. It is probable that this role had traditionally been held by the ruler's daughter, so Sargon was acknowledging and continuing local beliefs.

When Sargon's grandson NARAM-SIN (ruled ca. 2254–2218 B.C.) rose to the throne, he became the first Mesopotamian ruler to claim divinity* for himself. This change was important because it reflected the new idea that the king was the patron god of a united empire. Few kings after Naram-Sin claimed divinity, although his immediate successor, Shar-kali-sharri, and King SHULGI of Ur (ruled ca. 2094–2047 B.C.) did.

Under Shulgi's leadership, bureaucracies in Sumer and Akkad expanded greatly. Shulgi also introduced a system of messengers and road stations throughout the empire, standardized weights and measures, and introduced a new calendar. The introduction of more detailed record keeping for all phases of the economy and society meant that more officals loyal to the state rather than to a particular city or temple needed to be trained and employed. This centralized bureaucracy became a prominent feature of government.

A New Political Order. By the middle of the second millennium B.C.*, a new political order emerged, one in which powerful rulers known as Great Kings governed empires, such as the Babylonian and Assyrian empires. Administration was accomplished through a multilevel system of government, which consisted of the Great Kings, major vassals* where the royal house descended from the Great Kings' ancestors, and minor rulers. In conquered territories, kings often entrusted power to loyal supporters or members of the royal family, although they sometimes left local rulers in charge. Relationships between the king and these rulers were maintained through treaties, marriage arrangements, and other obligations, such as providing land in return for military support.

In this new political order, the king was the center of the government. Palaces served as the royal residence, the royal treasury, the site of state ceremonies, and the center of administrative activities. Palaces were large and impressive, reflecting their role in government and the prestige and authority of the king.

The Neo-Assyrian Empire. During the 1300s B.C., Assyria established itself for the first time as a territorial state. Beginning in the 800s B.C., Assyria began to expand by conquering its neighbors. The Assyrians established dominance in other states by having them send tribute* to the Assyrian king. However, the kings of these territories kept their thrones. This changed when Tiglath-pileser III became king in 745 B.C. and replaced the local dynasties with provincial governors.

* **tribute** payment made by a smaller or weaker party to a more powerful one, often under the threat of force

Government in Egypt

By about 3500 B.C., towns in Egypt's Nile River valley had gained control of strips of land along the river. Easy access along the Nile and the concentration of towns in the narrow river valley led to the formation of strong links among communities. This made it easier for a powerful ruler to bring large areas of the Nile Valley under his control, and kingdoms developed in Egypt.

Two major kingdoms emerged in Egypt: Upper Egypt and Lower Egypt. According to tradition, sometime between 3100 and 3000 B.C., King Menes joined the two regions into one great kingdom, with its capital at Memphis, and became the king of a united Egypt. Although the position and prestige of the king changed over time and not all kings ruled the whole land, the concept of kingship remained stable throughout Egypt's long history.

Kingship in Egypt. The Egyptian king was an absolute ruler who Egyptians believed was divine but inferior to the major gods. The king was the supreme high priest and, as some of his titles stated, the main link between Egyptians and their gods. As high priest, it was the king's duty to build and maintain temples and to see that religious rituals and ceremonies were conducted properly. In return, the gods assured the king—and the Egyptian people—peace and prosperity.

Although the king was an absolute ruler, the task of governing a large kingdom required help from others. He, or occasionally she, appointed various officials and scribes*, who carried out such administrative activities as collecting taxes, building temples and other public buildings, overseeing economic activities, maintaining law and order, and protecting Egypt's borders from attack. Although these tasks remained the same throughout Egypt's long history, the officials or institutions that carried them out changed over time as a result of political and social change.

Early Government Administration. The basic structure of government administration in Egypt took shape during the Old Kingdom period (ca. 2675–2130 B.C.). Governmental positions and institutions

Honorary Titles

Important officials in ancient Egypt often had many titles added to their names. Some titles indicated an individual's function, such as Overseer of the Great Mansions. Other titles reflected the individual's rank within a particular branch of the government. Some officials, however, had as many as 200 different titles. These names probably did not all refer to their functions and ranks. Many were honorary titles, perhaps awarded because of a particular accomplishment or contribution.

* **scribe** person of a learned class who served as a writer, editor, or teacher

Government

established during this period remained in place throughout ancient Egyptian history.

Administration centered around the king, who governed Egypt from his palace with the assistance of a group of high officials. The highest senior official, called the vizier, coordinated and supervised all governmental affairs. Two other senior positions were Overseer of All Royal Works, who organized and supervised the labor forces needed for royal building projects and agriculture, and Overseer of the Treasury, who collected, stored, and distributed goods in the state treasury.

Egypt was divided into provinces called nomes. Royal control over the nomes increased gradually, but local governments retained some degree of authority. The overseer of Upper Egypt acted as the central government's head of provincial affairs, while officials known as Great Overlords of the Nome served as a type of provincial governor.

Restructuring Government. During the period of instability that followed the end of the Old Kingdom, royal authority in Egypt broke down, and provincial rulers took on more responsibilities. This period ended in 1980 B.C., with the rise of the Eleventh Dynasty. This dynasty, the first in a period known as the Middle Kingdom (ca. 1980–1630 B.C.), established a new capital at THEBES and began to rebuild the country and restructure the government administration. However, another family, that of the Twelfth Dynasty, seized power and moved the capital far to the north to the area of LISHT.

The principal arm of the government was the White House, or treasury. It was the main storehouse and accounting and distribution center of national revenues. The treasury had a large bureaucracy that included officials throughout the empire.

The central government's control over the provinces was a delicate matter in the early years of the Twelfth Dynasty. Provincial rulers had become accustomed to some independence, and the central government exercised caution in dealing with them. The king maintained control by appointing all senior provincial administrators, or nomarchs. He also visited many provinces and helped settle local disputes. The provincial nomarchs continued to enjoy a large degree of freedom, however. They collected their own revenues, kept armed forces, and acted as local high priests. They strengthened their power by forming alliances with neighboring provinces and through marriage arrangements.

By the late 1900s B.C., the administrative structure of Egypt became more centralized. The vizier supervised Egypt's administrative life, and the treasury took control of provincial treasuries and became more important than ever. A labor bureau, known as the Office of the Provider of People, was established during this period and was responsible for registering and assigning the manpower to government projects.

Also, Egypt was divided into three main administrative units: District of the North, District of the South, and District of the Head of the South. Each district contained a number of nomes and was headed by several officials assisted by a large bureaucracy. At this time, other officials, known as councillors, were sent to the provinces on government business and carried out general administrative duties, such as supervising the construction of irrigation canals. During the 1700s B.C., the center of power shifted to a new dynasty at Memphis that could neither hold Egypt together nor prevent its invasion and conquest by the HYKSOS.

Ruling a Growing Empire. During the period known as the New Kingdom (ca. 1539–1075 B.C.), following the expulsion of the Hyksos, Egypt began to expand its rule over parts of the Levant* and to Nubia, the region to the south of Egypt. As the Egyptian empire grew, its rulers faced the new responsibility of governing conquered peoples, which led to changes in government administration.

The conquered territories had special administrations to oversee their government and affairs. The chief administrator for Nubia was a viceroy, a governor overseeing the land as the king's representative. In the Levant, local kings were overseen by a number of officials, titled Overseers of All Northern Foreign Lands, who were assisted by military commanders.

During the New Kingdom period, the central government revolved more than ever around the king. The palace was run by a number of officials, including the chief royal steward, who managed the vast royal estates throughout the country. There was one vizier for the north, stationed in Memphis, and one in the south, usually residing at Thebes. The

* **Levant** lands bordering the eastern shores of the Mediterranean Sea (present-day Syria, Lebanon, and Israel), the West Bank, and Jordan

Kingship was the main form of government in the ancient Near East. Kings, who were believed to hold power by the authority of the gods, were assisted by a group of officials who worked closely with him. The most senior official, called the vizier, coordinated and supervised all governmental affairs. This relief from Khorsabad shows King Sargon II of Assyria (center) with his vizier (left) and another high official.

Symbols of Power

Throughout much of Egyptian history, the king wore the Double Crown. This was a combination of the White Crown of Upper Egypt and the Red Crown of Lower Egypt, which symbolized the king's authority over the entire nation. The Blue Crown, which symbolized coronation and legitimate succession, was later combined with the Double Crown. On top of these crowns was the Uraeus, a rearing hooded cobra, the symbol of Wadjit, the goddess of Lower Egypt. Alongside the Uraeus was the neck and head of the vulture goddess, Nekhbet, of Upper Egypt.

* **aristocracy** privileged upper class

* **imperial** pertaining to an emperor or an empire

viziers worked closely with two overseers of the treasury, and they were assisted by officials. Among these were heralds, who represented the vizier around the country and maintained communication between the office of vizier and the various local branches of government.

The religious administration became very important in the New Kingdom. Much of the wealth from the provinces and territories went to the temples, and the priests gained control of large tracts of land as well. Temples had their own treasuries and other institutions, and temple administrations began to resemble those of the king's palace.

Later Changes in Government. Between about 1075 and 656 B.C., royal prestige and authority in Egypt declined, and the united kingdom was once again divided into northern and southern kingdoms, ruled by separate dynasties. By around 730 B.C., Egypt had fragmented into many small areas headed by rulers who used the title of king or claimed authority over a particular territory. The limited authority of these kings forced them to rely increasingly on their own families for help in governing. As a result, large numbers of well-established and experienced officials were replaced by loyal, but not necessarily competent, royal relatives.

Beginning in about 664 B.C., the government of Egypt began to improve. The Twenty-sixth Dynasty reunified the nation and divided it administratively into the two traditional areas of Upper and Lower Egypt. The new rulers appointed government officials, reorganized the navy, and increased revenues to the central administration. Many of the types of officials who had governed in previous centuries, such as viziers, once again became part of the central government. Provincial institutions were run by two governors, one for Upper Egypt and one for Lower Egypt. The next level of government consisted of 40 nomes (provinces), each headed by a nomarch. Below them were towns governed by mayors.

After ALEXANDER THE GREAT conquered Egypt in 332 B.C., he and his successors took over the Egyptian kingship. Most of the changes they put into effect occurred at the upper ranks, where Egyptian officials were replaced by Greco-Macedonians. At the local level, administrations remained largely unchanged, and Egyptian government continued to function much as it had over the course of more than 3,000 years.

GOVERNMENT IN ANATOLIA

Ancient ANATOLIA (present-day Turkey) consisted of city-states, each ruled by powerful families who formed an aristocracy*. By about 1500 B.C., the HITTITES had established their empire. They had transformed the kingship of city-states into an imperial* monarchy with the king as an absolute ruler. As in Mesopotamia and Egypt, other government institutions, such as a bureaucracy, developed to assist the king.

Hittite Kings. During the second millennium B.C., the ruler of the Hittite empire was known by many titles, including Great King—a title that was also used elsewhere. The king, who gained his authority from the gods who also protected him, was the chief priest of the national god. He was responsible for overseeing rituals and ceremonies.

DAILY LIFE

Plate 1
These mosaic plaques were found at a temple built by Egyptian king Ramses III
(ruled ca. 1187–1156 B.C.). From left to right, the figures portrayed are a Nubian, a
Canaanite, and a Libyan. These men were probably prisoners of war. Their clothing
and elaborate hairstyles suggest that they may have been aristocratic prisoners.

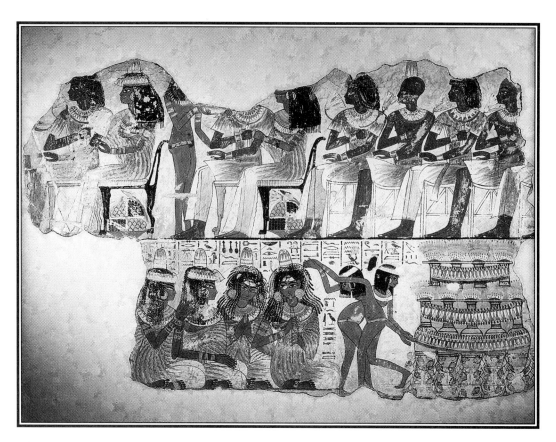

Plate 2

Once a year, the ancient Egyptians went to their relatives' tombs for a funerary banquet. Egyptians believed that during this meal, the living could communicate with the dead. Dating from the Eighteenth Dynasty (ca. 1539–1292 B.C.), this scene from a tomb painting at Thebes shows events at one such banquet. The seated figure at the far right of the lower panel plays a double flute. The two women to her right are dancing next to a stack of jars of wine.

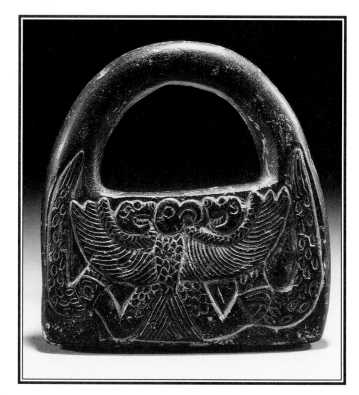

Plate 3

To ensure fairness in economic transactions, the people of the ancient Near East developed standards of weight. The handle weight shown here, which comes from Iran or Afghanistan, may have been used as a weight standard on a balance in a marketplace. Standing approximately 9 inches high, this particular weight was made of chlorite or steatite, both greenish stones, in the late third millennium B.C. Archaeologists have found similar handle weights from ancient Mesopotamia to the Indus Valley.

Plate 4

Many people of the ancient Near East believed that a king was given his power by the gods. It was then the king's duty to ensure that his people worshiped the gods properly, by observing holidays and practicing rituals. Dating from between 1200 and 1000 B.C., this 72-inch-high stela comes from Baluaa in Jordan (in the Levant). Carved from basalt, it portrays a king standing between a god and a goddess, who hold symbols of divinity.

Plate 5

Dating from perhaps as late as the 600s B.C., these figurines were carved in lapis lazuli and gold. Each of the figurines, which were found at a burial site in Karkamish, measures less than one inch in height, and each depicts a deity of the Hittite pantheon. The larger figure in the middle of the top row wears a winged disk on his head and holds the hieroglyph of his name.

Plate 6

Writings from the Egyptian Book of the Dead were often recorded on papyrus rolls, such as the one above. This papyrus dates from the Nineteenth Dynasty (ca. 1292–1190 B.C.) and portrays a judgment scene. Anubis (second from left), the god of the underworld, brings in the deceased and weighs the heart of the deceased against a feather representing truth. If the weights are not equal, a female monster named the "Eater," standing beneath the scale, will devour the deceased. Because the two are of equal weight, the deceased in this painting is presented to Osiris (seated at far right).

Plate 7

As part of their religious practices, the ancient Elamites made many offerings, especially of animal blood, to their gods. The two 3-inch-high figures of worshipers shown here date from the 1100s B.C. and were found at Susa, which was then part of Elam. The gold figure on the left is holding a kid, and the silver figure on the right is holding a small animal that may be intended for sacrifice.

Plate 8
These Sumerian statues dating from between 2900 and 2600 B.C. were excavated at Eshnunna. Known as votive (devotional) figurines, they represent worshipers and were placed on benches and ledges in temples to pray continually for the lives of the people who donated them. The clasped hands of the statues suggest prayer and a devotional attitude.

Plate 9
Found in Jordan and dating from the Iron Age (ca. 1200–500 B.C.), this model shrine resembles the typical temple facade found in the Levant in ancient times. Although scholars are unsure of its use, such a shrine may have been presented to a god in his temple, kept at home for private religious use, or placed in a tomb. It may also have contained figures representing the deity being worshiped.

Plate 10

A central myth in Egyptian religion concerns Osiris, the god of the dead; his sister and wife, the protector goddess Isis; and their son, the sky god Horus. The myth describes how Osiris is killed by his brother and how Isis and Horus avenge his death. This 3½-inch-high gold pendant portrays the three deities—Horus on the left, Isis on the right, and Egyptian king Osorkon II (reigned ca. mid-800s B.C.) in the form of Osiris in the middle. Horus and Isis are each raising a hand in a protective gesture toward Osiris.

Plate 11

Dating from the 800s B.C., this relief from Sippar depicts the Babylonian sun god Shamash viewing a display of respect from the three smaller figures on the left. Shamash represented justice to the ancient Babylonians. Like other peoples of the ancient Near East, the Babylonians believed that their laws came directly from the gods and that by following them, they were worshiping the gods properly. In return, they hoped the gods would be favorable to them.

Plate 12

Various aspects of agricultural life in Egypt are
depicted in this painting from the Theban tomb
of an Eighteenth Dynasty (ca. 1539–1292 B.C.)
official named Menna. In the lower panel,
workers are seen harvesting and collecting the
grain. In the center of the middle row, they are
shown separating seeds of wheat from their
husks. In the top panel, the grain is being delivered by boat to the tomb owner. The painting
also includes negative aspects. The people in
the center of the top row are being beaten,
perhaps for late or nonpayment of their taxes.

Plate 13

In the ancient Near East, women typically
performed most food preparation tasks,
such as pressing oil and grinding grain.
This terra-cotta figurine portrays a woman
carrying a churn, which was used to
make dairy products. Dating from around
3400 B.C., this figurine comes from southern Israel and may have had religious significance for the people who made it.

Plate 14

Seals such as the one from ancient Bahrain shown here held a place of importance in the ancient Near East. They were used to authenticate documents, to seal rooms or objects, and for religious purposes. Stamp seals found in Bahrain are markedly different from seals excavated elsewhere in the ancient Near East. This was probably a result of the Bahrainis' adapting the techniques of the wide range of peoples with whom they conducted trade.

Plate 15

Dating from around 1500 B.C., this Cycladic fresco from Thera depicts two children engaged in a boxing match. Other children's games included foot races, rope skipping, wrestling, tug-of-war, and leapfrog. However, children's activities were not limited to leisure activities. Youngsters were also expected to work with and for their families.

The king was also responsible for organizing, maintaining, and directing the army and for establishing friendly relations with other states, negotiating treaties, and arranging marriages between ruling families. Although the king sometimes carried out such military and diplomatic* activities himself, he also appointed representatives to act on his behalf. The king was the chief judge of the land, and he enforced the law, handed down decisions regarding crimes, and settled disputes.

* **diplomatic** concerning relations with foreign powers

Hittite Administration. The day-to-day work of the Hittite government was carried out by a royal bureaucracy, consisting of many officials, each responsible for a broad range of activities. The royal palace served as the central government, and local officials operated within a network of government institutions directly connected to the central authority. These institutions collected goods and revenues, sent wealth to the central government, and redistributed goods on the local level.

Within Anatolia, the administrative level directly beneath the king was that of the "Lands," nearby states subdued by the king that were governed by prominent members of the royal family. The next level consisted of royal appointees known as stewards, who governed the districts. "Lords of the watchtower" governed small territories in frontier regions, supervising a number of towns. Their responsibilities included watching the borders, organizing agriculture, maintaining royal buildings and temples, and administering justice within the areas under their control.

Over time, the Hittite empire included a changing array of conquered territories and kingdoms, some of which were incorporated into the central Hittite state. Others became vassal kingdoms that were generally ruled by members of the local ruling families. Their kings were bound by treaty to the Hittite king and were obligated to pay tribute, provide military assistance to Hittite armies, and protect the rights of the designated successor to the Great King.

Communication Between Kings

Rulers in ancient Mesopotamia often communicated by letter as part of diplomacy and foreign affairs. Kings often addressed each other as father, son, or brother to imply a certain type of relationship. For example, to address another ruler as father indicated that king's seniority or superiority. The word *brother* implied a equal relationship, while the term *son* signified a position of inferiority. Rulers could be very sensitive to these forms of address and might strongly resent one that they considered inappropriate.

GOVERNMENT IN THE LEVANT

Throughout ancient times, the Levant consisted of small political units headed by chieftains, military leaders, and kings. Some city-states in the region developed a type of government known as an oligarchy, where a small group of people rule together.

The city-states of the Phoenicians and Philistines had kingships. Evidence points to the existence of oligarchic rule in early Israel, where groups of elders held authority and made decisions for the community. They oversaw tax collection and were responsible for sending men and supplies to the army in times of war. Over time, these groups may have become advisers to the king.

In CANAAN, the king was considered the son of the patron god of the state. As the god's chosen representative, he had a duty to defend the god's territory, establish and enforce the law, and care for the people. He did this with the help of a palace administration centered at the capital city. This administration consisted of senior officials and a bureaucracy whose members were stationed all over the state.

* **cult** system of religious beliefs and rituals; group following these beliefs

Temples played an important role in society, both as a symbol of the gods and as part of the economic system. It was the king's duty to build temples and to appoint priests, prophets, scribes, and musicians to run the temples. The state cult* was the responsibility of the Canaanite government, and as the supreme authority over this cult, the king had many religious duties, including offering sacrifices and participating in other rituals.

GOVERNMENT IN IRAN

The kings of Persia in IRAN were believed to be the chosen representatives of the god AHURA MAZDA. As such, it was the king's duty to administer justice, and one of the most important components of justice was being faithful to the law of Ahura Mazda.

* **satrapy** portion of Persian-controlled territory under the rule of a satrap, or provincial governor

The Persian empire was created by CYRUS THE GREAT (ruled 559–529 B.C.). Cyrus established an imperial government for ruling the conquered territories. One of his successors, DARIUS I (ruled 521–486 B.C.), contributed greatly to the administration of the empire by organizing it into 20 satrapies*. Each satrapy was ruled by a governor called a satrap, a high-ranking Persian official who was required to pay taxes in the form of money, horses, and other items, as well as to provide ships or soldiers for the Persian army and navy. (*See also* **Assyria and the Assyrians; Babylonia and the Babylonians; Cities and City-States; Dynasties; Egypt and the Egyptians; Israel and Judah; Persian Empire; Phoenicia and the Phoenicians; Sumer and the Sumerians.**)

Graves

See *Burial Sites and Tombs.*

GREECE AND THE GREEKS

Greece is the part of Europe geographically closest to the Near East. Throughout history, the two areas have influenced each other as a result of close contact, through trade and war. The Greeks picked up ideas from the civilizations of the Near East and added many important elements of their own. Ever since, the world has learned from the unique Greek culture.

GEOGRAPHY

See map in Phoenicia and the Phoenicians (vol. 4).

Mainland Greece is at the southern end of Europe's Balkan Peninsula. Across the Ionian Sea to the west are Sicily and southern Italy. To the east, the AEGEAN SEA separates Greece from the Near Eastern peninsula of Turkey, which the ancient Greeks called ANATOLIA.

The Greek peninsula is almost divided into two parts by the Gulf of Corinth. On the smaller, southern part, known as the Peloponnese, the land is rough and hilly, with many valleys leading down to its long, rugged coastline. The northern section is more mountainous; its highest

* **headland** high land that juts out over a body of water

* **second millennium B.C.** years from 2000 to 1001 B.C.

peak, Mount Olympus, is almost 10,000 feet high. The coastline is indented with bays and headlands*. In general, the terrain in Greece is more rugged and the soil is less fertile than in many areas of the Near East.

The many islands of the Aegean Sea, which include the large island of CRETE and the Cyclades, are considered a part of Greece and are often called the Greek islands. However, until late in the second millennium B.C.*, they were influenced more by the civilizations of the Near East than by peoples from the Greek mainland. As the inhabitants of the islands had increasing contact with the peoples of the Greek mainland, they brought Near Eastern culture to the Greeks.

HISTORY OF ANCIENT GREECE

The islands of the Aegean Sea probably received their first settlers from Anatolia. These people brought techniques for farming, for making pottery, and perhaps for primitive metalworking from the ancient Near East. In Crete, settlers developed a unique culture called the MINOAN CIVILIZATION. Several kingdoms emerged on Crete, and each was centered around a magnificent palace. The islanders became a seafaring people and amassed great wealth from trade in the eastern Mediterranean region. The fact that they did not fortify their cities indicates that they were able to remain peaceful at first. Later in the second millennium B.C., however, early Greek mainlanders—known as the Mycenaeans—appear to have taken over the Minoan cities on Crete and built walls around them.

The Mycenaeans had probably entered the Greek mainland from the north. In about 1150 B.C., another Greek people, the Dorians, attacked the Mycenaeans on the mainland and also crossed the sea to Crete. The Dorians had stronger weapons and were able to bring down the developed settlements on the mainland, Crete, and around the Aegean. The invasions left the palaces and cities in ruins. This invasion began the period that modern historians call the Dark Age, which lasted from about 1150 to 800 B.C.

* **dialect** regional form of a spoken language with distinct pronunciation, vocabulary, and grammar

The Greek Language. By late in the second millennium B.C., the tribes on the mainland spoke early versions of Greek, a distinct Indo-European language. At the time, several dialects* of the Greek language were spoken and understood by the people of the region. The Minoans apparently did not speak Greek until the Mycenaeans brought it to Crete. This version of the language was written down in a script scholars call Linear B. After the Dorian invasion, their dialect of Greek became prevalent. By the 500s B.C., there were four main types of Greek dialects. The Greek language became more uniform during the Hellenistic* period, when people throughout the eastern Mediterranean and western Asia spoke a common dialect of Greek known as *Koine.*

* **Hellenistic** referring to the Greek-influenced culture of the Mediterranean world and western Asia during the three centuries after the death of Alexander the Great in 323 B.C.

The Rise of Greek Culture. There is no sign of any Dark Age buildings to rival the Minoan and Mycenaean palaces, and the art of writing probably died out during that period. However, a new culture was beginning to grow—one that, yet again, was picking up ideas from the peoples it had displaced.

Greece and the Greeks

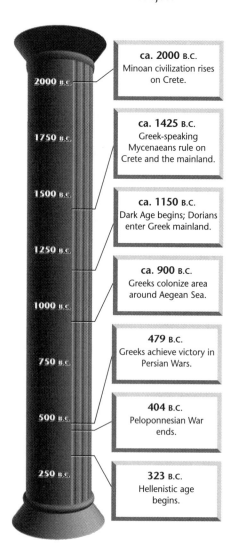

ca. 2000 B.C.
Minoan civilization rises on Crete.

ca. 1425 B.C.
Greek-speaking Mycenaeans rule on Crete and the mainland.

ca. 1150 B.C.
Dark Age begins; Dorians enter Greek mainland.

ca. 900 B.C.
Greeks colonize area around Aegean Sea.

479 B.C.
Greeks achieve victory in Persian Wars.

404 B.C.
Peloponnesian War ends.

323 B.C.
Hellenistic age begins.

Although the Mycenaeans had been conquered by the Dorians, stories of their earlier victories continued to be told, especially tales about their celebrated siege* of TROY, in Anatolia, around 1200 B.C. These stories were collected and written down at the end of the Dark Age. They evolved into two of the most celebrated works in world literature: Homer's *Iliad* and *Odyssey,* which interweave the exploits of Greek heroes and the plotting and planning of their gods.

The Near East continued to influence Greece during the Dark Age. Scholars have noted that the religion described in Homer's works is in some ways different from earlier Greek beliefs. For example, the gods act as a sometimes argumentative family, like gods in Babylonian myth, whereas Greek deities* were traditionally seen as individuals who did not belong to a larger group. This suggests that Greek views of the gods were shifting to be more in accordance with Near Eastern views.

By 900 B.C., Greeks had settled the islands of the central Aegean and sections of the west coast of Anatolia (East Greece). Between 750 and 550 B.C., Greek settlers spread to the west, establishing colonies in southern Italy (Magna Grecia), Sicily, southern France, and northern Spain. They also established colonies south across the Mediterranean in Libya in north Africa (Cyrenaica) and, in the northeast, ringing the shores of the Black Sea. These far-flung colonies allowed a variety of cultural influences, as well as great wealth, to circulate widely.

Greek cities, unlike those of the Near East, were small and independent. The citizens were rarely willing to cooperate with their neighbors, and they feuded almost as often as they traded. One consequence of this isolation was that Greek cities in Anatolia were unable to defend themselves alone and were quickly made subject to larger Asian empires—first Lydia in the 600s B.C., and then Persia after 546 B.C.

Classical Greece. The classical period of Greece began with the PERSIAN WARS, in which the Greeks repelled Persian invasions. The mainland city of Athens was the target of the first Persian invasion in 492 B.C. because Athens had sent forces to help some Anatolian cities reject Persian rule there. The Persians then launched major expeditions in 490 B.C. and 480 B.C., with the intention of subduing the Greek mainland.

The Greek victories in these wars led to the liberation of the cities of Anatolia, freeing them for expanded trade with the Greek mainland. It also gave Athens the opportunity, as the leading naval power that defeated the Persian fleet, to dominate sea trade. Athens gained great wealth and became the center of the vibrant Greek civilization that flowered during the next 50 to 100 years. This period produced major works of sculpture, architecture, philosophy, history, rhetoric*, and medicine and is considered to be the starting point of "Western" culture.

Athens's domination of the Greek world was resisted by Sparta, the chief city of the Peloponnese. Sparta had been the leading military force among the Greek cities for many years and resented Athens's attempt to expand. A series of battles, known as the Peloponnesian War, occurred between Athens and Sparta from about 431 to 404 B.C. Athens made several rash mistakes, allowing Sparta and its allies to break up Athens's power base. Athens remained the main center of a

still glorious culture but lacked the political influence that it had enjoyed before its defeat.

One of the allies who supported Sparta was the Persian empire—a long distance away, but still extremely wealthy. Persian influence was felt in Greece for the next 60 years or so, the Persians coming to the aid of different local cities as they fought each other for power.

Macedonia and the Hellenistic World. In 359 B.C., a new force emerged when the kingdom of Macedonia, to the north of Greece, gained a new king, Philip II. Philip saw the warring Greek cities to the south and sensed opportunity. In less than 25 years, Philip dominated all the northern cities of Greece, including Athens. Then, over a 13-year period, Philip's son ALEXANDER THE GREAT led a united Macedonian and Greek expedition all the way to India. This expedition crushed the ancient Persian empire and resulted in a new balance of power in the ancient Near East.

From this time on, the influence of Greek culture rivaled that of any of the Near Eastern civilizations. Philip had greatly admired Greek culture and taught his son to admire it as well. Thus, Alexander's conquests had the effect of spreading Greek culture across western Asia. After Alexander's death in 323 B.C., the vast Macedonian empire that he had created disintegrated into three large realms: Macedonia, Asia, and Egypt. Macedonian monarchs ruled all three lands—and though they warred with one another, all three of them provided fertile soils for further development and intermingling of Greek and Near Eastern cultures. These blends of Greek and local cultures resulted in what is broadly called Hellenistic culture. The roughly 300 years after Alexander's death, when Rome began to impose its own power across the Near East, is known as the Hellenistic age.

GREEK CIVILIZATION AND THE ANCIENT NEAR EAST

Ancient Greece provided unique and glorious contributions to the development of Western civilization, many of which owe part of their origins to the older, Near Eastern cultures. In social organization and politics, perhaps, the Greeks remained totally unlike the groups they came in contact with, but signs of Near Eastern influence exist in other cultural areas—from art and architecture to science and philosophy.

Society and Politics. Greek politics was very different from ancient Near Eastern politics. City-states* and lands in the ancient Near East were frequently large and almost always ruled by kings. Kingship was not unknown in Greece, especially in Mycenaean times, but during the classical period, several Greek city-states were democracies, meaning they were ruled by their citizens.

The most famous ancient Greek democracy, known as the Council of 500, was centered in Athens from around 508 to 322 B.C. The council, which was made up of citizens chosen by lottery, prepared legislation, and an assembly of Athenian citizens voted on the issues. The assembly included all qualified citizens of the city, typically fewer than 5,000 people.

Homer's Image of Egypt

In the *Iliad,* the Greek hero Achilles refuses to fight the Trojans for a long time. He says that he would not be willing to do battle even for all the wealth in Thebes:

Egyptian Thebes, where the houses overflow with the greatest troves off treasure, Thebes with the hundred gates and through each gate battalions— two hundred fighters—surge to war with teams and chariots.

Egypt, to the poets of Homer's tradition, was the very essence of wealth and power.

---

* **city-state** independent state consisting of a city and its surrounding territory

Not all inhabitants, such as foreign-born residents and slaves, were able to vote. In addition, Greek culture generally did not recognize any rights for women. The fact remains, however, that a pattern of Greek government was ruled by groups of people rather than by a single leader.

Architecture and Art. The most notable buildings of ancient Greek architecture were its temples and theaters. The temples were usually surrounded by a colonnade* that supported an overhanging stone roof. Though the careful details and proportions of these temples were a Greek creation, the influence of Egyptian monument building in stone was clearly felt; the Greeks had previously made temples from clay and wood and later switched to stone. Greek theaters, which were great semicircles with rows of seats carved into hillsides, were as unique as the plays that they housed.

The sculpture of Greece also borrowed techniques from Egypt. Typical statues at the end of the Dark Age were clay molded figures standing upright and looking straight ahead, with rigid looking bodies and limbs. Visits to Egypt during the 700s B.C. inspired Greek artists to create much larger works in stone. Around 480 B.C., Greek sculptors developed a new pose for the human body, one in which the body weight is unevenly distributed on the feet. In these sculptures, the head, torso, arms, and legs are gently and naturally turned and bent.

Mythology and Religion. The Greeks' religious beliefs were based on myths about their gods, whom they believed played certain roles in human activity. Different gods served different functions. Many of the characters in Greek mythology may have their origins in earlier stories from the ancient Near East. For example, certain myths about Aphrodite, the goddess of love and beauty, can be traced to a Syrian legend.

Greek cities also had their own patron gods and goddesses. The Greeks built magnificent temples for their deities, and priests and priestesses served in them to ensure that rituals were performed correctly.

Literature, Philosophy, and Science. Greek literature began with myth and with the stories of Homer and other writers. Athenians produced much of Greek literature: there were Athenian playwrights such as Sophocles, historians such as Thucydides, orators such as Demosthenes, and philosophers such as Plato. People who traveled to Athens from elsewhere also became prominent writers. The Greek historian HERODOTUS was born in Anatolia. The philosopher Aristotle came from Macedonia.

The list of ancient Greek contributors to Western culture includes many people. Hippocrates, born on the Aegean island of Cos (or Kos), is known as the father of modern medicine. Democritus, born in Thrace in northern Greece, was the man who coined the term *atom* to mean a particle of matter. Pythagoras, the mathematician from Samos, and Archimedes, the physicist from Sicily, are other well-known ancient Greeks. Greek philosophy provided the means to study and analyze the world in a way that had never been done before.

The tool with which Greece's contribution to culture was recorded was largely a product of the ancient Near East. The Greek ALPHABET—the

* **colonnade** row of regularly spaced columns or pillars

Small Change?

What could be more basic to our idea of trade than money? Yet during ancient times, trade took place either by barter, which means exchanging goods directly, or by using desirable metal objects such as silver bars. The first coins to be issued came from Lydia around 600 B.C. Lydian coins contained gold as well as silver and must have been used for large transactions only. It was in the cities of Greece and Anatolia that smaller, silver coins of different sizes were first used for buying and selling.

basis of many other alphabets—was developed from a writing system used by the Phoenicians, who lived in the area that is now Israel and Lebanon. (*See also* **Hellenistic World; Mediterranean Sea, Trade on; Mycenae and the Mycenaeans.**)

GUDEA

**ruled ca. 2144–2124 B.C.
Ruler of Lagash**

* **third millennium B.C.** years from 3000 to 2001 B.C.

* **city-state** independent state consisting of a city and its surrounding territory

* **patron** special guardian, protector, or supporter

In the late third millennium B.C.*, the ancient Sumerian city-state* of LAGASH was ruled by Gudea (goo•DAY•ah), who was more a governor than an independent king. During his reign, Gudea built and restored scores of temples, including a temple to Ningirsu, the patron* god of Lagash.

Gudea also supported the arts and literature. This is evident in the artistic and literary developments of the period as well as in the reemergence of Sumerian as a dominant written language. Among the most important artistic achievements from his reign are the cylinders of Gudea, the longest and most complex surviving early Sumerian literary work. The clay cylinders are inscribed with a hymn that describes the reconstruction of Ningirsu's temple—the Eninnu. In it, Ningirsu promises Gudea such material rewards as these:

> Prosperity shall accompany the laying of the foundations of my house. All the great fields will raise their hands for you, dikes and canals will crane their necks for you, and for you the water will rise to the high ground which the waters do not reach. Cream will be poured abundantly in Sumer in your time.

To build his temples, Gudea imported materials from distant lands. He also claimed to have made the Elamites and other inhabitants of Susa provide laborers to help build the temples. Many of the finished temples contained statues of Gudea, which portray the ruler standing or seated on a low stool. Dressed in a long robe, he often has a shaved head or wears a distinctive headdress decorated with fine curls. In all the statues, his hands are clasped together in reverence to the gods. These and other images of Gudea present him as an ideal ruler who was strong, wise, pious, attentive to divine command, authoritative, and protective of his people.

Gutians

See *Akkad and the Akkadians.*

HAIR

Archaeologists* working at sites in the ancient Near East have found bronze razors; combs made of wood, ivory, and bone; and curlers that were probably used for curling women's hair and men's beards. Wall paintings, carved panels, and statues offer evidence of the great variety of hairstyles worn over the millennia*. From these objects and artworks, it is clear that the men and women of the ancient Near East shaved, cut, curled, and arranged their hair.

Hair

* **archaeologist** scientist who studies past human cultures, usually by excavating material remains of human activity

* **millennium** period of 1,000 years; *pl.* millennia

* **Levant** lands bordering the eastern shores of the Mediterranean Sea (present-day Syria, Lebanon, and Israel), the West Bank, and Jordan

* **sixth millennium** B.C. years from 6000 to 5001 B.C.

* **first millennium** B.C. years from 1000 to 1 B.C.

It is not always known whether everyone in a particular society wore the styles represented in the surviving artworks. Scholars do know, however, that hairstyles often had a social significance. People's age, class, or role in society often determined their hairstyle. In Egypt, for example, children wore short hair, often with one long lock falling down the right side of the head. Grown royal children wore loose sidelocks over their wigs to highlight their relationship to their father, the king. Among the Babylonians of MESOPOTAMIA, a slave wore an *apputtum,* which was most likely a distinctive hairstyle. The law forbade barbers to shave away a slave's *apputtum* without the owner's permission. The barber's penalty for committing this crime was to lose a hand.

In many societies in the ancient Near East, long hair was considered a mark of beauty for both men and women. Kings, nobles, and other elite sometimes grew their hair long. Common people and slaves, on the other hand, often wore their hair shorter because they could not afford the care that long hair required.

Women's Hairstyles. Images from ANATOLIA (present-day Turkey), Mesopotamia, and the Levant* illustrate developments in women's hairstyles in these three regions. A figurine from the sixth millennium B.C.* shows a woman with long hair hanging down her back in a braid or plait. Other figurines depict women wearing long hair piled on their heads in topknots. A Mesopotamian goddess or priestess in an image from the fourth millennium B.C. (years from 4000 to 3001 B.C.) has long hair tucked behind her ears and falling past her waist. Women in other artworks, shown engaged in everyday activities such as weaving, wear their hair in braids.

Between 3000 and 2001 B.C., there was great variety in Mesopotamian women's hairstyles and headdresses. Women kept their hair long but rarely allowed it to hang down. Instead, they wore elaborate topknots or arrangements of braids on top of their heads. Some images show women with their hair contained in nets, scarves, coiled turbans, or headdresses of pleated cloth. An image from the first millennium B.C.* shows a queen of Assyria with curled, shoulder-length hair and a crown that resembles a miniature fortress.

Ancient artworks and the evidence found at burial sites suggest that some Canaanite and Israelite women wore wigs over their long hair. Before about 900 B.C., women in SYRIA and CANAAN parted their hair in the middle. Later they wore short hair with curled or braided bangs.

Royal Egyptian women wore wigs made of human hair, with vegetable fiber beneath the hair for extra fullness. Underneath the wigs, the head was often shaved or the hair cut quite short to prevent head lice. Wig styles seem to have reflected stages in women's lives rather than social class. Married women wore long-haired wigs, sometimes in a style that divided the hair into three parts. Unmarried women wore shorter hair that grazed the shoulders, with curls hanging beside the face. Women also wore special hairstyles during pregnancy, childbirth, and nursing.

Men's Hair and Beards. Mesopotamian artworks from the second half of the fourth millennium B.C. often depict a male figure that scholars call

As seen in this Eighteenth Dynasty wall painting from the tomb of Nebamun, wealthy and refined Egyptians often wore perfumed cones made of animal fat on top of their wigs. During the course of an evening, the fat would melt over the hair, face, and clothing, spreading the perfume.

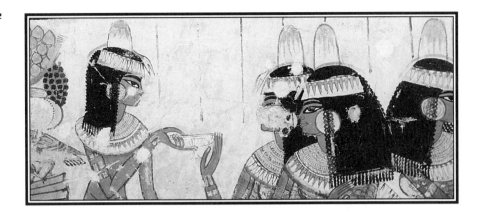

the priest-king. This figure wears shoulder-length hair held in place by a headband and has a full, thick beard. The same hairstyle and beard still appear in sculptures hundreds of years later. Later artworks show a greater variety of styles, though, including men without beards or wearing longer wavy or curly hair.

The variety and complexity of women's hairstyles may have influenced the hair fashions of Mesopotamian men during the third millennium B.C. A gold helmet found in a royal cemetery is decorated with a thick braid wrapped around the head and looped in a bun at the base of the neck. This style became associated with royalty and was also adopted in Persia. During the Early Dynastic period (ca. 2900–2700 B.C.), Sumerian men began to shave their heads and faces, but Akkadian, Babylonian, and Assyrian men kept long curly hair and curly beards. By about 2500 B.C., most men were clean-shaven. In some cases they kept their beards but shaved their heads.

During the Old Babylonian period (ca. 1900–1600 B.C.), kings were generally bearded and moustached, but other men might be beardless and have shaven heads. Assyrian kings had moustaches, thick, elaborately curled beards, and curled shoulder-length hair. During the same period, imperial Hittite men had long, straight hair and were clean-shaven. Syrian men depicted in Egyptian tomb paintings from the 1400s B.C. wear short beards and either shaven heads or shoulder-length hair held in place by a fillet, a strip of metal worn like a headband.

Ancient Egyptian art shows Canaanite and Israelite men with pointed beards covering their cheeks and chins but usually without moustaches. Art produced in Canaan sometimes shows noblemen and gods as clean-shaven, however. Israelite men are always portrayed with full beards and long hair tied back with linen bands. During the late first millennium B.C., some Israelites and Neo-Hittites adopted the Assyrian custom of arranging their beards in curls. Minoan men and women had long, wavy black hair, and the men were usually clean-shaven.

Egyptian men, like Egyptian women, often wore braided or plaited wigs over bald heads, shaven heads, or close-cropped hair. Some men kept mustaches, but they were rare. Wigs were considered attractive for both men and women. Priests were required to display their shaven heads when they were in the temple. Outside the temple, they, too, wore wigs. (*See also* **Clothing**; **Jewelry**.)

Hamitic Languages

HAMITIC LANGUAGES

Most of the major LANGUAGES of the ancient and modern Near East belong to a large family of languages that goes by several names. Scholars in the United States usually refer to this group of languages as Afro-Asiatic languages. In Europe, they are called Hamito-Semitic or Semito-Hamitic languages. This large language family includes more than 250 distinct languages and dialects*, which fall into five main branches, or subfamilies: Egyptian, Semitic*, Berber, Cushitic, and Chadic. Of these branches, Egyptian, Berber, Cushitic, and Chadic belong to the Hamitic family of languages.

The Egyptian subfamily consists of the ancient Egyptian language, which can be divided into two stages, each of which is characterized by certain differences in grammar and usage. The older form of Egyptian is called Older Egyptian, which was the language of all written texts from about 3000 to 1300 B.C. Older Egyptian, which can be further subdivided into phases that affect the writing system known as HIEROGLYPHICS, survived in formal religious texts until the A.D. 100s. The second stage of the Egyptian subfamily, known as Later Egyptian, remained in use from about 1300 B.C. to A.D. 1300. It also can be subdivided into several sublanguages: Late Egyptian, Demotic Egyptian, and Coptic Egyptian. Much of the greatest literature of ancient Egypt was written in Late Egyptian. Demotic Egyptian was in use from the 600s B.C. to the A.D. 400s. Coptic Egyptian, the language of Christian Egyptians, lasted from the A.D. 300s to the 1300s. It was replaced by Arabic, which remains the spoken and written language of Egyptians today.

The Berber subfamily includes modern Tuareg (spoken in the central Saharan region of Africa) as well as other languages and dialects of northern and northwestern Africa. Many groups that speak Berber also speak Arabic, and Arabic script is used to write the Berber languages. Written records in Berber do not appear until the A.D. 1800s. However, many scholars believe that these languages are descended from the language of ancient Libya, which appears on thousands of inscriptions dating from the 100s B.C.

Today about 15 million people in eastern Africa—from the Sudan to Ethiopia, Djibouti, Somalia, Kenya, and Tanzania—speak languages belonging to the Cushitic subfamily. The existence of this language group has been known to the West only since the A.D. 1600s. Although there is no written record of Cushitic in the ancient world, some of these languages show close ties with ancient Egyptian. A group of languages known as Omotic includes languages spoken in parts of southwestern Ethiopia. At one time, this group was considered part of the Cushitic subfamily, but scholars argue that it may not belong to the Afro-Asiatic family of languages.

The Chadic subfamily includes 140 languages and dialects that are spoken today by about 30 million people in central and West Africa. Among the most important of these is Hausa, a language of northern Nigeria and neighboring areas. Little is known about the relationship between modern Chadic languages and ancient languages.

The Semitic subfamily has existed in the ancient Near East since at least the fourth millennium B.C.* Spoken in Mesopotamia, Syria, the Levant*, and the Arabian peninsula, it included such languages as

Akkadian, Eblaite, Amorite, Ugartic, Aramaic, Old Canaanite, and Phoenician. Many Semitic languages are still used widely in western Asia and northern Africa, including Hebrew, Arabic, and Amharic—the language of Ethiopia. (*See also* **Indo-European Languages; Semitic Languages; Writing.**)

HAMMURABI

ruled ca. 1792–1750 B.C.
King of Babylon

The Code of Hammurabi, shown here, is one of history's oldest sets of written laws and is among the best-known artifacts of the Old Babylonian period (ca. 1900–1600 B.C.). The carvings at the top of the stela show King Hammurabi (on the left) receiving the rod and ring that symbolize kingship from the sun god, Shamash. The 282 laws are inscribed in cuneiform beneath the carvings as well as on the back of the stela.

Hammurabi (ha•muh•RAH•bee), also spelled Hammurapi, was the sixth king of the Amorite dynasty* of the city-state* of BABYLON. During his 43-year reign, he established one of the first sets of written laws in history, called the Code of Hammurabi. He also united most of MESOPOTAMIA under the rule of his kingdom, known as the Old Babylonian empire.

Hammurabi's ancestors were AMORITES, a tent-dwelling, nomadic* people from the Syrian desert, who first entered Mesopotamia late in the third millennium B.C.* Hammurabi's father, Sin-muballit, was the king of an Amorite dynasty that had been ruling Babylon for about 100 years. When Hammurabi inherited the throne from his father around 1792 B.C., he was still a young man. He had probably prepared for his responsibilities as king by performing some official duties in the government when he was younger.

Like previous Mesopotamian kings, Hammurabi began his reign by praising himself. He claimed that he had been destined to be the king since the beginning of time and proclaimed his dedication to justice in the laws he made for his people. Unlike earlier Mesopotamian kings, Hammurabi continued to proclaim his dedication to justice throughout his reign. A statue of Hammurabi presented him as the "king of justice," and Hammurabi spoke of having "established justice in the land" only months after he took the throne.

During the first years of his rule, Hammurabi built and restored temples, canals, city walls, and public buildings. He also honored the gods of Mesopotamia by dedicating shrines, temples, and cult objects to them in the cities and towns of his realm.

Around 1787 B.C., Hammurabi conquered the southern city-states of URUK and Isin, which had been controlled by his chief rival, King Rim-Sin of the city-state of Larsa. For the next 20 years, Hammurabi's kingdom did not engage in any major wars. During this time, Hammurabi concentrated on building and renovating temples, strengthening the walls of his cities in the north against possible enemies, and implementing justice within his land.

About 23 years after he had conquered Uruk and Isin, Hammurabi began a campaign to defeat Rim-Sin and seize Larsa. As part of his military strategy, he constructed a dam on the Euphrates River upstream from Larsa. Evidence suggests that he either released the waters suddenly to cause a devastating flood in Larsa or withheld the waters in order to cause drought and famine. Once Larsa was conquered, Hummurabi's kingdom became the dominant power in the region.

Around 1762 B.C., Hammurabi went to war against MARI, a powerful kingdom to the northeast. Mari had once been an ally of Babylon, and it

Hammurabi, Code of

* **dynasty** succession of rulers from the same family or group
* **city-state** independent state consisting of a city and its surrounding territory
* **nomadic** referring to people who travel from place to place to find food and pasture
* **third millennium** B.C. years from 3000 to 2001 B.C.

is not known why the two powers became enemies. The cause may have been a dispute over water rights or it may have been an attempt by Hammurabi to gain access to the overland trade route from which Mari derived its wealth. By conquering Mari, Hammurabi extended the power of the Old Babylonian empire farther up the Euphrates River. Two years later, Hammurabi began a campaign to defeat ESHNUNNA, a city-state east of the Tigris River. Using his strategy of damming the river waters, Hammurabi soon conquered Eshnunna.

Toward the end of his reign, Hammurabi became very ill and had to hand over his power to one of his sons before he died. Many Babylonian inscriptions have been discovered which say, "for the well-being of Hammurabi" and may date to the time of this illness. Around 1750 B.C., his son Samsu-iluna took over the throne, and Hammurabi died shortly thereafter.

Hammurabi's reign is regarded by many as a high point of Mesopotamian civilization. During this time, Mesopotamia made significant advances in the arts and in the study of astronomy and mathematics. Multiplication tables, tables of square and cube roots, and what we call the Pythagorean theorem were all known and used. (*See also* **Babylonia and the Babylonians; Hammurabi, Code of.**)

HAMMURABI, CODE OF

* **artifact** ornament, tool, weapon, or other object made by humans
* **stela** stone slab or pillar that has been carved or engraved and serves as a monument; *pl.* stelae
* **basalt** black or gray stone, often with a glassy surface
* **relief** sculpture in which material is cut away to show figures raised from the background
* **cuneiform** world's oldest form of writing, which takes its name from the distinctive wedge-shaped signs pressed into clay tablets
* **archaeologist** scientist who studies past human cultures, usually by excavating material remains of human activity
* **scribe** person of a learned class who served as a writer, editor, or teacher

One of the best-known artifacts* from ancient MESOPOTAMIA is a stela* that contains 282 laws set down by King HAMMURABI of BABYLON. These laws are collectively known as the Code of Hammurabi, one of the oldest sets of written laws in history. The stela, made of black basalt* and standing about eight feet tall, depicts in relief* King Hammurabi receiving rod and ring, symbols of kingship, from the sun god Shamash. The laws are engraved in cuneiform* beneath this relief as well as on the back of the stela from top to bottom. Archaeologists* think that originally there were at least two stone stelae containing these laws in Mesopotamia, parts of which were copied onto clay tablets by scribes* and their students. However, only one stela has been recovered to date.

Hammurabi decreed that his code was to be located in a public place, where people could read the laws or have them read out loud whenever they had a legal question. Historians believe that one copy of the code was kept in a temple next to a statue depicting Hammurabi as the King of Justice.

In ancient Mesopotamia, it was thought that the gods established the order of the world, that the king was the representative of the gods on earth, and that it was the king's job to implement justice on the gods' behalf. Consequently, the Code of Hammurabi served as a prescription for maintaining the divine order of the world.

The code includes laws about a variety of topics. Some of the legal issues covered by Hammurabi's laws included theft, murder, manslaughter, property damage, MARRIAGE, adoption, DIVORCE, trade, TAXATION, and the manumission* of SLAVES. Many of the laws in the Code of Hammurabi share similarities with other law codes of the ancient Near East. In fact, Hammurabi probably collected parts of older law codes from previous

* **manumission** act of legally freeing a person from slavery

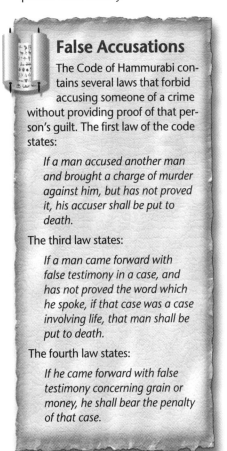

False Accusations

The Code of Hammurabi contains several laws that forbid accusing someone of a crime without providing proof of that person's guilt. The first law of the code states:

If a man accused another man and brought a charge of murder against him, but has not proved it, his accuser shall be put to death.

The third law states:

If a man came forward with false testimony in a case, and has not proved the word which he spoke, if that case was a case involving life, that man shall be put to death.

The fourth law states:

If he came forward with false testimony concerning grain or money, he shall bear the penalty of that case.

kings and included them in his code to prove his commitment to an ancient tradition of justice. The Code of Hammurabi shares common themes with the older Sumerian laws set forth by King Lipit-Ishtar of Isin (ruled ca. 1934–1924 B.C.), including the commitment to justice and the well-being of the people. The laws of MOSES in the Hebrew BIBLE also are similar to the Code of Hammurabi. However, the similarities are generally thought to be due to common cultural roots rather than a direct influence of Hammurabi's laws on the laws of JUDAISM.

Hammurabi's laws were more severe in their punishments than earlier Akkadian and Sumerian laws. One special characteristic of the Code of Hammurabi was the concept of "an eye for an eye," in which the perpetrator of a crime is punished by having that same crime inflicted on him. For example, the code states: "If a man struck another man's daughter and . . . if that woman has died, they shall put his daughter to death."

The Code of Hammurabi recognized three social classes: *awilum* (landowner), *mushkenum* (landless free citizen), and *wardum* (slave). Punishments for crimes varied according to the social class of the victim. For example, Law 200 states: "If a man has knocked out the tooth of a man of his own rank, they shall knock out his tooth." However, Law 201 states: "If he has knocked out a commoner's tooth, he shall pay one-third *mina* of silver."

Some historians believe that because many ancient Mesopotamian people could not read the cuneiform script used to write the laws and because the stela was probably not accessible to everyone, the Code of Hammurabi was used only by the elite and educated. Other historians believe that the laws were meant to serve as guidelines for future kings, in the hope that they would continue the traditions of their predecessor Hammurabi. (*See also* **Law.**)

HANGING GARDENS OF BABYLON

* **Hellenistic** referring to the Greek-influenced culture of the Mediterranean world and western Asia during the three centuries after the death of Alexander the Great in 323 B.C.

* **cuneiform** world's oldest form of writing, which takes its name from the distinctive wedge-shaped signs pressed into clay tablets

During the Hellenistic* period, the Hanging Gardens of Babylon, famed for their beauty and magnificence, were considered one of the Seven Wonders of the Ancient World. However, the gardens are not mentioned by ancient writers living during the time that they were said to have been built. Neither Babylonian cuneiform* tablets nor the inscriptions of Babylonian king NEBUCHADNEZZAR II speak of the gardens, though they do describe, in great detail, many building activities in Babylon. Moreover, the Greek historian HERODOTUS, who traveled to Babylon in the 400s B.C. and wrote about the region, does not mention the gardens.

Nevertheless, it is commonly believed that the gardens were built by Nebudchadnezzar for his wife, Amytis, who was from Media (in present-day Iran). It is said that the king built the gardens to resemble a mountain to please Amytis, who was homesick for the mountainous landscape of her homeland.

Although the mountainous shape of the gardens is generally agreed on, their size and their source of water are disputed. Diodorus Siculus, a historian writing during the 50s B.C., reported that the gardens were 75

Harbors

HARBORS

* **archaeologist** scientist who studies past human cultures, usually by excavating material remains of human activity

* **vaulted** having an arched ceiling or roof

feet in height. Strabo, a geographer writing a few years later, reported them to be even larger. It is unknown how the gardens were irrigated. Some ancient writers described pumps that were used to transport water from the EUPHRATES RIVER. Others suggested that the source of water was a well that was equipped with an endless chain of buckets.

Archaeologists* have searched for the remains of the Hanging Gardens of Babylon inside the walls of Nebuchadnezzar's palace and have discovered large underground walls, vaulted* rooms, and a well. These remains could be the original foundations of the gardens. Some archaeologists believe that the gardens were built in the area outside the palace near the Euphrates River because one of Nebuchadnezzar's inscriptions describes forming baked bricks into the likeness of a mountain in this region. A series of underground canals used for water supply and drainage were also found nearby and could have been used to irrigate the gardens.

More recently, it has been suggested that late classical writers, who were writing many hundreds of years after the gardens' construction, may have confused the enormous building activities of Nebuchadnezzar in Babylon with memories of a vast artificial garden in the city of Nineveh. This city was the famous capital of the Assyrians, who were known to have built irrigated terraces planted with trees from distant lands. Until new archaeological and textual discoveries are made, details about the Hanging Gardens of Babylon will remain unknown. (*See also* **Babylon; Gardens.**)

* **guild** association of professionals that sets standards and represents the interests of its members

A harbor is a sheltered coastal area where the waters are deep enough for ships to approach the shore. Harbors also enable ships to escape storms, anchor safely, and load and unload cargo. The ancient Near East had many excellent natural harbors as well as some that were improved by human efforts. Because these harbors were used by ships from all over the Near East, they become important centers of seafaring trade.

In ancient MESOPOTAMIA, the TIGRIS RIVER and the EUPHRATES RIVER were crowded with ships transporting goods. Like other bodies of water, the rivers in Mesopotamia had harbors that were used for docking and unloading cargo. These harbors attracted sailors from other lands, such as Dilmun (near present-day Bahrain), Magan (present-day Oman), and MELUKKHA (in present-day India), who came to buy and sell goods. During the 1800s B.C., societies of merchants or guilds* were formed in the wealthy port cities that surrounded the Mesopotamian harbors.

The NILE RIVER was the most commonly used route for transporting goods in ancient Egypt. However, one of the most famous trade expeditions in Egyptian history was launched from the harbor of Mersa Gawasis, located on the northwestern coast of the RED SEA. In about 1495 B.C., Queen HATSHEPSUT commissioned an expedition to Punt, a mysterious land of legendary wealth located along the southwestern coast of the Red Sea. The ships used for the expedition were carried in pieces overland from the city of THEBES to the harbor. After assembling the ships,

* **frankincense and myrrh** fragrant tree resins used to make incense and perfumes
* **ebony** dark, heavy, and highly prized wood from certain tropical trees

the sailors departed for Punt. Many months later, the ships returned loaded with frankincense and myrrh*, ebony*, IVORY, panther skins, and COSMETICS.

Some of the most important harbors in the ancient Near East were on the Mediterranean Sea. One particularly important harbor was in UGARIT, a city located on the Mediterranean coast of present-day Syria. The city's White Harbor, so-called because of the white cliffs surrounding it, was important because it was located between ANATOLIA (present-day Turkey) to the north and Canaan and Egypt to the south. In addition, the harbor was directly east of the island of CYPRUS, which had rich copper mines. This location led to seafaring trade with many cities, and as trade grew, so did Ugarit. However, the ships also brought disaster. Around 1200 B.C., invaders attacked from the sea and destroyed the city.

* **breakwaters** barriers to lessen the impact of waves, such as in a harbor; also called breakwalls or moles

Harbors were essential to the commercial empire of Phoenicia (present-day Lebanon). The Phoenicians made improvements to harbors at the cities of SIDON and TYRE. In the 1200s B.C., they built breakwaters* to protect the harbors from rough seas. These changes were among the first human-made improvements of harbors in history. (*See also* **Economy and Trade; Phoenicia and the Phoenicians; Shipping Routes; Ships and Boats.**)

HATHOR

* **cult** system of religious beliefs and rituals; group following these beliefs
* **predynastic** referring to the period before 3000 B.C., when Egypt's First Dynasty began

Hathor (HATH•awr) was a sky goddess and the universal mother goddess of ancient Egypt. She was most often pictured as a woman wearing a pair of cow's horns with a sun disk between them. She was also depicted as a lioness, snake, and tree goddess. Sometimes called the cow goddess, she was also represented as a cow or as a woman with a cow's head, horns, and ears.

It is not known whether Hathor had her own cult* in predynastic* Egypt, but it is clear that she was widely worshiped in ancient Egypt after that time. Temples and priestesses were dedicated to Hathor, and she was well represented in art and architecture, especially in tombs.

Hathor was the daughter of the sun god Ra and, in some ways, the mother of the falcon god HORUS. Her name literally meant "house of Horus." Because Horus symbolized the king, Hathor symbolized the mother of the king. Eventually, however, the role of Horus's mother was given to the goddess ISIS, and Hathor became Horus's wife.

* **deity** god or goddess
* **underworld** world of the dead

Hathor was primarily a benevolent, or helpful, deity*. She protected and assisted the dead in the underworld*, healed the sick, and helped women in childbirth. Her role in healing was probably based on a well-known story in which Hathor restores Horus's eyesight after he is injured during a battle. She was also associated with sexuality, wine, music, and dancing. Dances were held in her honor, and music was an important part of worship in her cult. Hathor was also occasionally considered a destructive deity. According to one myth, Hathor in the form of a fierce lioness nearly destroyed all of humanity before AMUN could trick her into stopping the slaughter. (*See also* **Egypt and the Egyptians; Gods and Goddesses; Religion.**)

Hatshepsut

HATSHEPSUT

ruled ca. 1472–1458 B.C.
Egyptian pharaoh

* **regent** person appointed to govern while the rightful monarch is too young or unable to rule

* **oracle** priest or priestess through whom a god is believed to speak; also, the location (such as a shrine) where such utterances are made

* **funerary** having to do with funerals or the handling of the dead

Hatshepsut, one of only four women to rule Egypt, adopted all the traditional titles and roles of the office. This red granite sphinx shows her wearing a false beard, one symbol of the Egyptian ruler's power. In most images, Hatshepsut was shown in a man's clothing because the position of a pharaoh was usually identified with men.

Hatshepsut (hat•SHEP•soot) was a queen of ancient Egypt who later proclaimed herself the kingdom's ruler, or pharaoh. She was one of only four women ever to rule Egypt in her own right. Hatshepsut was able to gain control of the throne largely because of her strong character and forceful personality.

Hatshepsut was the daughter of a pharaoh named Thutmose I. As was common among ancient Egyptian royalty, Hatshepsut married her half brother, Thutmose II, and they had a daughter named Neferura. Around 1492 B.C., Thutmose II succeeded Thutmose I as pharaoh, with Hatshepsut as his queen. After an unremarkable reign, he died unexpectedly around 1479 B.C. Because he had no sons with Hatshepsut, Thutmose II was succeeded by THUTMOSE III, his son by a minor wife and Hatshepsut's stepson.

Thutmose III was just a boy when he inherited the throne, so at first, Hatshepsut reigned as regent*. During that time, she gained power and the support of important royal officials. Then around 1472 B.C., after about seven years as regent, Hatshepsut had herself declared the ruler of Egypt by an oracle* from the god AMUN. She abandoned the titles of queen, which belonged to her as the chief wife of Thutmose II, and adopted all the pharaoh's traditional titles. In art and architecture, she was depicted wearing kingly dress, including the ceremonial false beard that was an ancient symbol of the king's power. However, it is not known whether she dressed as a man in real life. From then until her death about 14 years later, Hatshepsut ruled Egypt as the dominant partner in a co-reign with Thutmose III.

During Hatshepsut's reign, Egypt was involved in relatively little military activity. There are no records of military campaigns in Asia, and Egypt seems to have lost much of the ground that previously had been won in Asia. Nonetheless, Hatshepsut had a prosperous reign, as reflected by the impressive buildings and monuments that were constructed during her rule. She had the temple at Thebes renovated, including the addition of a chapel and four obelisks, each nearly 100 feet tall. She also cut a tomb for herself in the Valley of the Kings. Her best-known achievement is a magnificent funerary* temple she had built for herself at Dayr al-Bahri. The foundation of the temple stands today much as it must have looked in her time. Inscribed on its walls are the major events of Hatshepsut's reign, including the story of how Amun granted her the right to rule Egypt as pharaoh.

During Hatshepsut's reign, a man named Senenmut became one of the few commoners ever to gain prestige and renown in ancient Egypt. Senenmut was an influential man who held many important offices. He was the administrator of royal domains and tutor to Hatshepsut's daughter, Neferura. He also supervised the construction of the Dayr al-Bahri temple. (*See also* **Egypt and the Egyptians; Pharaohs.**)

HEALTH

The ancient Egyptians hoped that they would enjoy the twin blessings of "a good old age and a good burial." They believed that an ideal life lasted for 100 or 110 years—but it was the rare Egyptian who reached such an advanced age. Throughout the ancient Near East, people faced many health hazards, including disease and infection by parasites*. Although

* **parasite** organism that lives inside another organism and is often harmful to the host organism

* **plague** contagious disease that quickly kills large numbers of people

* **archaeologist** scientist who studies past human cultures, usually by excavating material remains of human activity

* **epidemic** spread of a particular disease within a population

* **domesticate** to adapt or tame for human use

* **migration** movement of individuals or peoples from one place to another

the diseases were caused by unclean water, poor sanitation, crowded living conditions, and dietary deficiencies, most ancients believed that diseases were the result of attacks by demons or other supernatural beings. In Akkadian (the language of the Babylonians), the term for plague was literally "the touch of god," often Erra. In the Hebrew BIBLE, plagues* are similarly referred to as "the touch." Consequently, most ancient Near Eastern peoples sought relief from these troubles in MAGIC and RELIGION.

Diseases and Ailments. More is known about the diseases and ailments of the ancient Egyptians than about those of any other Near Eastern culture. That is because of the Egyptian practice of preserving bodies. By examining MUMMIES and skeletons, as well as ancient medical texts, archaeologists* have been able to identify the problems that afflicted the people of ancient Egypt. Dental problems were common, especially wear on tooth enamel caused by sand in bread and other foods. Other health problems included broken bones, bone cancer, obesity, arthritis, lung diseases such as emphysema and tuberculosis, smallpox, polio, and parasitic diseases.

Medical texts from ancient MESOPOTAMIA suggest that eye diseases were common there, perhaps in part due to a diet poor in vitamin A. The Mesopotamians also suffered from many ailments of the digestive system, some of which were probably caused by intestinal parasites. Skin problems such as sores and rashes occurred frequently and may have been caused by the hot, dry, sunny climate as well as by certain infections.

Records left by the HITTITES of ancient ANATOLIA (present-day Turkey) mention ailments of the eyes, mouth, throat, and digestive system. They also refer to plagues—devastating epidemics* of disease.

Few references to health or illness appear in texts that survive from ancient IRAN. Health problems there were probably similar to those of neighboring Mesopotamia. It is clear, however, that people who suffered from some diseases with visible signs, such as skin ailments, were outcasts from society.

Health problems in SYRIA and CANAAN were much like those elsewhere in the ancient Near East. People combated infestations of insects such as lice by shaving and covering themselves with oil. Internal parasites such as tapeworms and whipworms, however, were not so easily defeated. The Hebrew Bible mentions illnesses among the ancient Israelites, including fevers, parasitic diseases, stroke, epilepsy, and skin diseases including leprosy. The Israelites believed that the plagues they suffered were caused by contact with other peoples. They also regarded a woman's infertility, or inability to bear children, as both an illness and something that lowered her social status.

Public Health. Many health problems in the ancient Near East were related to changes in lifestyle, such as domesticating* animals, which placed people in closer contact with animals and, consequently, the diseases they carried. Another change was the shift from the hunting-and-gathering life to settling in permanent communities in which people lived close together in large numbers. Greater population density allowed some diseases to flourish and to spread more easily. Finally, war, trade, and migrations* led to more contact among different populations. These events also spread diseases more widely.

153

The Mesopotamians recognized that some illnesses passed from person to person. They tried to prevent this spread by isolating sick people. Sometimes they moved the population of an entire village in the hope of preventing epidemics.

The social and physical conditions of people's lives also affected health. In some societies, food was unequally distributed among classes, so some people consumed more varied and plentiful food than others. Those whose food was insufficient or limited were more likely to suffer from conditions caused by a lack of nutrients.

Poor sanitation also contributed to public health problems. Water was necessary to life, but it could also bring disease. In Syria and Canaan, people collected rainwater in large containers called cisterns. Over time, water standing in these cisterns could become contaminated with disease-carrying organisms or with parasites. River water, too, could harbor health threats such as disease-causing parasites.

Contamination of drinking water by garbage or by human and animal wastes was one of the worst public health problems of the ancient world. Excavations in Egypt have shown that even the most luxurious homes, well built and maintained, were surrounded by heaps of garbage, open sewers, and thousands of flies.

Some cultures made efforts to dispose of human wastes effectively, although it is not clear whether they did so specifically to protect their health. In Mesopotamia, for example, some towns and cities had clay sewer pipes. Archaeologists have found clay pipes and drainage systems in several Hittite sites too, and some Hittite homes had toilets. Various cities in CANAAN also had drains, and remains of ancient toilets have been discovered in JERUSALEM.

Life Expectancy. It is difficult to determine how long people lived, on average, in the ancient Near East. Some of the best-preserved human remains come from Egypt, but even experts in the study of these relics do not always agree on life expectancy. Some experts suggest that Egyptians rarely lived more than 40 or 50 years, while others argue that those who survived into adulthood and did not die giving birth had a good chance of living to age 60. It must be remembered, though, that the mummies from which much of our information is gathered were almost always from Egypt's upper classes and do not represent Egyptian society as a whole.

Members of the privileged classes in Mesopotamia might live to age 70, although the average life expectancy of the ordinary farmer or laborer was undoubtedly much lower. Even for the privileged, however, existence was full of health threats. Accidents, famine*, and CHILDBIRTH, as well as illness, claimed a heavy toll in lives. Infant mortality, or the percentage of people dying before their first birthday, was also high in all ancient societies. (*See also* **Drought; Famine; Medicine.**)

Disease Prevention

This extract from an ancient Mesopotamian letter shows some understanding of disease transmission and prevention:

I hear that the woman Nanna is ill. . . . Give strict orders that no one drink from a cup she drinks from, that no one sit on a chair she sits on, and that no one sleep in a bed she sleeps in so that she does not infect [any more] of the women around her.

---

* **famine** severe lack of food due to failed crops

Hebrew

See *Semites; Semitic Languages.*

HEBREWS AND ISRAELITES

* **patriarch** male leader of a family or tribe

* **nomadic** referring to people who move from place to place in search of food and pasture

* **cuneiform** world's oldest form of writing, which takes its name from the distinctive wedge-shaped signs pressed into clay tablets

* **hieroglyphic** referring to a system of writing that uses pictorial characters, or hieroglyphs, to represent words or ideas

* **matriarch** female leader of a family or tribe

* **famine** severe lack of food due to failed crops

Where Are They Now?

In 722 B.C., the Assyrians conquered the kingdom of Israel and forced the ten northern Israelite tribes to relocate throughout the Assyrian empire. The people of these tribes blended into their new societies and were lost to history. However, many Jews continued to believe that their descendants would be found someday. One traveler in the A.D. 800s claimed to have found the tribes beyond the rivers of Ethiopia. From time to time, claims have been made that certain religious and ethnic groups—the Mormons, the Afghans, the Japanese, and the indigenous people of North America—are descendants of these lost tribes.

The term *Hebrew* is generally used to refer to the patriarch* Abraham (also called Abram) and his descendants—a nomadic* tribespeople who worshiped the god YAHWEH. The traditional history of these people—beginning with Abraham's migration from MESOPOTAMIA to CANAAN—is told in the Hebrew BIBLE. The term *Hebrew* itself is rarely used in the Bible, in most cases only by other people in their references to or about Abraham or his descendants. Some historians believe that the name *Hebrew* may have come from a people who lived in Canaan during the Late Bronze Age (ca. 1600–1200 B.C.) and were referred to in cuneiform* and Egyptian hieroglyphic* texts as *Khabiru*. Others suggest that the term *Hebrew* derives from the name Eber, the name of one of Abraham's ancestors.

The term *Israelites* refers to the descendants of Abraham and his immediate family—considered the patriarchs and matriarchs* of Israel. According to the Hebrew Bible, Abraham's grandson Jacob, who was renamed Israel by Yahweh, had 12 sons. Their descendants were later organized into 12 tribes, each named for one of Jacob's (Israel's) sons or grandsons. Together, these tribespeople came to be known as the children of Israel or the Israelites.

Biblical History. According to the Bible, Jacob and his family fled to Egypt to escape a famine* in Canaan, and there their descendants eventually became slaves. A leader named MOSES led them out of captivity on a 40-year journey through the desert back to Canaan, which Yahweh had promised to them as their homeland, the Promised Land. During the Exodus, as this journey was called, Yahweh revealed the TEN COMMANDMENTS to Moses on Mount Sinai. The Israelites then completed the journey to Canaan, where they began a new phase of their history.

Once back in Canaan, the Israelites came into conflict with Canaanite peoples and the PHILISTINES, a people who had come from the eastern Mediterranean and settled in Canaan. To combat the Philistines, the Israelite tribes united under King Saul. The Bible describes a series of wars in which the Israelites overcame these groups. After Saul died in battle against the Philistines, his son-in-law DAVID, a former outlaw, became king. David conquered JERUSALEM, which had been under foreign control but was situated between lands held by the southern and northern Israelite tribes, and made it Israel's capital. During the reign of SOLOMON, David's son and successor, Israel became an empire that stretched from Syria to Egypt. Solomon also built a splendid temple and palace in in the city of Jerusalem.

Still, the Israelite kingdom was fragile. Some tribes objected to the taxes and forced labor that paid for and built the new structures, and tensions existed between the northern and southern tribes. After Solomon's death, the kingdom was divided into a northern kingdom called Israel and a southern one called Judah, whose people were the Judeans, or, in modern English, Jews. After the split, the histories of the kingdoms of ISRAEL AND JUDAH were separate.

What Modern Historians Believe. No contemporary archaeological* evidence exists to support the story of the patriarchs and early Israelites as told in the Bible. Historians are divided on the accuracy of

Hebrews and Israelites

* **archaeological** referring to the study of past human cultures, usually by excavating material remains of human activity

* **Semitic** of or relating to people of the Near East or northern Africa, including the Assyrians, Babylonians, Phoenicians, Jews, and Arabs

* **Levant** lands bordering the eastern shores of the Mediterranean Sea (present-day Syria, Lebanon, and Israel), the West Bank, and Jordan

* **city-state** independent state consisting of a city and its surrounding territory

* **bureaucracy** system of officials and clerks that perform government functions

* **cult** system of religious beliefs and rituals; group following these beliefs

biblical accounts because this text was compiled many centuries after the events occurred. Moreover, it was compiled by editors whose intentions may have been to strengthen national and religious unity by emphasizing the shared past of the Israelite people. Notwithstanding its problems, the Bible is considered a starting point for discussing the early history of the Israelites and for archaeological investigations.

Although historians know that the Israelites were a Semitic* people, they know little of their history before 1100s B.C. At the time, the Levant* was undergoing social and political change, perhaps caused by population movements and invasions of the SEA PEOPLES. City-states* were falling, urban culture was weakening, and people were on the move. Some historians believe that the Israelites settled in the thinly occupied highlands of Canaan during this period. Others, however, have suggested that the Israelites may have originated among segments of the Canaanite population.

After arriving in Canaan, the Israelites began to shift from a nomadic lifestyle to permanent settlement and agriculture. At first, they occupied the northeast region of present-day Israel, but they eventually moved down the hills and into more fertile regions. They tended to form new settlements in areas outside the territories of the old city-states. Archaeological evidence from the region does not easily support the idea of the sudden or violent changes resulting from the battles with other groups as described in the Bible. Instead, the Israelite expansion may have involved gradual blending with other groups as well as conflict. Over time, the Israelites came to share many customs, traditions, and cultural elements with their Canaanite neighbors, although they maintained a separate identity.

Some historians also think it is unlikely that the empire of David and Solomon existed as described in the Bible. The lack of historical evidence about David and Solomon suggests to some scholars that their achievements may have been more modest than described in the Bible. A few others even question whether the united monarchy existed. Instead, they suspect that the kingdoms of Israel and Judah emerged separately between 900 and 800 B.C. and that later Jewish historians claimed there had been a united kingdom in order to link the people of the two kingdoms to a common heritage.

Government and Economy. The Israelites had established settled communities by 1200 B.C. Divided into tribes, they were headed by a tribal chief who came forward at times of crisis. It is unclear what role the leaders played in day-to-day governance. The tribes recognized their shared identity as "children of Israel" and were united mainly by their religion, the worship of Yahweh.

After the Israelites adopted kingship as their system of government, a bureaucracy* developed within the monarchy to handle the administration of the royal estates, tax collection, and defense. The state cult* was also a function of the monarchy. The king had supreme authority over the cult and performed such duties as offering sacrifices and ordering the people to religious meetings. There were also two classes of priests: the Levites, who were in charge of temple maintenance, and the Kohens, who performed sacrifices and rituals.

The economy of the early Israelites was based on agriculture, and ownership of land was the basis of wealth and social status. Farmers either developed or adopted from neighboring cultures several technical advances that helped them cultivate the hilly, dry land. They dug cisterns (reservoirs) in rocks where they could store rainwater and built terraces* to plant crops on steep hillsides. Their principal crops were grain, olives, and grapes. Although they had taken up farming, and eventually urban living, they did not abandon raising livestock. They maintained herds, primarily sheep and goats but also some cattle. Craftspeople produced pottery, including cooking pots with handles and jugs with spouts. Metalworkers produced tools and weapons of bronze, which was gradually replaced by the use of the more abundant and stronger iron. The Hewbrew Bible describes trade in foreign luxury goods under King Solomon, but archaeological evidence supports only modest trade in the region.

* **terrace** artificial level platform of earth, supported by an outer wall, dug or built into the side of a hill; terraces may be stacked on top of each other like stairs

Society. In the period before the establishment of the monarchy, Israelite settlements differed from the earlier Canaanite cities in that they did not have large temples or palaces, nor were they surrounded by walls. Settlements fell into three types: villages, towns or villages with buildings circling an open center, and farmsteads that consisted of individual buildings or small clusters of buildings in walled compounds. During the early years of the monarchy, the village pattern of settlement gave way to cities and towns. These were usually surrounded by a thick defensive wall pierced by a single GATE. Many cities had systems of wells, pools, and tunnels to distribute water.

Differences in the size and quality of buildings were not extreme, suggesting that the differences between social classes were not great. There were free farmers or herders who worked their own land and whose individual wealth and social status depended on the amount of land they controlled. In addition, some individuals may have been recognized as having higher status because of birth, performance in battle, or for other reasons. Slaves occupied the lowest social class. The majority of people, however, were free peasants.

Two kinds of education existed among the Israelites. One was the traditional ancient Near Eastern system of home schooling, in which parents taught children practical skills, social customs, and religious and moral matters. The other was a formal system devoted to training in writing. In the schools in this system, professional scribes* were trained to perform such functions as writing letters and keeping records. The scribes trained in this manner became an essential part of the religious tradition, responsible for copying sacred and legal documents and for teaching the law.

* **scribe** person of a learned class who served as a writer, editor, or teacher

Alphabet and Language. The Israelites spoke Hebrew, a Semitic* language that is closely related to Phoenician and Moabite (from the kingdom of Moab in present-day Jordan). As a spoken language, Hebrew was replaced by Aramaean by the 300s B.C. It existed only as the language of Jewish religious traditions and worship until it was revived in the A.D. 1800s and 1900s.

The early Hebrew alphabet that was used before the 500s B.C. was based on early Northwest Semitic traditions. It was an aleph-beth, having

* **Semitic** of or relating to a language family that includes Akkadian, Aramaic, Arabic, Hebrew, and Phoenician

157

signs only for consonants. A later form of Hebrew alphabet, called Classical or Square Hebrew, was based on the Aramaic alphabet.

Culture. Very little is known about the culture of the early Israelites. Aside from some settlements uncovered by archaeological excavations, few physical objects can be dated with certainty to the era before the divided monarchy.

While the Israelites placed great importance on their distinct and unique identity, in truth, they shared many cultural and artistic elements with other peoples who lived in Canaan. Despite the official devotion to Yahweh, Israelites were exposed to other cults, and some worshiped other gods—such as the Canaanite deities BAAL and Asherah—instead of, or in addition to, Yahweh.

The architecture of the Israelites expanded from residential structures to include public buildings such as palaces and temples. In the south, they were influenced by Egypt and built structures modeled on Egyptian palaces, with rooms arranged around a central courtyard. In the north, a different type of public building appeared. It consisted of two rectangular rooms and a porch supported by two columns, a style influenced by Syrian architecture.

Much art in the ancient Near East concerned images of gods and goddesses. However, making images of Yahweh was forbidden by the religion of the Israelites. As a result, the surviving artworks of the Israelite period tend to be sculptures of guardian lions or other animals from gateways or public buildings.

The Israelites had a rich tradition of poetry. The biblical PSALMS are among the best-known examples of Israelite poetry. Such poems were often set to music. Among the Canaanites, music was both a folk art and part of temple worship. The Israelites probably shared this musical tradition; the Bible contains references to singing and playing musical instruments, and King David is said to have been talented at music. (*See also* **Judaism and Jews; Mosaic Law; Patriarchs and Matriarchs of Israel.**)

The Question of the *Khabiru*

In the 1300s B.C., Canaan was occupied by small kingdoms and city-states whose documents refer to a class of people called the *Khabiru* (sometimes *Habiru* or *Hapiru*). The terms referred to social outcasts, including refugees, outlaws, and other people outside the mainstream of society. Rulers sometimes used the term as an insulting way to refer to their enemies. Some modern scholars, noting the similarity between the terms *Khabiru* and *Hebrew,* suggested that these documents contain early mentions of the Hebrews. However, because the connection cannot be proved, most scholars believe instead that the term refers to a miscellaneous social class rather than a particular nation or people.

HELLENISTIC WORLD

* **dynasty** succession of rulers from the same family or group

* **Levant** lands bordering the eastern shores of the Mediterranean Sea (present-day Syria, Lebanon, and Israel), the West Bank, and Jordan

The term *Hellenistic* (he•luh•NIS•tik) refers to the Greek-influenced cultures throughout the lands of the eastern Mediterranean and western Asia during the period between the death of ALEXANDER THE GREAT in 323 B.C. and the conquest of Egypt by Rome about 300 years later. The word comes from *Hellas,* the Greek word for Greece. Alexander, himself a Macedonian, admired Greek culture and initiated the spread of Greek ideas throughout the areas he conquered, from Egypt and ANATOLIA (present-day Turkey) in the west to the borders of India in the east.

After Alexander's death, the lands he conquered did not remain a single empire. His generals began to fight among themselves, and eventually, three important dynasties* were established. The lands from Syria to India fell to Seleucus I, founder of the SELEUCID EMPIRE; Egypt and the southern Levant* became the domain of the Ptolemies; and the Antigonids ruled MACEDONIA.

Settlers from Macedonia and Greece moved to the new empires in large numbers. These colonists built numerous cities, which were laid out to resemble traditional Greek city-states*. The colonists also brought their language with them, and Greek became the language of government and commerce. In addition, coins of the type used in Greece, especially Athens, were now minted in large quantities throughout the Hellenistic world, and these helped promote trade.

The Hellenistic colonies were ruled by the central state authority of their land or by his local representative. For example, the Seleucids divided their territory into smaller administrative units ruled by military governors responsible to the king, a system similar to the satrapies* of the Persian empire. This blending of Greek culture with that of the ancient Near East was typical of many aspects of life during the Hellenistic period.

The decline of the Greek-influenced world began when the Romans conquered Macedonia and Greece in 148 B.C. At this time, the Seleucids also began losing power to the Parthians in IRAN. By 63 B.C., the Seleucid state had ceased to exist, and the Romans ruled those parts of their former empire not already conquered by the Parthians. Egypt, the last surviving Hellenistic power, became a province of the Roman Empire in 30 B.C., marking an end to the Hellenistic world. (*See also* **Greece and the Greeks; Ptolemy I.**)

* **city-state** independent state consisting of a city and its surrounding territory

* **satrapy** portion of Persian-controlled territory under the rule of a satrap, or provincial governor

See map in Alexander the Great (vol. 1).

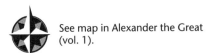

HERODOTUS

**lived ca. 484–430 B.C.
Greek historian**

* **city-state** independent state consisting of a city and its surrounding territory

* **archaeologist** scientist who studies past human cultures, usually by excavating material remains of human activity

Herodotus (hi•RAH•duh•tuhs), a Greek writer of the 400s B.C., was the first major historian of the ancient Near East. His work is simply called the *History,* which means "inquiry" in Greek. In the *History,* he sought to give an account of the PERSIAN WARS between the Greeks and the Persians and the events leading up to them. Most of what is known about the Persian Wars comes from his writings. Herodotus's writings are also a major source of information about the history and legends of the ancient Near East.

Herodotus was born in Halicarnassus, a Greek city-state* in Caria in southwest ANATOLIA (present-day Turkey), which was under Persian rule at that time. As a youth, he was banished from the city for his opposition to the Persian regime. He then traveled widely and lived in several places, including Athens and Thurii, a Greek colony in southern Italy.

During these travels, Herodotus collected numerous stories, which he later included in the *History.* He organized his work by beginning with an account of the rise of the PERSIAN EMPIRE. He wrote about the lands that were conquered by Persia, including Egypt and MESOPOTAMIA, supplying details about the customs, religions, and histories of each land's people. He then described the Persian Wars, including Persia's attack on Greek city-states, the major land and sea battles, and the surprising victory of the Greeks against the much larger Persian army.

Later historians, including some from the ancient world, have found errors in some of Herodotus's work. However, modern archaeologists* have found that some of his accounts of places and events are supported by their own findings. Herodotus's detailed descriptions of ancient Near

Eastern social customs—which he often tells with great enthusiasm because they were so different from his Greek customs—are still enjoyed by modern readers. (*See also* **History and Historiography.**)

HIEROGLYPHICS

The term *hieroglyphics* (hy•uh•ruh•GLI•fiks) refers to a system of writing in which picture symbols represent ideas and sounds. The term was derived from the Egyptian expression "god's words." First developed in Egypt around 3000 B.C., the system continued to be used for INSCRIPTIONS on monuments, wall paintings, and religious texts until the A.D. 300s. Other systems of hieroglyphics, possibly inspired by the Egyptian, were used in Crete during the Middle Bronze Age, in Hittite Anatolia in the Late Bronze Age, and in Neo-Hittite north Syria in the Iron Age. Decoding each of these different forms of hieroglyphics became a key to understanding much about these ancient cultures.

Hieroglyphic Symbols. Egyptian hieroglyphics was based on a set of about 700 signs, including pictures of living beings and objects, gods, goddesses, people, animals, human and animal body parts, plants, celestial bodies, buildings, furniture, and vessels. Each of these signs was used as a logogram, phonogram, or determinative, to convey the message to the reader.

Basic Egyptian vocabulary was expressed by logograms (derived from the Greek words for "word" and "writing"), where the sign literally means what it depicts. Scribes* used the sign in the shape of a house to mean house, or the sign in the shape of a head to mean head.

Phonograms (from the Greek words for "sound" and "writing") were used to sound out a word, most often because no suitable logogram existed. Individual signs might represent one, two, or even three consonants. Vowels are not expressed in this system. The sounds represented by the signs were usually related to the name of the object shown by the sign. For example, because the Egyptian word for house was *per* or *par,* the sign in the shape of a house could represent the sound *p-r* in a word, even if that word had nothing to do with a house. Among the phonograms, there was a set of 24 symbols, each representing the sound of a single consonant. These symbols included all but one of the consonant sounds in spoken Egyptian. Still, the Egyptians never developed hieroglyphics into an alphabetic system of writing, in which symbols standing for single sounds are combined to create words.

When phonograms are used to "spell" out a word, the word is usually followed by a determinative, a sign that gives the reader a visual clue (it was not read) to the meaning of the preceding word. For example, the picture of a house might follow the word for a building, room, house, or tomb, or the picture of a seated god might follow the name of a god. A special determinative was the cartouche—an oval enclosing a person's name—which indicated that the person named was an Egyptian ruler. To help the reader decide whether a sign was a logogram (which is to be read) or a determinative (which is just a visual clue), the scribes often placed a vertical line after a logogram.

* **scribe** person of a learned class who served as a writer, editor, or teacher

Hittite Hieroglyphics

In addition to the Egyptians, the Hittites also developed a hieroglyphic script, during the second millennium B.C. The script first appeared on Hittite Old and Middle Kingdom seals at Boğazköy. It was initially used on royal seals and was later used to write identifying labels on sculptures. Over time, however, Hittite hieroglyphics was increasingly composed in the Luwian language, instead of Hittite. By about the 700s B.C., the Hittite hieroglyphic tradition had come to a close.

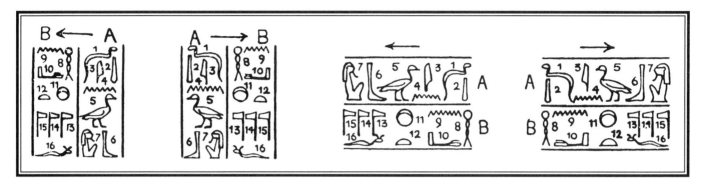

Egyptian hieroglyphics were written and read both from left to right and from right to left. This chart shows the same sentence arranged in four ways with arrows showing the direction of the text. The numbers mark the sequence of the signs.

In translating hieroglyphics, linguists first identify the phonograms (1, 3, and 4), logograms (2 and 11), and determinatives (7) in the script. Then they transliterate the characters into Roman letters—2 is *mdw*, 5 is *gb*. The Roman letters are transcribed into Egyptian consonant sounds, which are translated into English. The sentence here reads "To say the words by Geb with his Ennead." Geb was the Egyptian god of the earth and Ennead refers to a divine family.

An example from English shows how the system worked. Suppose a word contained the phonograms *w-sh-ng t-n* (remember that hieroglyphics did not include vowels). If the phonograms were followed by the picture of a sitting man, the reference would be to a person, George Washington. If they were followed by the symbol for a village, the word would refer to a place, Washington, D.C. Hieroglyphics was generally written from right to left with the heads on human and animal signs facing right. In monuments and wall paintings, the sequence could be different for artistic reasons. In all cases, however, the text was always read from the direction in which the human and animal heads faced.

Changes to Hieroglyphics. In use for more than 3,000 years, Egyptian hieroglyphics evolved over time. During the Old Kingdom period (from about 2675 to 2130 B.C.), there were about 1,000 signs. This number declined to about 750 during the time of the Middle Kingdom (ca. 1980–1630 B.C.) and New Kingdom (ca. 1539–1075 B.C.). From about 300 B.C., the number of signs increased to several thousands. The new signs included combinations that created new meanings by taking advantage of the fact that hieroglyphics was based on pictures. For example, scribes had used a rectangular box open on one side to indicate the sound /m/ and a crawling snake for the sound /f/. In later years, these signs were combined by placing the snake symbol inside the open box. The result was two new signs for words. If the snake faced the closed end of the box, as though it had just crawled in, the symbol meant "to enter." If it faced the open end, the meaning was "to exit."

Because each symbol had to be carefully created on the surface individually, hieroglyphics was a difficult system to adopt easily. Consequently, scribes derived other ways of writing the Egyptian language from hieroglyphics. They developed another form of writing called hieratic, which first appeared around 2600 B.C. In the 600s B.C., another cursive form of hieroglyphics was also developed. Called demotic, this form was a shorthand and simplified version of hieratic, which it mostly replaced.

Deciphering Hieroglyphics. In the A.D. 300s, Egypt, then a part of the Roman Empire, became Christianized. Under the influence of the Christian church, a new system of writing based on the Greek alphabet was adopted. Hieroglyphics and the hieratic and demotic scripts were abandoned, and the meaning of the symbols was forgotten. Hieroglyphic

texts on monuments were still visible, though, and European scholars and travelers tried to understand what these scripts meant. Their attempted explanations were often fanciful—and completely wrong.

The key to understanding hieroglyphics came in the early 1800s, after the discovery of the ROSETTA STONE. This monument, which dates from about 200 B.C., contains inscriptions in three scripts: ancient Greek and demotic and hieroglyphic Egyptian. French scholar Jean-François Champollion determined that the three inscriptions all contained the same text. By comparing the Greek to the hieroglyphics, Champollion developed the basic principles to decipher* hieroglyphics, enabling later scholars to understand other Egyptian writings. (*See also* **Alphabets; Decipherment; Egypt and the Egyptians; Languages; Writing.**)

* **decipher** to decode and interpret the meaning

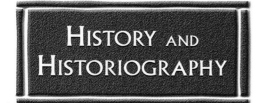

HISTORY AND HISTORIOGRAPHY

* **artifact** ornament, tool, weapon, or other object made by humans

* **annals** record of events arranged chronologically by year

* **coronation** act or ceremony of crowning a leader

* **scribe** person of a learned class who served as a writer, editor, or teacher

Historiography is the writing of history. Modern historians write history by examining ancient inscriptions, manuscripts, texts, artifacts*, and other sources and use that information to try to reconstruct a record of human activities. Their aim is to get a true understanding of people in earlier times.

The peoples of the ancient Near East recorded their histories in various kinds of written documents, such as INSCRIPTIONS, KING LISTS, CHRONICLES, and annals*. These sources contain two types of history. The first type documents recent events: battles, coronations*, or other important events that were recorded soon after they occurred. The second type presents events and people from the remote past. The dividing line between these two types of histories is often unclear. Yet in the ancient Near East, the recording of recent events was distinct from the recording of the remote past, both in terms of the kind of information they contained and the reasons for writing.

The audience for historical works also varied in the ancient Near East. Some works were intended to be read to the public, while others were of interest to only a small group of people, such as scribes*. In some cases, historical texts were created for a god rather than for humans. Texts such as these were often put in inaccessible places because they were meant only for the gods.

TREATMENT OF RECENT EVENTS

When peoples of the ancient Near East recorded recent events, they primarily relied on eyewitness accounts. The purpose of recording history was to preserve the story of important events, especially triumphs and accomplishments, for future generations. The main focus of such accounts was usually the king. Historical records included not only references to specific public events but also information about the king's life, character, and achievements.

Mesopotamia. In ancient Assyria and Babylonia, the recent events that were recorded were almost always about the activities of the king.

Among the earliest texts were simple inscriptions crediting the king with building temples. Over time, these inscriptions developed into lengthy texts praising the king for constructing temples and palaces.

Babylonian inscriptions dealt almost entirely with royal building activities. Assyrian texts, however, placed greater emphasis on their king's military campaigns. Some Assyrian texts are in the form of annals, which were written by royal scribes and listed the king's wars in chronological order. Based on field records, these were the official version of events that would become the source for future historical texts. Nevertheless, the purpose of Assyrian texts, and texts from other Near Eastern cultures, was not to create an accurate record of events. Instead, the texts were intended to glorify the king and recount his conquest of the kingdom's enemies.

Another type of historical writing in ancient Mesopotamia was "letters to the gods." These special texts were usually written for presentation at public gatherings to celebrate an important military victory. Addressed to a god, they praised the king for his great victory and honored the soldiers who fell in battle. An interesting feature in some of these texts is that they included details about the geography and customs of foreign lands.

Egypt. As early as about 2600 B.C., the Egyptians developed a chronological method for recording important recent events. At first, these texts simply recorded the names of kings and the years of their individual reigns. Beginning with the Middle Kingdom (ca. 1980–1630 B.C.), these records included information on government activities.

The ancient Egyptians also wrote inscriptions on the tombs of high-ranking officials. The autobiographical texts listed the achievements of

In ancient times, people recorded histories to preserve the story of important events, such as military triumphs. This relief from the Assyrian palace at Nineveh shows two scribes (third and fourth from left) recording the events, booty, and number of enemies slain during a military campaign in Babylon. Note the pile of heads lying at their feet.

History and Historiography

* **stela** stone slab or pillar that has been carved or engraved and serves as a monument; *pl.* stelae

the deceased as well as his titles and honors and how he earned them. Officials also installed stelae* with inscriptions that detailed the accomplishments of important leaders. Both types of inscriptions were major sources of historical information for later generations of Egyptians.

By the 1900s B.C., some royal inscriptions in Egypt reflected important changes in historiography. Instead of just recording events, these inscriptions described the circumstances that existed when the events occurred. This was important because it helped explain not only what happened but also why it happened.

Beginning in the 1500s B.C., Egyptian kings produced inscriptions that contained narratives of their military conquests. Based on field records and other sources, these inscriptions included detailed descriptions of some military campaigns and overviews of others. The inscriptions served an important purpose. They helped the king prove that he was the rightful heir to the throne because of his victories over foreign armies. Victory, the Egyptians believed, was proof that the king had the support of the gods. Some of the inscriptions also contained highly poetic stories of battles.

The Hittites. Most ancient Hittite texts contain accounts of recent events and were presented in royal inscriptions. The earliest of these texts describe events that occurred around the 1700s B.C. The Hittites continued to record their history until the end of their civilization in the 1200s B.C. They maintained two types of inscriptions, and each took the form of public pronouncements of the king.

Annals, which reported the king's military activities year by year, were one type of Hittite royal inscription. These texts describe the king's "manly deeds" and were meant to impress the reader and justify the king's succession to the throne. Some annals cover a greater time frame than a king's individual reign and record the activity of other Hittite princes and generals. In this way, they are very different from Assyrian and Egyptian annals, which focused exclusively on the achievements of the king. Hittite annals also contain information on military campaigns, such as explanations of strategy and the reasons for undertaking or delaying actions.

A second type of Hittite text dealing with recent history contained justification for past actions. This emphasis on accountability is distinctive to Hittite historiography. The earliest example of such a text is the "Political Testament" of KHATTUSHILI I. Addressed to nobles and officials, this text explains that the king's unusual selection of a grandson as heir was due to the evil behavior of certain members of the royal family. The king cites events from the past (although not in chronological order) in support of his decision. The use of past historical events to justify current actions became a significant feature of Hittite historiography.

An Egyptian Historian

One of the few named individuals who might be considered a historian in ancient Egypt was a priest named Manetho. In about 280 B.C., Manetho compiled a list, written in Greek, of all Egyptian kings from the beginning of Egyptian history to his own time. He divided the list into 30 dynasties, giving the name and length of reign of each ruler as well as information about him. For example, Manetho claimed that the first Egyptian king, Menes, "was taken by a hippopotamus and died." Only fragmentary copies of Manetho's work have survived. However, these fragments have been important sources for scholars trying to confirm the succession of Egyptian kings. Moreover, scholars still use Manetho's division of Egyptian rulers into 30 dynasties.

* **Levant** lands bordering the eastern shores of the Mediterranean Sea (present-day Syria, Lebanon, and Israel), the West Bank, and Jordan

Syria and the Levant. In ancient Syria and the Levant*, recent history was recorded in memorial inscriptions, which include royal inscriptions written in an autobiographical style. Memorial inscriptions dating from the 1200s B.C. to 700s B.C. are found throughout the Levant. The inscriptions were dedicated to a god and contain details about the king's

relationship to the god as well as accounts of his achievements. Generally composed late in a king's reign or after his death, these inscriptions are not presented in chronological order. They served mainly as a memorial to a ruler and his accomplishments.

Memorial inscriptions often refer to a troubled period of civil* disorder or foreign domination that was ended by the ruler. For example, the stela of King Mesha (ca. 800s B.C.) describes how he liberated his people from Israelite domination and praises him for constructing temples and other buildings.

No memorial inscriptions have been found from the kingdoms of IsRAEL AND JUDAH. However, some of the books in the Hebrew BIBLE contain accounts of military and other activities by kings that resemble memorial inscriptions found elsewhere in the Levant. The Hebrew Bible also specifically refers to the existence of the annals of the kings of Israel and Judah. Biblical narratives about King David may have been based on eyewitness reports of the events. Indeed, the succession story of David found in the book of Samuel and the book of Kings in the Hebrew Bible is regarded by some experts as the foremost example of Israelite historiography because of its accurate presentation of the Israelite monarchy.

TREATMENT OF THE REMOTE PAST

Historiography dealing with the remote past serves to explain the present in terms of a society's origins. This approach relied heavily on mythology, and it presented history largely in religious terms rather than relating actual events that took place. As time passed, however, records became more accurate and detailed.

Mesopotamia. Chronology, or the sequence of events, is an indispensable part of presenting the remote past. Chronologies developed in Mesopotamia in response to the practical need for dating administrative documents. In Babylonia, it led to the creation of a system in which each year was named for an important event that occurred during the previous year, such as a military victory or the dedication of a temple. These year names enabled scribes to trace the chronology of Babylonian kings. Chronologies eventually spanned thousands of years, providing a history of the remote past for later generations. The Assyrians also devised a similar system of *limmu* lists, where each year was named for an important official.

The Mesopotamians also used king lists as a chronological record. Such lists were used to understand the remote past, including the origins of kingship and the state. The Sumerian king list, first produced during the second millennium B.C.*, extended into the distant past and included references to mythical events and godlike kings. In this way, Sumerian history reached back to the time of human origins. The Assyrian king list, first compiled in the 1200s B.C., also reached back into the distant past. Once the king list was established, the Assyrians continued to add the names of new rulers.

Another group of texts dealing with the remote past were chronicles. Like annals, these works presented a precise chronology dated according

* **civil** relating to the state or its citizens

* **second millennium B.C.** years from 2000 to 1001 B.C.

to the reigns of kings. A single chronicle might cover the reigns of several kings, and series of such texts extended over many years. By the 600s B.C., chronicles had become quite precise and detailed in their accounts. As with annals, they focused on the king, but they were not written to justify his actions. Instead, they recorded the activities of successive rulers with a great deal of objectivity and concern for factual accuracy.

Egypt. Around the 2300s B.C., the Egyptians compiled annals covering a period of about 700 years, and they preserved this information on a stone monument known as the Palermo Stone. This artifact is believed to have originally contained the names of all the kings of Old Kingdom Egypt and the years each ruled, along with one or more important events for each year.

A text similar to the Palermo Stone, called the "Turin Canon of Kings," dates from the 1200s B.C. Although only fragments of this papyrus text remain, it originally contained a list of all the kings of Egypt, with the lengths of their reign. It extends into the distant past and deals with the role of gods and spirits in early Egyptian history.

The Hittites. The Hittites did not develop a way of recording the remote past comparable to that of the Mesopotamians or Egyptians. Their civilization was shorter, and they did not have any interest in long-range chronology or king lists. In texts that do deal with history beyond one or two generations, accounts of the past are used to lend force to arguments concerning matters such as treaties.

Only one text treated the remote past extensively: the *Edict of Telipinu.* This text served to regulate succession to the throne, and it did so by setting forth the history of the monarchy to show the importance of a strong kingship to the survival of the state.

The Levant. Apart from the Hebrew Bible, texts that deal with the remote past of the Levant are scant. King lists exist from a few cities in the region, and the works of later historians refer to annals. Other than this, information is not dated and does not resemble the annals or chronicles elsewhere in the ancient Near East.

The writers of the Hebrew Bible used ancient sources such as annals, chronicles, and king lists in creating their histories. Biblical writers also used materials based on oral tradition and mythology to reconstruct the history of Israel and its people and to extend it back to the origins of humans and the world. Because the Hebrew Bible is a religious document as well as a historical one, some later editors may have changed dates and facts to support certain religious beliefs.

The Hebrew Bible went beyond any other history written in the ancient Near East in the scope of its presentation of the history of a nation and people. Rather than focusing on the role of kings, its focus is on the origins and destiny of the people as a whole. Moreover, it makes no distinction between the recent past and the remote past in terms of the activity of God in civil and human affairs. (*See also* **Archaeology and Archaeologists; Books and Manuscripts; Epic Literature; Herodotus; Libraries and Archives; Writing.**)

The Historian of Babylon

In the late 300s and early 200s B.C., a Babylonian priest named Berossus wrote a three-volume work, the *Babyloniaca,* that traced the history and culture of Babylonia from the creation of the world to his own time. Although only fragments of this work survive, it was widely used by early Greek historians as a source of information on ancient Mesopotamia. For hundreds of years, Berossus was recognized as the ultimate authority on the history of Babylonia. Written in Greek, Berossus's work may have been a token of gratitude and support to the Greek-speaking kings who restored order to Mesopotamia after the death of Alexander the Great and the breakup of his empire.

Hittites

HITTITES

The Hittites (HIT•tyts) lived in ancient ANATOLIA (present-day Turkey), where they flourished from about 1700 to 1200 B.C. During that time, they became a major political force in the Near East.

HISTORY

Anatolia is divided by mountains, which made it difficult for any ancient power to gain control of the entire region. Anatolia's early history, then, was marked by the development of independent states, including the early Hittite state.

The Old Kingdom. The early Hittite rulers aimed to control the trade in metal ore and metal products. King KHATTUSHILI I (ruled ca. 1650–1620 B.C.) made KHATTUSHA in north-central Anatolia, the capital and renamed himself after the city. The city's location on a plateau made it easy to protect from enemies and a good stronghold from which to launch attacks. Khattushili quickly began an effort to expand the territory he controlled. He defeated a force to the north and a kingdom named Arzawa to the west. He then turned south toward SYRIA, where most trade routes met. He died before he could conquer Syria, but his successor, Murshili I, continued the effort. He quickly took the important Syrian city of Halab (Aleppo) and, in about 1595 B.C., the more important city of Babylon.

Shortly thereafter, Murshili returned to Khattusha because the government there was too weak and disorganized to control the new conquests. However, he was assassinated by a brother-in-law, and during the next century, weak rulers led the Hittites. The Hittites lost Syria and Arzawa, and tribes from the northwest were able to chip away at Hittite lands to within a few miles of Khattusha. Nevertheless, the capital remained a symbol of Hittite power and potential.

Tudkhaliya I took the throne around 1450 B.C., and Hittite fortunes seemed to improve. He quelled nearby unrest, then retrieved Arzawa and acquired some additional land. He made a peace treaty with Egypt. After he died in about 1420 B.C., however, the situation had worsened again, and the armies of the Hittites' Anatolian enemies seized more and more Hittite lands. Hittite fortunes fell so low that in a letter to the king of Arzawa, Amenhotep III of Egypt wrote, "I have heard . . . that the land of Khatti [as the Hittite kingdom was called] is dead."

The Hittite Empire. The Hittites' fortunes were soon reversed. Around 1380 B.C., SHUPPILULIUMA I—the great-grandson of Tudkhaliya—rose to the throne. He first consolidated his empire in the north and west. He then advanced into Lebanon and Syria and took KARKAMISH, a city on the west bank of the Euphrates River. This was a vital conquest because Karkamish was a hub of trade. Shuppiluliuma's success broke the power of Mitanni, the kingdom of the HURRIANS of Syria. Shuppiluliuma then sent an expedition to Egypt, but victory there was costly. Captive prisoners brought with them a plague*, which soon killed the Hittite king and his son and desired successor.

Murshili II, another son of Shuppiluliuma, ascended the throne around 1339 B.C. He reconquered Arzawa in the west, quieted unruly

* **plague** contagious disease that quickly kills large numbers of people

In Hittite Anatolia, married gods and goddesses and their children were assumed to have the same relational dynamics as human families. Consequently, Hittites prayed to the favorite daughter of a powerful god and goddess and asked her to plead on their behalf. This Hittite lead mold depicts a divine couple with their children.

Hittites

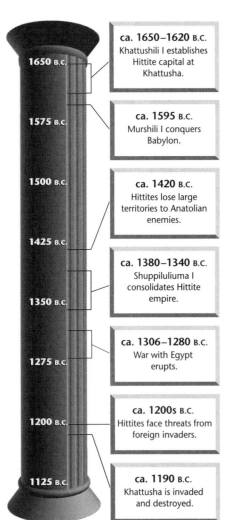

* **pharaoh** king of ancient Egypt

* **archaeologist** scientist who studies past human cultures, usually by excavating material remains of human activity

* **diplomat** person who conducts negotiations or relations with foreign kingdoms, states, or nations

* **pastoralist** person who herds livestock to make a living

ca. 1650–1620 B.C.
Khattushili I establishes Hittite capital at Khattusha.

ca. 1595 B.C.
Murshili I conquers Babylon.

ca. 1420 B.C.
Hittites lose large territories to Anatolian enemies.

ca. 1380–1340 B.C.
Shuppiluliuma I consolidates Hittite empire.

ca. 1306–1280 B.C.
War with Egypt erupts.

ca. 1200s B.C.
Hittites face threats from foreign invaders.

ca. 1190 B.C.
Khattusha is invaded and destroyed.

tribes in the north, held Karkamish against an Assyrian attack, and kept Syria under Hittite control. He maintained internal stability, and neither Egypt nor Assyria attacked during his reign. During the reign of his son Muwattalli II (ca. 1306–1282 B.C.), war with Egypt erupted when Egypt tried to take over Syria. The Egyptian and Hittite armies fought a battle at Qadesh, but Syria remained in Hittite hands.

Shortly thereafter, the Assyrians, whose power increased as a result of the defeat of the Hurrians, began threatening the Hittites from the east. KHATTUSHILI III (ruled ca. 1275–1250 B.C.) countered the threat by signing a peace treaty with Egypt. He also gave his daughter in marriage to the pharaoh*. This kept the Assyrians in check—if they attacked the Hittites, they would also be fighting Egyptian armies.

The Hittites also faced challenges on the west by a power named Ahhiyawa, whose kings resided at Mycenae. Tudkhaliya IV (ruled ca. 1254–1220 B.C.) tried to counter this threat by capturing Cyprus and taking tighter control of trade in the Mediterranean. Nevertheless, this was the beginning of the end. There was unrest on all sides of the empire, and dissent within. The once great empire was now too disorganized to protect itself when its lands were invaded in the late 1200s B.C., perhaps by the SEA PEOPLES. Around 1190 B.C., Anatolian enemies, from perhaps the north, invaded and burned Khattusha to the ground.

CULTURE

Excavations at Khattusha have yielded more than 10,000 CLAY TABLETS. They have helped archaeologists* reconstruct who the Hittites were and how they lived. The tablets have also provided scholars with information on the government, economy, religion, and literature of the Hittites.

Government and Laws. The Hittites were ruled by hereditary kings. Succession passed from father to son, but it could be any son, not necessarily the oldest. The king was in charge of the operation of the government and of all the administrators he appointed. He was also the land's chief priest and presided over the empire's religious events. The king was seen as acting in the place of the gods, protected by them but ruling the land that belonged to the chief god. He was commander in chief of the military and chief diplomat* and was expected to join his troops on the battlefield. The king was also the highest judge in the land, and the most serious crimes were brought before him.

The Hittites had a code of laws that consisted of 200 paragraphs of text on clay tablets. The laws defined crimes as homicides, kidnappings, sorcery, and sexual offenses; set rules for marriages, wages, and prices of goods; and prescribed punishments, including fines, banishment, and death. Two versions of the code have been found, one dating from about 1650 B.C. and the other from between 1350 and 1200 B.C. The later version contains some changes in the punishments assigned to various crimes.

Economy. Most Hittites were small-scale farmers and pastoralists*. They raised oxen, sheep, goats, horses, mules, donkeys, pigs, and dogs.

* **deity** god or goddess

This map shows the extent of the Hittite Empire just before its collapse, around 1200 B.C. Despite geographical barriers such as mountains, which made expansion difficult, the Hittite rulers eventually brought most of Anatolia, as well as areas of north Syria, under their control.

Some animals were used as workers—oxen for plowing, horses to pull chariots, mules to carry loads. Goats and sheep produced milk, which the Hittites consumed directly or made into cheese. They also cultivated wheat, barley, and oats for bread, cake, and cereal and grew fruits and vegetables, including grapes for raisins and wine. Food producers were obliged to give part of what they produced to the government as a tax. Some farmers worked on lands owned by another individual or an institution such as a temple. Captives and slaves could be sent to Hittite villages to work the fields, a major help in a land that often suffered a shortage of workers.

The Hittites were skilled in metalwork, fashioning objects from copper, tin, bronze, and iron. There were a variety of craftspeople: potters, leatherworkers, weavers, blacksmiths, beekeepers, carpenters, sculptors, gold- and silversmiths, and glassmakers. Most of these crafts workers were controlled by the palace or temple.

Religion. Hittite religious traditions drew on those of other peoples. The Hittites had so many deities* that they said they had "a thousand gods." When the Hittites adopted the gods of other peoples, they also adopted the prayers and phrases addressed to these gods in the original languages. The important gods were the storm god TESHUB and the sun goddess Khepat. Hittite myths and legends reflect Hurrian traditions,

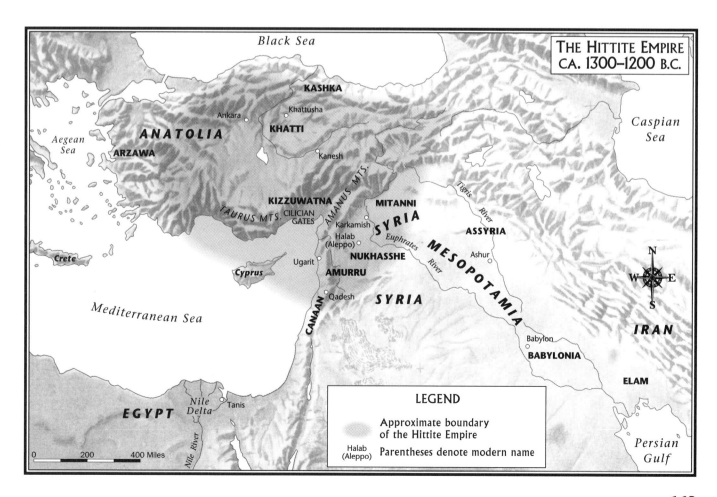

Hittite Queens

Hittite queens had a measure of power and prestige. Pudukhepa, wife of Khattushili III, had an administrative role. She and King Ramses II of Egypt carried on a vigorous correspondence full of mutual respect. Even the gods listened to Pudukhepa. When her husband was ill, she implored the goddess Lelwani to make him well. Lelwani answered the prayers: Khattushili lived to be 70. Lelwani apparently favored Pudukhepa, though. She lived to be 90.

* **cuneiform** world's oldest form of writing, which takes its name from the distinctive wedge-shaped signs pressed into clay tablets

including the Kumarbi Cycle, a three-part story of KUMARBI and his desire for power in heaven and his battle with his son Teshub.

Official festivals occurred monthly, along with seasonal festivals in the spring and fall. The king, queen, or a prince presided. A statue of the deity was offered food and drink, clothing, and entertainment from musicians, acrobats, and athletes.

The Hittites believed in an AFTERLIFE and considered it necessary to follow the proper death and burial rituals for a smooth transition from the world of the living to the world of the dead. The Hittites also believed that their dead ancestors reached from beyond the grave to provide strength to the family. A grandfather was thought to pass his powers to his grandsons. For this reason, from about 1500 B.C. on, grandsons took the name of their grandfathers when reaching the Hittite throne.

Literature and Mythology. Hittite literature was greatly influenced by Mesopotamian traditions. It was from Mesopotamia that the Hittites adopted the cuneiform* writing system, and the achievements of Mesopotamian culture had an impact on Hittite writing. Like others, Hittite kings left often glorified accounts of their achievements. They considered it important to be recognized and remembered as mighty warriors and wise rulers. They also wrote official proclamations that provided instruction on how to organize the state or punish crimes.

The Hittites are better known for their architecture than their art. Their capital at Khattusha contained at least 30 temples, some administrative and royal buildings, and many homes and workshops. The city was surrounded by high walls with towers, seven gates, and a moat. (*See also* **Assyria and the Assyrians; Egypt and the Egyptians; Government; Khatti; Law; Metals and Metalworking; Neo-Hittites; Religion.**)

Holy Land

See *Israel and Judah.*

HORSES

* **domesticated** adapted or tamed for human use

* **cavalry** soldiers who fight on horseback

* **nomadic** referring to people who travel from place to place to find food and pasture

Horses were domesticated* in the ancient Near East around 3000 B.C., much later than SHEEP, GOATS, and CATTLE. Valued primarily for their labor rather than for their meat or hides, horses played an important role in warfare. The armies of many ancient Near Eastern empires contained horse-drawn CHARIOTS and mounted cavalry*. Horses also played a role in transportation and farming and were represented in art and RELIGION.

Horses were probably introduced into the ancient Near East from a region in Central Asia north of the Black and Caspian Seas. By 2000 B.C., horses had been domesticated in Iran, Anatolia, and northern Syria. Horses were not commonly used in Mesopotamia until the 1800s B.C. They did not reach Egypt until about 1600 B.C.

Horses were probably first used as pack animals for carrying goods or pulling wagons. Nomadic* peoples of Central Asia rode horses as early as the third millennium B.C. (years from 3000 to 2001 B.C.), and some groups became accomplished horsemen. Riding horses in the ancient Near East was uncommon until horses were introduced into warfare.

Among the first groups in the Near East to develop horse-drawn chariots for use in warfare were the people of Mitanni, a HURRIAN kingdom in northwestern Mesopotamia, and the HYKSOS. By about 1600 B.C., the use of horse-drawn chariots had spread throughout Mesopotamia and into Egypt. Among the earliest peoples to fight and hunt on horseback were the HITTITES, the Babylonians, and the Assyrians. Such horseback riding led to the development of mounted cavalry.

The use of horses in warfare greatly increased their importance to Near Eastern societies. People developed specialized gear for both riding and harnessing horses to chariots and wagons. Horse breeding and training became important activities, and certain groups became known for their skills as horsemen and breeders. The KASSITES and Phrygians were among the first to breed horses systematically and successfully. They bred horses for specific characteristics, such as size, and kept detailed records of horses and their pedigrees, or ancestry.

Only wealthy people could afford to own and raise horses. Horses became a symbol of status and prestige. In many societies, charioteers were members of the highest social classes. The demand for horses in warfare was high and contributed to a thriving trade. Nubian horses, a particularly large and strong type bred in Nubia (present-day Sudan) and Egypt, were especially in demand by the Assyrians to pull their large chariots.

Horses made suitable gifts for monarchs, and they were often used in ceremonial processions. In both art and religion, horses symbolized such characteristics as power, wealth, and sexuality. The Kassites considered the horse to be a sacred animal, and the Greeks sometimes sacrificed white horses to the gods. Horses also figured in ancient MYTHOLOGY. A creature with the body of a horse and the head, arms, and torso of a human was popular in Assyria, Babylonia, and eventually Greece, where it was called a centaur. In the Hellenistic* period in Babylonia, a leaping winged centaur, with bow and arrow drawn, came to represent the astrological sign Sagittarius. Persian mythology includes a story about a battle between an evil black horse and a good white horse. (*See also* **Animals; Animals, Domestication of; Animals in Art; Transportation and Travel; Wars and Warfare.**)

* **Hellenistic** referring to the Greek-influenced culture of the Mediterranean world and western Asia during the three centuries after the death of Alexander the Great in 323 B.C.

HORUS

Horus (HOHR•uhs) was one of the most important gods of ancient Egypt and was the kingdom's first state god. The name *Horus* meant "the high" or "the distant one." As the god of the sky, Horus was depicted as a hawk, falcon, or a man with a hawk or falcon's head. Early in Egyptian history, Horus became the symbol of divine kingship. He was identified with the king, who was considered a living manifestation of the god.

Horus was the son of OSIRIS, king of the gods, and ISIS, the mother goddess (although some say HATHOR was the mother of Horus). According to

Horus, was one of the most important gods in ancient Egypt. As the sky god, Horus was usually depicted as a hawk or falcon, or as in this relief, a man with a hawk or falcon's head. Egyptians considered their king the living manifestation of Horus, who was also the king of the gods.

an ancient Egyptian legend, Isis secretly raised Horus in the marshes of the Nile Delta, where she used her magical powers to protect him from all kinds of dangers, especially scorpions, snakes, and crocodiles. Isis also protected Horus from his uncle, the god SETH, who had killed Osiris and tried to take over his position as king of the gods. Later Horus challenged Seth to the throne, and after many years of battle and with support from the other gods, Horus finally won. He became king of the gods and of humanity and was considered the reincarnation of Osiris. At that time, Osiris came to symbolize Egypt's dead kings, and Horus was identified with the living king.

During one of Horus's battles with Seth, Horus's eye was ripped out but was healed by the goddess Hathor. The representation of the restored eye, known as the Eye of Horus, became one of the most important religious symbols in ancient Egypt. It was a sign of protection and was often worn as an amulet (object thought to possess magical powers) on necklaces or placed in tombs. Since Horus was the sky god, the Eye of Horus also symbolized the sun. In addition, the Eye of Horus represented all that was complete, good and holy. This included the concept of kingship, the power and strength of the king, and the salvation of the cosmos. (*See also* **Egypt and the Egyptians; Gods and Goddesses; Religion.**)

HOUSES

* **deity** god or goddess

* **eighth millennium B.C.** years from 8000 to 7001 B.C.

See color plate 8, vol. 3.

I n the ancient Near East, the house not only sheltered a family but was also the center of its daily activities. The grand structures of PALACES AND TEMPLES were houses built on a larger scale for kings and deities*. Although much of our knowledge of the ancient past comes from the excavated remains of the more impressive structures, the daily life of the ancient world took place within the humble walls of the houses in which generations of ordinary folk were born, lived, and died.

Mesopotamia. The oldest known houses in MESOPOTAMIA, dating from the eighth millennium B.C.*, have been found at the sites of Qermez Dere and Nemrik in the north. These houses are single round rooms built partly underground. In the western Zagros Mountains, the people who inhabited the sites of Jarmo and Tell Maghzaliyeh built rectangular multiroomed houses around 6750 B.C. By the second half of the fifth millennium B.C. (4500 to 4001 B.C.), two regional styles emerged in Mesopotamia. In the north, at such sites as Tell Arpachiyah, people built a type of round house called a *tholos,* made of pressed mud on a stone foundation. These houses consisted of just one room, sometimes with a rectangular chamber attached at the side. In the south, a typical house had a three-part structure with a single large central room and a row of smaller chambers on either side, such as those found at the sites at Chogha Mami and Tell es-Sawwan.

After 3200 B.C. or so, as large urban centers developed, a new house form consisting of a central unroofed courtyard with rooms on all sides became the standard. This style remained in use for thousands of years and became the basis for later architecture in Mesopotamia. Temples, palaces, and ordinary houses were built around central courtyards. The form was not rigid, however. In crowded urban settings, some houses had rooms on only two or three sides of the courtyard. (City houses were next to each other and shared outer walls.)

The houses of the wealthy included bathrooms and chambers where household goods could be stored. Sometimes they contained a room that served as a shrine to gods and ancestral spirits. Some larger houses had a second story. Houses in Mesopotamia were always made of mud brick—mud, straw, and water mixed and dried in the sun. Sometimes stone was used for foundations. Wood was scarce and expensive. Beams and doors made of wood were considered precious parts of a house and were carefully listed in bills of sale or in wills.

Anatolia. Archaeologists* working in ANATOLIA (present-day Turkey) have uncovered the remains of very early houses dating from between 9000 and 6000 B.C. The remains consist of fieldstone foundations that supported mud-brick walls. The structures varied little in size and stood side by side with no spaces between them. Houses at ÇATAL HÜYÜK were apparently entered by climbing a ladder from the ground to a roof shared by all the structures and then by descending another ladder through a hole in the roof of the individual house. Elsewhere in Anatolia, people built houses with entrances at ground level.

The HITTITES forged an Anatolia-based empire in the middle and late second millennium B.C. (period from 2000 to 1001 B.C.). They, too, built houses of mud brick, perhaps reinforced with wood, on stone foundations. Wooden beams supported flat roofs that were packed with mud and twigs. A typical house might have a forecourt or open space in front, with two rooms behind it. Other rooms could be added as needed. There could be a second story, entered by means of a wooden ladder from the courtyard. A house built on a hillside might contain storage rooms under one part of the building and residential spaces on the upper level. Houses had hearths for fires and areas for bathing.

* **archaeologist** scientist who studies past human cultures, usually by excavating material remains of human activity

Mud brick was used for building houses throughout the ancient Near East. This picture is an aerial view of Rumeilah, al-Ain oasis, a settlement on the Arabian Peninsula, dating from the Iron Age (ca. 1200–500 B.C.). The houses consist of 1 to 4 narrow rooms, measuring from 7 to 13 feet in width and up to 17 feet in length. Many of these rooms had fireplaces.

Houses

Egypt. The ancient Egyptians were more likely to demonstrate wealth and social status in the richness of their family tombs than in their houses. Most houses were fairly small and simple. Still, wealthy people did have larger homes than common folk. One high-ranking official's home had 28 rooms on the ground floor. Such country estates often included gardens as well. The paintings that decorate Egyptian tombs show scenes from the idealized world of these country estates rather than the cramped reality of the ordinary Egyptian's life.

Most Egyptians had simple homes. Because work was done outside, the needs for indoor space were not great. The main elements of a house were a large room for eating and entertaining, small rooms for sleeping and washing, and areas that served as kitchens, workshops, and storage spaces. Small windows, which could be covered with wooden grilles or reed mats to shut out dust, were designed for ventilation and light.

The city of AKHETATEN (dating from the 1300s B.C.) contained a large area of ordinary workers' houses built close to each other on narrow streets. A partly roofed area at the front of the house was used for keeping livestock and for such tasks as grinding grain. Behind it was the main living room. Smaller chambers at the rear of the house were used for sleeping or storage. In some houses, the kitchen was located in a back courtyard, while in others it was on the roof. Some houses had a chamber on the roof for women and young children.

Iran. In the fourth millennium B.C. (years from 4000 to 3001 B.C.) site of Tepe Sialk on the northern Iranian plateau, people built multiroom houses. Erected on stone foundations, the houses had walls made of molded rectangular brick and were decorated with buttresses (stone or brick structures to support the wall) and alcoves. The doors were less than three feet high and narrow; windows looked out onto the streets, which wound through the town separating estates from each other. The interiors were decorated in red or occasionally in white; the dead were buried beneath the floors.

The city of Susa in southwestern Iran was the capital of the Elamite kingdom during the years between about 2000 and 646 B.C. Excavations there have yielded royal and religious buildings, as well as the houses of some important citizens. These were like little palaces organized around a central courtyard. Visitors reached the courtyard by passing through a series of rooms in a zigzag arrangement. The reception room in such a house was a long rectangle, perhaps measuring 80 feet wide and 16 to 17 feet long. It contained a chimney specifically designed for heating, different from the hearths and chimneys used for cooking. This type of heating system was unknown in nearby Mesopotamia.

The Levant. The region that consists of present-day Syria, Lebanon, the West Bank, Jordan, and Israel was one of considerable cultural mixing and ethnic diversity, resulting in many styles of homes. Still, some features were standard from about 3500 to 500 B.C. A typical house was built of sun-dried mud bricks on two or three layers of stone foundation. Floors were usually of packed earth, although some houses had floors plastered with mud or paved with stone. The ceiling and the flat roof were made of wooden beams and reeds packed with mud.

Beware of the Dog

The ancient Mesopotamians believed that by keeping spirits of ill will out of their houses they could protect themselves from disease and misfortune. On the walls of their houses they hung small clay tablets with quotations from mythical works and certain tablets that contained blessings for the owner of the house that were believed to ward off the plague. People also buried small statues they believed had protective qualities under the doors, in the bedrooms, and along the walls of their houses. Some of these figurines were of dogs and bore inscriptions such as, "Don't think it over, [but] bite!" These hidden statues served as a household's spiritual watchdogs.

See color plate 13, vol. 3.

To create more living space in crowded towns, people began building houses with upper levels. In Canaanite houses, these levels were reached by staircases inside an enclosed courtyard, while Israelite houses had ladders leading to the roof or upper levels. The family's private chambers were usually located in the rear of the upper level. Activities such as washing and cooking were performed on the terrace, which was formed by the roof of the lower level. The ground floor of the house might contain shops, craft workshops, and storage rooms.

Houses in the city of Ugarit on the north Syrian coast had rooms of varying sizes. The number of rooms depended on the status and wealth of the owners. All of the houses, however, had small central courtyards, living spaces on the upper floor or floors, and windowless rooms on the ground floor for storage and possibly also to serve as workshops. Nearly every house also contained a family tomb built into the basement and usually entered through its own door. Tombs were within the house because houses were expected to remain in the same family's hands over time.

Israelite sites dating from 1100 to the 580s B.C. feature houses built to a standard rectangular pattern. The entrance led into a large courtyard open to the sky. To the left, part of the courtyard was roofed. Here cooking, baking, washing, and household chores such as spinning and weaving took place. To the right was a storeroom equal in size to the roofed part of the courtyard. A doorway at the rear of the central courtyard, opposite the entrance, led to a room used for dining, sleeping, and entertaining guests. Some of these activities may also have taken place on an upper level, which was reached by a ladder. The residents may have kept livestock in one or more of the ground-floor rooms. (*See also* **Architecture; Bricks; Building Materials; Furnishings and Furniture; Stone.**)

HUMAN FORM IN ART

* **stylized** referring to art style in which figures are portrayed in simplified ways that exaggerate certain features, not realistically

* **millennium** period of 1,000 years; *pl.* millennia

* **relief** sculpture in which material is cut away to show figures raised from the background

In portraying people, artists of the ancient Near East tried to show them realistically but not as individuals. That is, the people depicted in art are recognizably human, but they are idealized or stylized* to emphasize certain features rather than to show characteristics unique to the individual person being portrayed. Artists used the size and posture of a figure and the positioning of other humans in their artworks to make a point about the status of the people they portrayed.

Egyptian and Mesopotamian artists each had standard ways of presenting human figures, which they followed over the course of several millennia*. This style was more rigidly followed in Egypt. In Mesopotamia, where different peoples dominated the region from time to time, there was more variety.

Portraying the Human Body. The Egyptian style used in painting and reliefs* was standard in Egypt for about 3,000 years. People were portrayed with the head in profile and with one entire eye visible. The shoulders and chest faced forward, while the hips, legs, and feet returned to a profile view. When humans are shown facing left, the right hand appears on the left arm and the left hand appears on the right arm. Both feet rest on a baseline.

Wooden writing boards like the one shown here were used throughout Egypt to make sketches. This board from the Eighteenth Dynasty shows the 18-square system used by the Egyptians to draw human figures in correct proportion. The artist has sketched a figure of King Thutmose III. He has also drawn a quail chick and has practiced drawing arms.

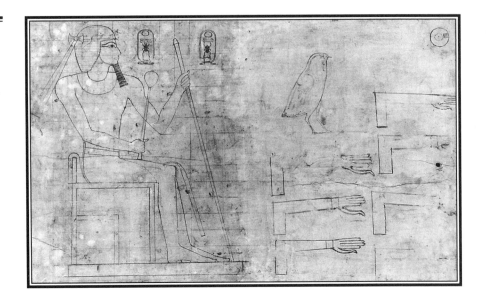

Egyptian artists used mathematical calculations to determine the proportions of the body parts. Egyptians used a grid of 18 squares that stretched from the baseline to the hairline. From the sole of the foot to the ankle was 1 square, from the ankle to the kneecap was 5 squares; and so on. These proportions changed over time, but the general principle of following strict guidelines continued. The combination of profile and frontal views along with the use of standard proportions give Egyptian art its distinctive look.

No evidence of a formal system of proportions exists for Mesopotamian art. Still, many scholars believe that similar guidelines existed. In Mesopotamian art, as in Egyptian, human figures were shown in a combination of profiles and frontal views. These combinations would be impossible to see in real life, but they allowed the artists to make images that conveyed the human body. In early Sumerian art, as in a processional scene from the royal tombs of Ur, the head and legs are in profile but the body from the shoulders to the hips is depicted in a frontal view. The style was followed down to Assyrian times, where it appears in the magnificent scenes of battles and lion hunts that decorated the palaces of Assyrian kings.

In full-body sculpture, also called sculpture in the round, the human figure is three-dimensional and freestanding. The viewer can walk around the statue and see the figure from all sides rather than the two-dimensional view in a painting or relief. Whether the subject was shown standing or sitting on a throne, the front of a statue looked like the front of the person: head facing forward, with the eyes in the front; torso facing forward; and legs and feet pointing straight ahead.

The art of ancient Syria and the Levant* was influenced by that of the Egyptians and Mesopotamians. During the Early Bronze Age (ca. 3000–2200 B.C.), inland Syria borrowed techniques and traditions from Sumer. For example, statues in Syria portray worshipers dressed in Sumerian garments. Sculptures from Phoenicia during the Iron Age (ca. 1200–500 B.C.) showfigures wearing Egyptian costumes and headdresses. Although they

* **Levant** lands bordering the eastern shores of the Mediterranean Sea (present-day Syria, Lebanon, and Israel), the West Bank, and Jordan

* **fresco** method of painting in which color is applied to moist plaster so that it becomes chemically bonded to the plaster as it dries; also, a painting done in this manner

* **propaganda** communcation deliberately shaped or slanted toward a particular viewpoint

* **hierarchy** division of society or an institution into groups with higher and lower ranks

The Medium Makes the Message

The material used to create art had an impact on how humans were portrayed. A temple from the Kassite period of Babylonian history, dating from about 1400 B.C., illustrates this idea. In this temple, reliefs were created by combining a series of bricks, each carved to hold part of the final image. Because the bricks were a standard size, the sizes of different parts of the body were determined by the height of the bricks. The legs of the people shown were made extra long so that the figure filled the height of the wall being decorated. A Persian relief used the same principle of manipulating form to fit a space, albeit in the opposite way. Artists working on this relief shrank some of the figures so they would fit underneath a nook in the wall.

* **indigenous** referring to the original inhabitants of a region

borrowed from other cultures, the people of Syria and the Levant also added their own contributions to the portrayal of the human form.

Unlike the rest of the ancient Near East and perhaps because of their isolation, the Minoan artists of Crete portrayed people engaged in sports or leisure activities rather than in scenes of battle or worship. The Minoans are especially known for their frescoes*. In them, they portrayed the human form in more natural poses than did the Egyptians or Mesopotamians. The sculptures produced by the Minoans were generally miniature rather than life size or large. Two examples from around 1600 B.C. are female figures—snake goddesses—who are seminude and hold snakes in front of them. Later, during the 600s B.C., Crete and Greece were influenced by Egyptian art, and their sculptures assumed the proportions and formal poses of Egyptian figures.

Idealized Forms. Ancient paintings and sculptures typically were not accurate pictures of a particular person. In reality, people were short and tall, fat and thin, ugly and beautiful. However, art at this time was not depicting reality as seen by the human eye. Humans were shown in ideal ways. In Egyptian art, men had broad shoulders and looked muscular, and women were smaller and had a slighter build. The size difference reflected the fact that Egyptian society was male-dominated.

Generally, there was little attempt to depict physical changes that would reveal age. In Egypt, however, artists drew lines on the neck to indicate folds that came with aging. Older people might also be portrayed as fatter, although this could also symbolize wealth. In addition, Egyptians used colors symbolically to indicate age or other attributes. Red skin was used to portray men, and yellow was used for women, a technique borrowed by the Minoans of Crete. Gods were painted in blue or gold.

Throughout the ancient Near East, many paintings, reliefs, and sculptures were ordered made by a ruler. In these cases, art served as propaganda*; it was one way the ruler made clear the power and authority of being king. A statue of GUDEA, leader of the Mesopotamian city of Lagash, emphasizes his shoulders and chest to show his power, and his clasped hands reveal religious devotion and justice. In group scenes, the king was always the largest figure and tended to be in the center. Further, in some cultures, a king shooting a bow was shown with the bowstring passing behind his head so as not to pass in front of his face. As people's status decreased, so did their size. At the lowest rung were enemies, who often were shown lying down or crouching in submission. In the Persian reliefs at the palace at Persepolis, the hierarchy* is obvious. King DARIUS I sits enthroned at the center, larger than life and larger than anyone else. Persian nobles of equal rank are smaller but all the same size. Nonnobles are smaller still.

Some images were styled to emphasize the particular traits of different groups of people. An Egyptian painting from the 1280s B.C. shows four groups of people—those of Egypt, Libya, Nubia, and the Levant. Each is depicted in characteristic clothing and hairstyle. A similar example comes from the palace at Persepolis. Reliefs showing 20 different peoples who lived in the PERSIAN EMPIRE decorate the staircase leading to the audience hall of the palace. Each figure, whether Mede, Scythian, Persian,

Humor

* **tribute** payment made by a smaller or weaker party to a more powerful one, often under the threat of force

or Ionian, appears in indigenous* dress and carries some object associated with his homeland as tribute* to the king. (*See also* **Art, Artisans, and Artists; Bas-Reliefs; Sculpture.**)

HUMOR

Every culture has its own sense of humor—the perception and expression of the ridiculous or amusing. Still, all cultures share some ideas about what is humorous. Humor breaks taboos, referring publicly to things considered private, such as sex and bodily functions. It ridicules people by pointing to truths they prefer to ignore, or it embarrasses people by presenting them in an unfavorable light. Whatever the situation, the object of humor is to provoke laughter and to entertain.

Humor was common in ancient Near Eastern LITERATURE, and many examples of jokes and humorous sayings or episodes have been found in many texts. Numerous surviving examples of ancient Near Eastern humor deal with the breaking of taboos, such as bodily functions. One Babylonian poem scolds a woman: "Why did you break wind and feel mortified? Why did you stink up your boyfriend's wagon like a wild ox?" Sexual behavior is another favorite subject. For instance, a Babylonian poem includes a humorous episode in which a widowed queen must deal with sexual frustration.

Literatures of the ancient Near East are also rich in stories in which someone is outwitted or put to shame by a person less clever or at a disadvantage. One well-preserved Babylonian story, for example, tells of how a poor man named Gimil-Ninurta tricks the mayor of NIPPUR into giving him a fine meal, new clothes, and a pound of gold.

* **piety** faithfulness to beliefs

One type of humor common in Egypt and Mesopotamia involved depicting animals behaving like humans. This humorous Egyptian papyrus from the 1300s B.C. shows several animals engaged in human activities and occupations. An antelope and a lion are playing a board game; a fox is herding deer; and a cat is herding poultry.

Social satire, a type of humor in which the humorist makes fun of certain professions or classes of people, was also common. Just as people today tell jokes about lawyers, an Egyptian joke makes fun of a potter, remarking that although he is covered with earth, he is still among the living. In a Sumerian satire, a priest is ridiculed for his piety*. When his boat sinks, he hopes that the river god will enjoy his cargo. When he slips and falls, he is not sure that he should get up because it was the will of the gods that he should fall.

They also produced witty sayings and proverbs. One example of Babylonian wisdom offers this advice: "Do not buy an ox in the springtime, do

not choose a girl on a holiday. Even a bad ox will look good in that season, a bad girl just wears good clothes for the occasion."

A type of humor that was common in Mesopotamia and Egypt centered on animals behaving like humans. Various human weaknesses are revealed in humorous stories about conceited dogs and wily foxes. This type of humor also was portrayed in art. For example, a series of Egyptian drawings show a group of mice asking a cat pharaoh* for peace and an army of mice laying siege* to a cat fortress.

Ancient Near Eastern literature also contains comic characters usually found in folklore around the world, including the trickster, the wise fool, the country bumpkin, and the deceived lover, whose actions and failings reflect the human condition. (*See also* **Animals in Art; Poetry.**)

* **pharaoh** king of ancient Egypt
* **siege** long and persistent effort to force a surrender by surrounding a fortress or city with armed troops, cutting it off from supplies and aid

HUNTING

* **domesticate** to adapt or tame for human use
* **anthropologist** scientist who studies human cultures

People throughout the ancient Near East hunted animals, but the role of hunting changed over time. Before people developed AGRICULTURE and domesticated* animals, hunting was a survival strategy, and wild game was a food resource. While people continued to hunt for food after adopting food-producing strategies, hunting took on another role. People also hunted for sport, and in several cultures, the royal hunt was used to enhance the status of the king.

Anthropologists* use the term *hunter-gatherers* to describe people who live by hunting wild game, FISHING, and gathering wild food such as fruits and seeds rather than by growing crops or herding animals. Before the beginnings of controlled food production, all people were hunter-gatherers. In prehistoric Egypt, for example, people living along the NILE RIVER hunted hippopotamus, giraffe, antelope, and buffalo and also fished and gathered turtles and shellfish.

People eventually began to domesticate some of the animals they had once hunted, such as SHEEP, GOATS, and CATTLE. Other game animals such as deer and antelope, however, were never domesticated. The dog and the cat, two domesticated animals, became the hunter's helper. An Egyptian stone carving dating from around 2400 B.C. shows a hunter pursuing several antelope with the help of three trained dogs. Hunters sometimes used a cat to make geese and other fowl fly up out of the reeds so that they could more easily be killed or captured.

After the rise of agriculture and the ensuing growth of urban civilization, hunting became a pastime instead of a necessity, at least for some people. Egyptian tomb paintings often show noble families on fishing and bird-hunting excursions in the reed marshes along the Nile.

The kings of Assyria in northern MESOPOTAMIA liked to be portrayed as strong, brave, and skillful hunters who were victorious over the fiercest beasts. King Tiglath-pileser I, for example, claimed to have slayed 4 wild bulls, 10 elephants, and 920 LIONS. A successful hunt meant that the king enjoyed divine favor. It also demonstrated the ruler's personal qualities and symbolized the protection he gave his people. Assyrian royal hunts were carefully managed, however. Often, captured wild lions were released into royal game parks so that the king could kill them under controlled conditions. The practice of having royal parks continued in the PERSIAN EMPIRE.

Hurrians

In ancient times, hunting was a recreational sport as well as a food-producing strategy. Wild game was an important food source throughout the ancient Near East. This Assyrian relief from a palace at Nineveh, dating from the 600s B.C., shows a man trapping deer in a net.

* **bas-relief** kind of sculpture in which material is cut away to leave figures projecting slightly from the background

Assyrian kings decorated their palaces with some breathtaking bas-reliefs* of hunting scenes. A relief from the palace of Ashurnasirpal II at Nimrud shows the king hunting bulls and lions from a chariot. The most vivid hunting scenes are carved into the walls of the palace of King Ashurbanipal at Nineveh. One scene shows the king stabbing a lion standing on its hind legs. This motif was adopted as the royal SEAL of Assyrian kings.

* **scribe** person of a learned class who served as a writer, editor, or teacher

Images of these hunts were often spectacular. Wall paintings show Amenhotep III of Egypt and his court hunting antelope from chariots, with a royal scribe* keeping count of the king's kills. Amenhotep also slew more dangerous game, such as wild bulls and lions. (*See also* **Animals; Animals in Art.**)

HURRIANS

* **Fertile Crescent** semicircular area of rich farmland that stretches from Egypt across the southeastern coast of the Mediterranean Sea down to the Persian Gulf

* **third millennium** B.C. years from 3000 to 2001 B.C.

The Hurrians (HUR•ee•uhnz) were one of many peoples who migrated to the Fertile Crescent* from the surrounding hills. Sometime before the end of the third millennium B.C.*, Hurrians arrived in northeastern MESOPOTAMIA. From there, they worked their way westward into SYRIA, establishing a number of kingdoms, including the kingdom of Mitanni, which grew into a major power in the ancient Near East during the 1400s and 1300s B.C. Hurrian culture, which had absorbed many Mesopotamian elements, was also a major influence on the literature and religion of the HITTITES, a people who inhabited north Syria and ANATOLIA (present-day Turkey).

Origins and Migrations. The language of the Hurrians suggests that they originated in eastern Anatolia or a region near the Zagros Mountains of northwestern IRAN. This is because the Hurrian language is most closely related to the language of URARTU, a kingdom that historians know arose in eastern Anatolia.

Hurrians in the Hebrew Bible

Does the Hebrew Bible record inter-actions between Hurrians and He-brews? Many American scholars believe that a people called the Horites—who appear in the book of Genesis—were Hurrians. Although some European scholars disagree, those who support the identification of the Horites with the Hurrians point out that the Hurrians are known to have been numerous along the Syrian coast. They may well have moved south from there into regions where they would have come in contact with the Hebrew population.

* **dynasty** succession of rulers from the same family or group

* **archaeologist** scientist who studies past human cultures, usually by excavating material remains of human activity

The Hurrians established a number of king-doms in Mesopotamia and Syria, including the powerful kingdom of Mitanni. This bronze lion said to be from the city of Urkesh dates from about 2000 B.C. It contains an inscription in the Hurrian language.

Historians believe that the migration of Hurrians occurred over a long period of time. From about 3000 B.C. onward, small groups of Hurrians left their homeland and migrated westward. By around 2200 B.C., small Hurrian states existed along and between the upper reaches of the Tigris River and the Euphrates River in northern Mesopotamia.

By around 1700 B.C., the Hurrians had expanded westward into northern Syria. In fact, many texts in their language have been found at ALALAKH, located just north of the present-day Syrian border along the Mediterranean Sea. However, the Hurrian heartland was in northern Mesopotamia. It was in this region that the Hurrians established the powerful kingdom of Mitanni.

The Kingdom of Mitanni. The oldest known references to Mitanni are found in Egyptian texts dating from the late 1500s B.C. These texts also contain the names of the kings of Mitanni, but only after the early 1400s B.C. However, these royal names are not Hurrian. They are related to the Indo-European language-speaking groups that conquered northern India in the second millennium B.C. (years from 2000 to 1001 B.C.). Consequently, some historians believe that Indo-Europeans, along with groups of Hurri-ans, entered northern Mesopotamia from the east and founded Mitanni. An Indo-European dynasty* ruled the kingdom, although the majority of the population was Hurrian, and Hurrian was the spoken language.

Mitanni became the dominant power in northern Syria after the Hit-tites lost control of the area around 1500 B.C. In the mid-1400s B.C., Mi-tanni came into conflict with Egypt, which also wanted to expand its rule into Syria. Under King Saushtatar, Mitanni not only survived this conflict but also acquired new territory on the borders of the Hittite empire. Saushtatar ruled from the capital city, Washukkani, which modern ar-chaeologists* have not yet located.

During the 1400s B.C., Mitanni reached the height of its power. By around 1420 B.C., the Mitanni kingdom had grown, stretching from the Mediterranean Sea to northern Iran. Shortly thereafter, Mitanni estab-lished peaceful relations with Egypt. During this time, as a gesture of peace, Mitanni kings sent their daughters to become the wives of the rulers of Egypt.

During the reign of King Tushratta in the 1300s B.C., Mitanni began to lose power. The Hittite empire had emerged as a serious threat, and it con-quered Washukkani. By around 1350 B.C., after the Hittites had seized much Mitanni territory, one of Tushratta's sons killed him in disgust. Fol-lowing attacks by the Assyrians in its major cities, Mitanni became part of the Hittite empire.

Hittite control over Mitanni did not last long. Assyria, which referred to the Hurrian kingdom as Khanigalbat, had become stronger and more aggressive, and eventually the Assyrian empire overwhelmed the last remnants of the former kingdom of Mitanni. The Assyrians dispersed the Hurrian population, settling new groups in the region, and the Hurrian language gradually disappeared. However, Hurrian culture greatly influ-enced those parts of the Hittite empire that remained free from Assyrian rule. The Hittites worshiped the Hurrian storm god TESHUB and adopted the Hurrian literary work called the Kumarbi Cycle into their mythology.

Hyksos

HYKSOS

* **nomadic** referring to people who travel from place to place to find food and pasture

* **Levant** lands bordering the eastern shores of the Mediterranean Sea (present-day Syria, Lebanon, and Israel), the West Bank, and Jordan

* **archaeological** referring to the study of past human cultures, usually by excavating material remains of human activity

* **indigenous** referring to the original inhabitants of a region

* **delta** fan-shaped, lowland plain formed of soil deposited by a river

* **sinew** tough cord of tissue that attaches muscles to bones

* **pharaoh** king of ancient Egypt

* **tribute** payment made by a smaller or weaker party to a more powerful one, often under the threat of force

The Hyksos (HIK•sahs) were a nomadic* group from west Asia who ruled Egypt from about 1630 to 1523 B.C. The word *Hyksos* is the Greek pronunciation of an Egyptian term meaning "shepherd kings." The exact origins of the Hyksos are not known. Some historians think they were HURRIANS who came from SYRIA, while others believe they were AMORITES who came from the Levant*.

The Hyksos Takeover. Most of the information on the Hyksos takeover of Egypt comes from writings of the Egyptian priest Manetho, who lived in the 200s B.C., and from archaeological* excavations. According to Manetho, the Hyksos invaded Egypt from the east, destroying cities and temples and oppressing the population. In reality, the Hyksos takeover may have been more gradual and less forceful than Manetho suggested. Archaeological evidence indicates that there was a large presence of immigrants from west Asia in the eastern Nile Delta as early as 2000 B.C. and that the number of immigrants increased over the next 300 years.

At first, the west Asian immigrants appear to have peacefully coexisted with the indigenous* Egyptians. Egypt was already ethnically diverse, and the immigrants were probably accepted into Egyptian society without prejudice. However, when Egypt's central government weakened around 1700 B.C., some of the west Asian immigrants may have decided to take advantage of the situation and seize control of power. First, they created a series of small states in the eastern delta*, with a center of power at the city of Avaris, which is the only known Hyksos city in Egypt. Then around 1640 B.C., they captured the city of MEMPHIS. This event, according to Manetho, marked the beginning of the Fifteenth Dynasty, which consisted of a succession of six Hyksos kings who ruled Egypt for almost a century.

It is not surprising that the Hyksos were able to seize control of Egypt. They had superior weapons and methods of warfare that gave them a further advantage over the Egyptians, who were already weakened by internal problems. Egyptian soldiers used wooden bows and arrows with stone arrowheads. They also fought nearly naked and on foot. In contrast, the Hyksos used compound bows made of wood, horn, and sinew* that could send their bronze-tipped arrows twice as far as the Egyptian arrows. They also wore armor and leather helmets for protection, and they fought from horse-drawn CHARIOTS. In short, the Egyptians were no match for the Hyksos.

Once in power, the Hyksos kings presented themselves as traditional Egyptian pharaohs*. They used Egyptian titles in their royal court, adopted the Egyptian system of writing called HIEROGLYPHICS, and retained the general structure of the Egyptian government. However, unlike traditional Egyptian pharaohs, the Hyksos ruled most of Egypt outside the delta only indirectly. In those regions, the Hyksos allowed the local kings to remain in power as long as they were willing to acknowledge the authority of, and pay tribute* to, the Hyksos kings.

Driving Out the Hyksos. Although the local kings of THEBES in central Egypt grudgingly acknowledged the authority of the Hyksos rulers, there was growing resentment toward them. Around 1575 B.C., King Seqenenre II of Thebes rebelled against the Hyksos. Seqenenre did not succeed in his rebellion and was killed in battle. His successor Kamose, continued the fight. He eventually recaptured much of the Nile Valley. Later Kamose tried to capture the Hyksos capital of Avaris but failed.

King Kamose was succeeded by his younger brother AHMOSE, the first king of the Eighteenth Dynasty and the founder of the New Kingdom. Because Ahmose had adopted Hyksos weapons and methods of warfare, he was able to capture Memphis, which completed the recapture of the Nile Valley. Around 1530 B.C., Ahmose captured Avaris and pursued the Hyksos out of Egypt and into the Levant, where the Hyksos had a stronghold. Eventually, the Hyksos surrendered, and the Levant came under Egyptian rule.

Although the Hyksos were driven out of Egypt after ruling for a relatively short time, they had a lasting impact on Egypt. As a result of Hyksos influence, the Egyptians created a permanent professional army and improved their military technology, allowing them to create their empire. The Hyksos also had an influence on Egyptian music, language, and religion. (*See also* **Egypt and the Egyptians; Weapons and Armor.**)

HYMNS

* **deity** god or goddess

* **piety** faithfulness to beliefs

* **pharaoh** king of ancient Egypt

Hymns are poems addressed to deities* or rulers that praise, celebrate, make requests, and give thanks. Hymns are found in the LITERATURE of many ancient Near Eastern cultures, including those of the Sumerians, Egyptians, Israelites, and Greeks.

Of the surviving 130 royal hymns from ancient Sumer, some address the gods, seeking their protection and blessings for the king. Others praise the king, who is presented as a god and an ideal human being. The hymns, which were recited in court, praise the king's power and authority, beauty and strength, wisdom and piety*, and justice and achievements. Among the finest Sumerian hymns are those written for SHULGI, a great king of ancient UR.

Ancient Egyptian literature contains several hymns, including those to OSIRIS, prayers of the goddess ISIS for her baby, hymns to the gods AMUN and Ra, and those of the pharaoh* AKHENATEN. Many Egyptian hymns are prayers of thanksgiving, such as one in which the artist Nebre thanks Amun for healing his son. The Egyptian BOOK OF THE DEAD contains hymns of mourning. Ancient Egyptian hymns were sung or recited during sacred ceremonies, and many of these works have been preserved.

Hymns were also common in ancient Israel and Greece. The largest collection of hymns from ancient Israel is found in the Hebrew BIBLE in the book of Psalms. The book contains numerous songs of praise, addressed to God. Greek hymns begin with the name of the deity to whom the work is addressed. They were important in religious ceremonies and as an accompaniment to dancers. One of the oldest surviving Greek hymns is addressed to the god Dionysus by his women followers. (*See also* **Prayer.**)

Iconography

ICONOGRAPHY

* **deity** god or goddess

Iconography is the use of imagery or traditional illustrations selected to convey the meaning in a work of art. Easily recognizable visual images of the gods and rulers served to help people recall the powers of a deity* or king. People of the ancient Near East believed that gods and goddesses, who had created societies, had ultimate power over them, and if displeased, could destroy them. Kings were seen as the gods' chosen representatives. The portrayal of deities and kings in art reminded

Symbols were the most striking element in Mesopotamian religious art. Simple images, such as celestial events, animals, and tools of the land, were used as direct substitutes for individual gods and goddesses. Occasionally, a single deity might have more than one such symbol, or in rare instances, a particular symbol might stand for more than one deity.

184

people of their role and helped keep them united in their beliefs and purposes as a society.

The ancient Mesopotamians and Egyptians often used animal imagery to symbolize their gods. For instance, during the Akkadian Empire (ca. 2350-2193 B.C.), the goddess ISHTAR was portrayed as a lion. Egyptian iconography consisted of a mixed form in which gods typically were depicted with an animal head on a human body. In the Egyptian Late

PRINCIPAL SYMBOLS OF MESOPOTAMIAN DEITIES

	Symbol	Deity represented*
1	solar disk	Utu/Shamash, sun god
2	winged disk	Utu/Shamash, sun god; Ashur, state god of Assyria; Ninurta, war god
3	cross	Possibly Utu/Shamash, sun god
4	crescent	Nanna/Sin, moon god
5	eight-pointed star	Inanna/Ishtar, goddess of passion, love, and war
6	seven dots or seven stars	Sebittu, the seven gods
7	lightning	Symbol of storm gods throughout the ancient Near East
8	triangular-headed spade	Marduk, state god of Babylonia
9	plough	Ningirsu, city god of Girsu
10	barley stalk	Shala, goddess of agriculture
11	stylized tree	Possibly a general symbol of fertility
12	vase with streams	Possibly a general symbol of fertility; Enki/Ea, wisdom god; Marduk, state god of Babylonia
13	horned cap	Anu, sky god; Ashur, state god of Assyria
14	stylus	Nabu, scribal god
15	lamp	Nusku, fire god
16	"omega"	Associated with the mother or birth goddesses; Inanna/Ishtar, goddess of passion, love, and war
17	lozenge	Possibly Inanna/Ishtar, goddess of passion, love, and war
18	bull	Associated with storm gods
19	lion	Inanna/Ishtar, goddess of passion, love, and war; Ninlil, goddess of Nippur
20	horse	Utu/Shamash, sun god
21	horse head	(unknown)
22	dog	Gula, goddess of healing
23	turtle	Enki/Ea, wisdom god
24	scorpion	Ishkhara, goddess of love and healing
25	horned snake	Ishtaran, city god of Der; Ningishzida, god of the underworld
26	striding bird	Papsukkal, messenger god
27	bird with back-turned head	Harbe, Kassite god
28	bird on high perch	Shuqamura and Shumalia, twin gods
29	bird on low perch	Ninurta, war god
30	(snake-)dragon	(unknown)
31	lion-dragon	Ishkur/Adad, storm god
32	goat-fish	Enki/Ea, wisdom god
33	double lion-headed scepter	Nergal, god of the underworld
34	lion-headed staff	Nergal, god of the underworld
35	eagle-headed staff	Zababa, patron god of Kish
36	ram-headed staff	Enki/Ea, wisdom god
37	crook	Amurru, god of the nomads
38	ring-post with streamer	Inanna/Ishtar, goddess of passion, love, and war
39	ring-post without streamer	Possibly Enki/Ea, wisdom god
40	ring-post	Possibly Utu/Shamash, sun god

*"/" separates Sumerian and Babylonian names of deities

Period (664-332 B.C.), the gods could be represented by more than one animal image. For example, the goddess HATHOR was shown as a cow, a snake, a lioness, or as woman with a cow's head. This way of displaying their gods occurs as early as 3000 B.C.

Ancient people sometimes portrayed their gods in human form. When shown as humans, the gods were usually portrayed with an object that came to symbolize the deities themselves. For example, the HITTITES of ANATOLIA portrayed the storm god holding a lightning bolt and the moon god with a crescent moon on his hat. In ancient Mesopotamia, the sun god might have rays coming out of his upper body and be shown rising between mountains. During and after the Akkadian Empire, Mesopotamian gods were commonly shown wearing a headdress with sets of horns—the greater the number of sets, the more major the god. When appearing in a scene with people, gods in human form were distinguished by their larger size.

Other ancient peoples also used symbols for their gods. The Persians depicted their chief god, AHURA MAZDA, as a human within a winged disc. Unusual in the ancient world was the Israelite god YAHWEH, who was not depicted by his worshipers. A passage in the Hebrew Bible (Deuteronomy 4:12, 15) says that Yahweh has no form, no shape that can be shown. Other Near Eastern cultures also had gods that were not symbolized.

Imagery and symbols were also used to represent rulers in the ancient Near East. In Mesopotamia, the king could be recognized in art by the garments, headgear, and weapons he was wearing. To the ancient Mesopotamians, these served more as identifiers than did actual physical features. Hittite kings in art were also recognizable through their dress.

Other figures appear in Near Eastern art, from those of nobility and high ranking officials to conquered peoples. Such people were portrayed in ways that reflected their situations. For example, captives were shown with their arms bound. The ancient people who viewed such art would have been able to identify who or which group the figures represented based on how they were portrayed. (*See also* **Gods and Goddesses; Human Form in Art.**)

INCENSE

Incense is a substance made from the sap, wood, bark, roots, or fruit of certain plants. When burned, it releases a fragrant or spicy odor. In the ancient Near East, incense was used for religious purposes and was an important article of trade. Two of the most important forms of incense were frankincense and myrrh*.

The ancient Babylonians burned incense while offering prayers or sacrifices and consulting oracles*. They also believed that they could read the future from the smoke rising from burning incense. Incense was also important to the Egyptians, who used it daily in rituals to their gods. The ancient Israelites believed that incense had miraculous powers, and they made daily OFFERINGS of incense to please their god YAHWEH and to protect the priests. Only priests could offer incense to Yahweh, and its use for nonreligious purposes was forbidden. The Greeks burned incense as an offering to the gods and for protection against DEMONS.

Incense also played an important role in funerary rites and was used in embalming* dead bodies. The use of incense at funerals may have

* **frankincense and myrrh** fragrant tree resins used to make incense and perfumes

* **oracle** priest or priestess through whom a god is believed to speak; also, the location (such as a shrine) where such utterances are made

* **embalming** treating a corpse with oils or chemicals to preserve it or slow down the process of decay, usually after body fluids have been removed

arisen as a way of masking the disagreeable odors of decomposing bodies. Still, it also had religious signifance. Burning incense was believed to purify the dead, and the rising smoke represented the soul of the deceased rising to heaven.

Ancient peoples also believed that incense had divine powers. They used it as a medicine to cure diseases and heal wounds. People also used certain kinds of incense as PERFUME, believing that it made them divinely beautiful or transferred them to a higher level of life.

Incense was also an important item in Near Eastern trade. The demand for frankincense and myrrh, which came primarily from southern Arabia, encouraged trade between that region and the kingdoms in the FERTILE CRESCENT. Trade routes also ran between Egypt and Syria and other regions in the Near East. So much wealth was involved in the incense trade that it often had political consequences. The Assyrians and Babylonians expanded their empires, in part, to gain greater control over the incense trade. (*See also* **Cosmetics; Death and Burial; Economy and Trade; Oracles and Prophecy; Rituals and Sacrifice.**)

INDO-EUROPEAN LANGUAGES

Indo-European languages are today the most widely spoken family of languages in the world. In use from western Europe through Central Asia to India, they are also the dominant languages in the Americas and in Australia. While most of the languages of the ancient Near East were HAMITIC LANGUAGES, a few of the languages of that region belonged to the Indo-European language family.

The idea that certain languages were all part of an Indo-European language family first took shape around A.D. 1800. Scholars at that time began to recognize similarities between Greek, Sanskrit (an ancient language of India), Latin (the language of the Romans), and a number of other languages. The research of linguists, or language experts, was later combined with archaeological* evidence, allowing scholars to trace the development of Indo-European languages as well as the relationships among them.

The Indo-European language family includes ten main language groups, or subfamilies, two of which are no longer spoken. The groups are Anatolian, Indo-Iranian, Greek, Italic, Germanic, Armenian, Tocharian, Celtic, Balto-Slavic, and Albanian. Indo-European languages share common roots for several words, certain grammatical forms, and patterns of sounds. Yet the languages also have many differences that reflect their individual development, which occurred over thousands of years.

Development of Indo-European Languages. All ancient and modern Indo-European languages are thought to have descended from a common parent language, sometimes called Proto-Indo-European. The origins of that language are unknown, but scholars are quite certain that it began to divide into several distinct languages as early as the 4500s B.C.

The home of the Indo-European languages is thought to be in the region north of the Black Sea. By the third millennium B.C.*, people from that region had begun to migrate, spreading different Indo-European dialects* throughout Europe and Asia. Soon these dialects developed into distinct languages, many of which have been preserved in written records.

* **archaeological** referring to the study of past human cultures, usually by excavating material remains of human activity

* **third millennium** B.C. years from 3000 to 2001 B.C.

* **dialect** regional form of a spoken language with distinct pronunciation, vocabulary, and grammar

Inheritance

Mystery of an Extinct Language

Two Indo-European language groups have become extinct: Anatolian and Tocharian. While scholars know quite a bit about Anatolian and the people who spoke it, Tocharian is more of a mystery. Known only since A.D. 1908, the Tocharian languages were an isolated group of Indo-European dialects once spoken in remote areas of northwestern China. The Tocharian dialects were strikingly different from the Iranian languages spoken by people in surrounding regions. Instead, they showed similarities to some of the Indo-European dialects spoken in Europe. Scholars do not know how Tocharian came to this remote area nor how it disappeared. Some experts suggest that the Tocharians migrated to China from Europe as early as the third millenium B.C. Until more evidence is found, however, the origin and disappearance of the Tocharian language group will remain a mystery.

Indo-European Languages of the Near East. The majority of Indo-European languages developed in areas outside the Near East, primarily in Europe. For example, the Italic subfamily today includes the so-called Romance languages*. The Germanic languages include German, English, and the languages of Scandinavia, while the Balto-Slavic subfamily consists of Russian, Polish, and other languages of eastern Europe and areas near the Baltic Sea. Only three subfamilies of Indo-European languages were spoken in the ancient Near East: Anatolian, Indo-Iranian, and Greek.

The Anatolian subfamily of languages, now extinct, was one of the oldest Indo-European language groups in the ancient Near East. These languages were spoken in ANATOLIA and northern SYRIA as early as the second millennium B.C.* The best-known Anatolian language is Hittite, which was spoken in the northwestern parts of the region. Hittite was written in a CUNEIFORM system adapted from that used in MESOPOTAMIA. Hittite texts date from the 1600s to about 1200 B.C.

Another Anatolian language, Luwian, was spoken in southern Anatolia and northern Syria. Forms of this language were written in both cuneiform and a HIEROGLYPHICS system. Scholars believe that the Luwians borrowed cuneiform from Mesopotamia but that they created the hieroglyphic system on their own. Surviving texts in the Luwian language date from between 1400 and 200 B.C.

Closely related to Hittite and Luwian is Palaic, a language spoken in areas north of the Hittite heartland in central Anatolia. This language was extinct by the 1300s B.C. Other ancient Anatolian languages—all spoken in western Anatolia—include Lydian, Lycian, Pisidian, Sidetic, and Carian. Little is known of these languages except that they were written in a script closely related to Greek.

A second group of Indo-European languages is Indo-Iranian. This group contains two main subgroups. The first, Indo-Aryan, which includes Sanskrit, was spoken in India, Pakistan, and Iran. The second subgroup are the Iranian languages, including Avestan, the sacred language of Zoroastrians, spoken in Iran as early as the first millennium B.C. (years from 1000 to 1 B.C.), and Old Persian, the language of the PERSIAN EMPIRE.

Historically, Greek is one of the oldest and most important Indo-European languages. Various forms of Greek have been spoken in Greece from at least the 1600s B.C. One of the oldest known forms of ancient Greek was Mycenaean, which dates from about the 1200s B.C. Later dialects—Arcadian, Aeolic, Doric, and Ionic—were spoken on the Greek mainland, on the islands of the AEGEAN SEA, and in western Anatolia.

By the 400s B.C., a dialect known as Attic became popular among the Greeks. During the Hellenistic* period, the Attic Greek language and culture spread far beyond the borders of Greece. Modern Greek is descended from earlier forms of the language. Meanwhile, ancient Greek remains an important language for learning about the ancient world. (*See also* **Ethnic and Language Groups; Languages; Semitic Languages; Sumerian Languages; Writing.**)

Inheritance

See *Family and Social Life; Law.*

INDEX

Index

Index

Index

Index

Index

Djoser, **2:40**
dynasties of, 2:44–45
Hatshepsut, **2:152**
Hyksos, **2:182–83**
Khufu, **3:33–34**
king lists, 3:35
Necho II, **3:132–33**
Nefertiti, **3:133–34**
Nitokris, **3:141**
Pharaohs, **3:178–81**
Piye, 3:147
Ptolemy I, **4:19–20**
queens, 4:24
Ramses II, **4:26–27**
Ramses III, **4:27**
Sety I, **4:76–77**
Taharqa, **4:114–15**
Thutmose III, **4:124**
Tutankhamen, **4:133–34**
El, **2:66**, 2:130
in Baal cycle, 1:99
Canaanite worship of, 1:139
Elam and the Elamites, **2:66–70**, 2:81
archaeological discoveries of, 1:63
in Babylonian history, 1:105
dynasties of, 2:45
family and social life of, 2:88
feasts and festivals of, 2:92–93
geography of, 2:66–67
gods and goddesses of, 2:67, 130, 4:33
history of, 2:67–70, 3:6
language of, 2:34, 36, 3:49
priests of, 4:14
Proto-Elamites, 2:67
religions of, 2:67, 3:7–8, 4:33
Susiana and, 4:108
women's role in, 2:67, 4:164
Elba, **2:47**
Elburz Mountains, 2:120
Ellil. *See* Enlil
Empire(s)
armies of, 1:73–75
communication within, 2:11
idea of, 1:22
Employment. *See* Work
Enkheduanna, 1:21, 4:138 *(illus.)*
Enki, 1:110, 2:14
Enki and Ninmakh, 1:110, 3:125
Enlil, **2:70**, 2:127
in Babylonian pantheon, 1:110
in creation myths, 2:14
cult of, at Nippur, 3:140
Enmerkar, 2:19–20, 4:5
Enmerkar and the Lord of Aratta, 2:75
Entertainment, **2:70–73**. *See also*
Feasts and festivals
banquets, 2:72
dance, **2:24–26**, 71–72
feasts and festivals, **2:91–94**
games, **2:110–12**
Kumarbi Cycle for, 3:39
music and musical instruments, **2:71–72**, **3:119–21**
sports, 2:72–73
storytelling, 2:73

Enuma Anu Enlil, 1:94, 96, 3:62, 4:96
Enuma Elish, 1:48, 110, 2:14, 3:71, 125
Envelopes, clay, 2:1, 4:28, 66
Environmental change, **2:73–75**
Ephermerides, 1:96
Epic literature, **2:75–76**
Aqhat, Epic of, 1:138, 3:126
Atrakhasis, Epic of, 1:48, 110, 3:125
in Babylonia, 1:111
Curse of Akkad, 1:18
Ea in, 2:45
Enuma Elish, 1:48, 110, 2:14, 3:71, 125
Gilgamesh, Epic of, **2:122–23**
Gilgamesh and Khuwawa, 4:5
Iliad, 3:121
Keret, Epic of, 1:138, 3:126
Odyssey, 3:121
poetry as, 4:5
Epic of Aqhat, 1:138, 3:126
Epic of Atrakhasis, 1:48, 110, 2:97, 3:125
Epic of Creation. See Enuma Elish
Epic of Gilgamesh, **2:122–23**
Anu in, 1:48
dreams in, 2:41
Great Flood in, 2:97
Ishtar myth in, 3:12
netherworld in, 1:5
title of, 3:59
walls of Uruk in, 1:175
Epic of Keret, 1:138, 3:126
Eratosthenes, 3:70
Ereshkigal, queen of the dead, 1:5
Eridu, **2:76–77**
Erra, 1:110–11
Erra Myth, 1:110, 3:125
Esarhaddon, **2:77**
and Ashurbanipal, 1:82
death omen of, 1:94–95
reign of, 1:90
Eshnunna, **2:77–78**
divorce in, 2:39
laws of, 3:52, 73 *(illus.)*
Palace of Governors, 1:65, 3:158–59
Eshtan, 2:129
Etana, 1:119
Ethiopia. *See* Nubia and the Nubians
Ethiopian language, 4:73
Ethnic and language groups, **2:78–84**
Anatolian, 2:82
Arabian, 2:83
Canaanite, 2:82–83
Egyptian, 2:65, 80–81
Iranian, 2:81–82
Mesopotamian, 2:78–79
Ethnoarchaeology, 1:59
Eunuchs, **2:84**
Euphrates River, **2:84–85**, 2:118, 4:38–39
changes in, 2:74, 4:137
flooding of, 1:9, 2:99, 4:153–54
harbors on, 2:150
and irrigation, 3:9
Mesopotamian dependence on, 2:98

shipping routes on, 4:79
trade routes along, 4:128
Evans, Sir Arthur, 2:17, 3:39, 109
"evil eye," 4:160
Excavations. *See* Archaeological sites
Exorcisms, 1:5
Extispicy, 3:153–54
Eye of Horus, 2:172
Ezra, 3:26

F

Fabrics. *See* Textiles
Faience, **2:85–86** *(illus.)*
Faiyûm Depression, 2:57, 3:137–38
Falcons in art, 1:118
Family and social life, **2:86–89**
of Anatolians, 2:87
of Babylonians, 1:108–9
burial customs, 1:127
of Chaldeans, 1:158
childbirth, **1:162**
children, **1:163–64**
dance, **2:24–26**
divorce, **2:39–40**
economy's effect on, 2:49
of Egyptians, 2:65–66, 86–87, 89
of Elamites, 2:88
entertainment, **2:70–73**
feasts and festivals, **2:91–94**
games, **2:110–12**
gender and sex roles in, **2:116–18**
gradual disasters and, 2:39
of Hittites, 2:87
houses, **2:172–75**
influence of cities on, 1:171
inheritance and, 2:88–89
Iranian, 2:88
of Israelites, 2:87–89
legal rights in, 3:51
Lycian, 2:87
marriage, **3:74–75**
merchant families, 3:92
Mesopotamian, 2:86, 89
naming, 3:128
nomadic, 3:145
of peasants, 3:169
of Persians, 2:88
polygamy, **4:5–6**
pregnancy, **4:12–13**
women, role of, **4:161–64**
Famine, **2:90–91**, 3:138
Farmer's Almanac, 1:10
Farming. *See also* Agriculture; Gardens
animal husbandry with, 1:43
by Aramaeans, 1:52
and canals, 1:140–41
cattle, **1:150**
in Crete, 2:15
as economic foundation, 2:47
effect of, on climate, 2:6
in Egypt, 1:155
and irrigation, **3:8–11**
of Israelites, 2:157
in the Levant, 1:155

198

Index

Index

location of, 2:170 (map)
Luwians and culture of, 3:62
magic and, 3:68, 69
marriage among, 3:74 (illus.), 75
military force of, 4:152–53
Mitanni and, 2:181
music and dance of, 2:71
mythology of, 2:170, 3:126
navy of, 3:130
Neo-Hittites and, 3:134–36
Old Kingdom of, 2:167
palaces of, 3:161
peasant labor in, 3:169
poetry of, 3:60
prayers of, 4:12
priests of, 4:13, 14, 16
queens of, 4:24–25
religions of, 2:169–70, 4:34
sculpture of, 4:58
servants of, 4:74
Shuppiluliuma I, **4:83–84**
slavery of, 4:87
social institutions of, 4:89–90
sports of, 2:73
temples of, 3:163
theology of, 4:122
women's role in, 4:162–63
writing of, 4:171
Hogarth, David George, 1:63–64
Hole, Frank, 3:142, 143
Holy wars, 4:150
Homer, 2:140, 142, 4:132
Honey, 1:44
Horoscopes, 1:95, 4:177–78
Horostepe, 1:38
Horses, 1:40, **2:170–71**
    in cavalry, 1:152
    domestication of, 1:42
    uses of, 1:44, 4:61
Horus, 2:128–29, **2:171–72** (illus.)
    birds representing, 1:47, 118
    in creation myths, 2:14
    Hathor and, 2:151
    and Ishtar, 3:13
    priests of, 4:16
    Seth and, 4:76
"house" (family as), 2:86
Houses, **2:172–75**. See also Palaces;
    Temple(s)
    in Anatolia, 1:70
    Aramaean royal compounds, 1:53
    burial under floors of, 1:128
    at Çatal Hüyük, 1:70, 148
    construction of, 4:165
    courtyard houses, 1:65
    in Egypt, 1:67
    furnishings and furniture, **2:106–10**
    in Mesopotamia, 1:64–65
    Mosaic Law concerning, 3:115
    of peasants, 3:169
    of Philistines, 3:183
    in Ugarit, 1:68
Human form in art, **2:175–78**
    combined with animals, 1:47–48
    of Crete, 2:17
    Egyptian, 2:64

Greek influence on, 2:142
    on Narmer Palette, 1:114
Human rights, 4:85–86
Humor, **2:178–79**
    in animal art, 1:40, 47
    in literature, 3:60
Hunter-gatherers, 2:179, 4:167
Hunting, **2:179–80**
    art depicting, 1:45, 46
    chariots for, 1:161
    domestication of animals and,
        1:41–42
    of lions, 3:57
    transition to farming from, 1:7
Hurrians, 2:79, **2:180–81**
    Khepat, **3:33**
    Kumarbi, **3:39**
    language of, 3:49
    migration of, 3:105
    Mitanni established by, 3:97
    Teshub, **4:117–18**
Hyksos, **2:182–83**
    Ahmose's defeat of, 1:12–13
    in Canaan, 1:138
    Phoenicians and, 3:184–85
Hymns, **2:183**
    of Egypt, 3:59
    Mesopotamian, 3:59
Hymn to Aten, 1:97

I

Ice Ages, 2:5
Iconography, **2:184–86**
Idrimi, statue of, 3:5–6
Iliad, 2:140, 141, 3:121, 4:5, 132
Ilion/Illium. *See* Troy
Imdugud, 1:47, 119
Imhotep, 2:130, 4:20
Immortals (Persian army troops),
    1:74–75
Inanna, 2:127
Inar, 2:129
Inara, 2:129
Incantations, 3:68, 69
Incense, **2:186–87**
Incubation, 2:41
India
    Aryans, 1:81
    number systems of, 3:148–49
Indo-Aryan language, 2:188
Indo-European languages, **2:187–88,**
    3:48–49
Indo-Iranian languages, 2:188
Indra, 2:129
Inheritance
    family and social customs about,
        2:88–89
    laws concerning, 3:52–54, 4:164
    of priesthood, 4:13
    property rights and, 4:17
    in Scythia, 4:62
Inscriptions, **3:1–6**
    alphabet contributions from, 1:28
    Anatolian, 3:5

Assyrian conquests described in,
    1:83
    at Azatiwadiya, 3:135
    in Bahrain, 1:113
    Behistun inscription, **1:115–17**
    bilingual, for decipherment, 2:33
    on clay tablets, 2:2 (illus.)
    Egyptian, 3:4
    format of, 3:1–2
    as historical records, 2:163–65
    Hymn to Aten, 1:97
    Iranian, 3:4–5
    from the Levant, 3:5–6
    as literature, 3:60
    materials and methods for, 3:2
    Mesopotamian, 3:2–4
    pillar of Xanthus, 3:5
    and Rosetta Stone, **4:41–43**
    royal, 1:164–65, 2:2, 3
    Treaty of Naram-Sin, 3:4
    types of, 3:1
Insect plagues, 2:38
Inshushinak, 2:130
The Instruction of Amenemope, 4:18
Instructions of Shuruppak, 4:18
Instruments, musical, 3:120–21
Investment, in trading missions, 3:93
Iran, **3:6–8**
    Achaemenid dynasty, 2:45
    afterlife beliefs in, 1:6
    Ali Kosh, 3:173
    animals in art of, 1:45–46
    archaeology and archaeologists in,
        1:62–63
    Aryans in, **1:80–81,** 3:7, 106
    Behistun inscription, **1:115–17**
    building materials in, 1:127
    burial sites and tombs in, 1:131
    climate of, 2:120
    clothing of, 2:8–9
    domesticated animals in, 1:42
    dynasties of, 2:45
    early inhabitants of, 3:173
    Elam and the Elamites, **2:66–70**
    Elamites, 2:81
    ethnic and language groups in,
        2:81–82
    family and social life in, 2:88
    geography of, **2:120,** 3:6
    gods and goddesses of, 2:130,
        4:33–34
    government of, 2:138
    health in, 2:153
    history of, 3:6–7
    houses in, 2:174
    Manneans, 3:6–7
    Medes, 2:82, 3:7, **3:80–83**
    mining in, 3:108
    mythology of, 3:126
    nomads in, 3:143, 145 (illus.)
    Persian Empire, 2:82, 3:7,
        3:171–76
    religions of, 3:7–8, 4:33–34
    sculpture of, 4:59
    social institutions in, 4:90–91
    Susa and Susiana, **4:108–9**

Index

Index

Index

Hittite, 2:170
horses in, 2:171
Iranian, 3:126
Isis and Osiris, 3:125
Israelite, 3:125–26
King Minos in, 3:111
Kumarbi Cycle, 3:39, 4:117–18
of the Levant, 3:125–26
lions as symbols in, 3:58
Macedonians in, 3:67
Marduk in, 3:71
Mesopotamian, 3:125
Minotaur in, 3:111
netherworld in, 1:5
Osiris and Isis, 3:157
Poseidon in, 3:111
role of, 3:124–25
sphinx in, 4:94
theology in, 4:122–23
Theseus in, 3:111

N

Nabateans, 1:51
Nabonidus, **3:126–27**
and Cyrus the Great, 2:23
Neo-Babylonian empire under,
1:103 *(map)*
reign of, 1:106
Nabopolassar, **3:127**
and arranged marriages, 3:74
ethnicity of, 1:159
reign of, 1:106
Names, personal, **3:128–29**
in Babylonia, 1:110
of Chaldeans, 1:158
given to babies, 1:162
Namma, 2:127
Nanna. *See* Sin (god)
Naram-Sin, **3:129–30**
and Enlil's temple, 1:21
government under, 2:132
inscriptions about, 3:2
reign of, 1:18
in Sargon's dynasty, 2:44
victory stela of, 1:17 *(illus.)*, 21
Narmer Palette, 1:113–14
Narunde, 2:130
Natural disasters, **2:37–39**
Natwatwa twins, 2:129
Naval power, **3:130–31**
of Assyrians, 4:152
in Persian Wars, 3:177–78
Navigation, 3:88
Neanderthal peoples, 4:111
Nearchus, 1:25
Nebayot tribe, 1:49
Nebuchadnezzar I, 1:105
Nebuchadnezzar II, **3:131–32**
and Hanging Gardens of Babylon,
2:149–50
rebuilding by, 1:100
reign of, 1:106
Necho II, **3:132–33**
Necromancy, 1:6, 3:69, 4:160

Necropolises, 1:128
Nefernefruaten, Queen, 1:15
Nefertari, Queen, 1:1, 2:111 *(illus.)*,
4:144
Nefertiti, Queen, 1:15, **3:133–34** *(illus.)*
Nefrusobek, 3:37
Negahban, Ezat, 1:131
Negev Desert, 2:121
Nehemiah, 2:84, 3:26
Nemrik, 2:172
Neo-Assyrian empire, 2:133, 4:40
Neo-Babylonians, 3:159
Neo-Hittites, **3:134–36**
Neolithic period
Çatal Hüyük, **1:148–49**
economy in, 2:49
Transcaucasia, 1:151
Nephthys, 2:128
Nergal. *See* Erra
Nerik, 2:129
Netherworld, 1:5
Nile River, 2:56–57, 118–19,
3:137–38, 4:38–39
archaeological sites along, 1:59
farming along, 1:9–10
flooding of, 1:10, 141–42, 2:38, 42,
74, 97–100, 4:153–54
and irrigation, 2:61–62, 3:10–11
as Nubian trade route, 3:145
Opet festival at flooding of, 3:63
shipping routes on, 4:79
Nineveh, **3:139–40**
library in, 1:83
roads in, 4:40
Sennacherib and, 4:74
Ninkhursag, 1:110
Nintu, 4:13
Ninurta, 2:127, 3:124 *(illus.)*, 159
Nippur, **3:140**
magic in, 3:68
map of, 3:70
orchards and gardens in, 1:175
plan of, 1:171 *(illus.)*
temple Eshumesha at, 3:159
Nitokris, **3:141**
Nofret, Lady, 2:12 *(illus.)*
Nomads and nomadism, **3:141–45**
Amorites, 1:33
animal husbandry and, 1:43
in Arabia, 1:49
Aramaeans, **1:51–54**
in Central Asia, 1:154
pastoral nomadism, 3:104–5, 141
Scythians, 4:61
tent camp archaeological site, 3:142,
143
"norms," 4:121
Nubia and the Nubians, 2:81,
3:145–47
Abu Simbel, 1:1 *(illus.)*
Kush, 3:39–41, 3:146–47
Meroë, 3:39–41
pyramids of, 3:146 *(illus.)*
in the Sudan, 4:100
Taharqa, **4:114–15**
Ta Sety, 3:146

Numbers and numerals, **3:148–49**
Nut, 2:14 *(illus.)*, 128
Nuzi, **3:149–50**, 4:161

O

Oases, 2:120
Obelisk of Manishtushtu, 1:20
Obsidian, 1:108, 151, **3:150–51**
Occupations. *See* Work
Octavian, 2:4
Odyssey, 2:140, 3:121, 4:132
Offerings, **3:151–52**
burial, 1:130–32
for the dead, 1:5, 2:29, 3:151–52
food and drink, 4:32, 37
goats for, 2:126
to gods and goddesses, 3:151, 4:33
(illus.)
of incense, 2:186
ritual offerings, 4:37
wine as, 4:159
Old Persian language, 2:34, 188,
3:48–39
Old Testament. *See* Bible, Hebrew
Olives, **3:152–53**
Oman Peninsula, 1:62, **3:153**
Omens, **3:153–54**
death omen of Esarhaddon, 1:94–95
and divination, 3:155
eclipses as, 1:94–95
for foretelling future, 1:94, 3:153–54
and medicine, 3:84
natural events as, 1:94, 3:154
weather as, 1:94
Omri, 1:11–12, 3:15
Onomastics, 3:129
Opet festival, 2:92, 3:63
Oracles and prophecy, **3:154–57**
in Hebrew Bible, 1:117
Isaiah, **3:12**
Jeremiah, **3:17**
The Potter's Oracle, 4:10
Oral tradition, 3:58
Ordeals, 3:52
Osiris, 2:128–29, **3:157**
in creation myths, 2:14
cult of, and Abydos, **1:1–2**
and Ishtar, 3:13
Seth and, 4:76
unrecorded stories of, 3:125

P

Paints, 4:145
Palaces, **3:157–61**
art depicting animals in, 1:46
in Assyria, 1:93
bas-reliefs in, 1:114–15
in cities, 1:175–76
of Crete, 2:16, 3:110, 111
at Djoser's burial site, 2:40
in Egypt, 1:66
functions of, 3:157, 158

Index

Index

Index

Index

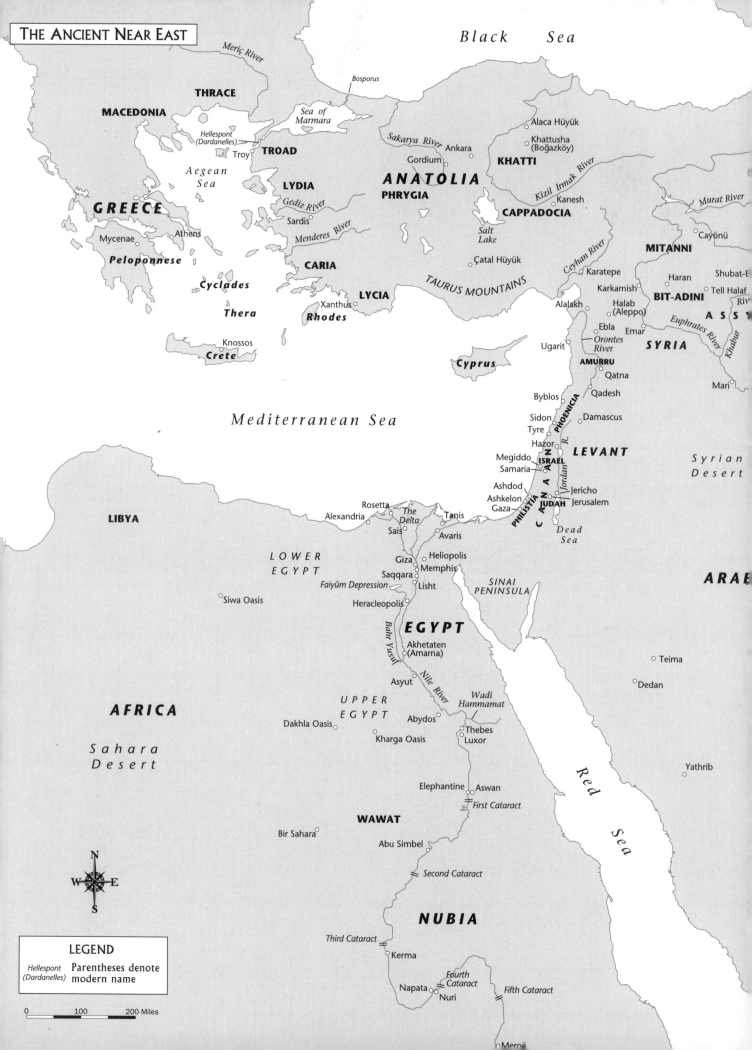

THE ANCIENT NEAR EAST

Meriç River

Black Sea

Bosporus

THRACE

MACEDONIA

Sea of Marmara

Alaca Hüyük

Khattusha (Boğazköy)

Sakarya River Ankara

KHATTI

Hellespont (Dardanelles) Troy TROAD

ANATOLIA

Aegean Sea

LYDIA PHRYGIA Gordium

Kizil Irmak River Kanesh

Murat River

GREECE

CAPPADOCIA

Çayönü

Gediz River Sardis

Salt Lake

MITANNI

Menderes River

Haran Shubat-E

Mycenae Athens

Çatal Hüyük

Karatepe Tell Halaf Riv

Ceyhan River Karkamish BIT-ADINI

Peloponnese

TAURUS MOUNTAINS

Alalakh Halab (Aleppo) ASS¥

CARIA

Cyclades

Ebla Emar *Euphrates River* *Khabur*

LYCIA

Thera

Ugarit *Orontes River* SYRIA

Rhodes Xanthus

AMURRU Qatna

Mari

Knossos

Cyprus

Byblos PHOENICIA Qadesh

Crete

Sidon Damascus

Mediterranean Sea

Tyre Hazor LEVANT

Syrian Desert

Megiddo ISRAEL

Jordan R.

Samaria CANAAN

Ashdod Jericho

Rosetta *The Delta* Ashkelon Jerusalem

Alexandria Tanis Gaza PHILISTIA JUDAH

Sais Avaris *Dead Sea*

LIBYA

ARAB

Giza Heliopolis

Saqqara Memphis

Faiyûm Depression Lisht *SINAI PENINSULA*

Siwa Oasis Heracleopolis

EGYPT

Bahr Yusuf

Teima

Akhetaten (Amarna)

Dedan

AFRICA

Nile River Asyut

Wadi Hammamat

Sahara Desert

UPPER EGYPT

Dakhla Oasis Abydos

Thebes Luxor

Kharga Oasis

Red Sea

Yathrib

Elephantine Aswan

First Cataract

WAWAT

Bir Sahara

Abu Simbel

Second Cataract

N
W E
S

NUBIA

Third Cataract

0 100 200 Miles

Kerma

Fourth Cataract

Napata *Fifth Cataract*

Nuri

Meroë